NING

CHELTENH
&
GLOUCE
College of High

ƆAN

Recent advances in the field of computer vision are leading to novel and radical changes in the way we interact with computers. It will soon be possible to enable a computer linked to a video camera to detect the presence of users, track faces, arms and hands in real time, and analyse expressions and gestures. The implications for interface design are immense and are expected to have major repercussions for all areas where computers are used, from the work place to recreation.

This book collects the ideas and algorithms from the world's leading scientists, offering a glimpse of the radical changes that are round the corner and which will change the way we will interact with computers in the near future.

Roberto Cipolla was a Toshiba Fellow at their Research and Development Centre in Kawasaki in 1991–92 before joining the Department of Engineering at the University of Cambridge in 1992 as a Lecturer and a Fellow of Jesus College. He became a Reader in Information Engineering in 1997. IIis research interests are in computer vision and robotics. He has authored more than 100 papers and has written one book and edited three others. He has won two international prizes and four national prizes for scientific contributions in these areas.

Alex Paul Pentland is the Academic Head of the MIT. Media Laboratory and the Toshiba Professor of Media Arts and Sciences. In 1987 he founded the Perceptual Computing Section of the Media Laboratory, a group that now includes over fifty researchers in computer vision, graphics, speech, music, and human–machine interaction. He has published more than 180 scientific articles in these areas. He has won awards from the AAAI for his research into fractals; the IEEE for his research into face recognition; and *Ars Electronica* for his work in computer vision interfaces to virtual environments. *Newsweek* magazine has recently named him one of the 100 Americans most likely to shape the next century.

COMPUTER VISION FOR HUMAN–MACHINE INTERACTION

Edited by
Roberto Cipolla and Alex Pentland

CAMBRIDGE
UNIVERSITY PRESS

PUBLISHED BY THE PRESS SYNDICATE OF THE UNIVERSITY OF CAMBRIDGE
The Pitt Building, Trumpington Street, Cambridge CB2 1RP, United Kingdom

CAMBRIDGE UNIVERSITY PRESS
The Edinburgh Building, Cambridge CB2 2RU, UK http://www.cup.cam.ac.uk
40 West 20th Street, New York, NY 10011-4211, USA http://www.cup.org
10 Stamford Road, Oakleigh, Melbourne 3166, Australia

First published 1998

Printed in the United Kingdom at the University Press, Cambridge

Typeset by the author

Typeset in Computer Modern 10/13pt, in LaTeX

A catalogue record for this book is available from the British Library

ISBN 0 521 62253 0 hardback

Contents

Foreword: Out of Sight, Out of Mind
N. Negroponte   *page* vii

Preface   ix

Part one: New Interfaces and Novel Applications   1

1   Smart Rooms: Machine Understanding of Human Behavior
    A.P. Pentland   3

2   GestureComputer – History, Design and Applications
    C. Maggioni and B. Kämmerer   23

3   Human Reader: A Vision-Based Man-Machine Interface
    K. Mase   53

4   Visual Sensing of Humans for Active Public Interfaces
    K. Waters, J. Rehg, M. Loughlin, S.B. Kang and
    D. Terzopoulos   83

5   A Human–Robot Interface using Pointing with Uncalibrated
    Stereo Vision
    R. Cipolla and N.J. Hollinghurst   97

Part two: Tracking Human Action   111

6   Tracking Faces
    A.H. Gee and R. Cipolla   113

7   Towards Automated, Real-time, Facial Animation
    B. Bascle, A. Blake and J. Morris   123

8   Interfacing through Visual Pointers
    C. Colombo, A. Del Bimbo and S. De Magistris   135

v

9   Monocular Tracking of the Human Arm in 3D
    E. Di Bernardo, L. Goncalves and P. Perona   155

10 Looking at People in Action – An Overview
    *Y. Yacoob, L. Davis, M. Black, D. Gavrila, T. Horprasert
    and C. Morimoto*   171

Part three: Gesture Recognition and Interpretation   189

11 A Framework for Gesture Generation and Interpretation
    J. Cassell   191

12 Model-Based Interpretation of Faces and Hand Gestures
    *C.J. Taylor, A. Lanitis, T.F. Cootes, G. Edwards and
    T. Ahmad*   217

13 Recognition of Hand Signs from Complex Backgrounds
    J.J. Weng and Y. Cui   235

14 Probabilistic Models of Verbal and Body Gestures
    *C. Bregler, S.M. Omohundro, M. Covell, M. Slaney,
    S. Ahmad, D.A. Forsyth and J.A. Feldman*   267

15 Looking at Human Gestures
    M. Yachida and Y. Iwai   291

    Acknowledgements   313
    Bibliography   317
    List of contributors   345

Foreword: Out of Sight, Out of Mind

N. Negroponte

Face it. Butlers cannot be blind. Secretaries cannot be deaf. But somehow we take it for granted that computers can be both.

Human-computer interface dogma was first dominated by direct manipulation and then delegation. The tacit assumption of both styles of interaction has been that the human will be explicit, unambiguous and fully attentive. Equivocation, contradiction and preoccupation are unthinkable even though they are very human behaviors. Not allowed. We are expected to be disciplined, fully focused, single minded and 'there' with every attending muscle in our body. Worse, we accept it.

Times will change. Cipolla, Pentland *et al*, fly in the face (pun intended) of traditional human-computer interface research. The questions they pose and answers they provide have the common thread of concurrency. Namely, by combining modes of communication, the resulting richness of expression is not only far greater than the sum of the parts, but allows for one channel to disambiguate the other. Look. There's an example right there. Where? Well, you can't see it, because you cannot see me, where I am looking, what's around me. So the example is left to your imagination.

That's fine in literature and for well codified tasks. Works for making plane reservations, buying and selling stocks and, think of it, almost everything we do with computers today. But this kind of categorical computing is crummy for design, debate and deliberation. It is really useless when the purpose of communication is to collect our own thoughts. Under such conditions what you say is often far less important than how you say it. Gesture and facial expression are signal, not noise as some might have them, and sometimes so powerful that words are incidental.

Your face is your display. This display is wired so tightly to what you say, it is almost impossible to turn it off. Watch somebody talking on the telephone: they smile, frown, grimace – for whose benefit? In fact, turning off facial expression is an art form, well known to poker players.

The machine vision community has been object oriented (in its way). Separating figure from ground, finding edges or locating limiting contours has been about 'things.' Classical problems have been dominated by autonomy. The goal has been for computers to inspect, distinguish or locate anything from cracks to cliffs. Research has been driven by factory automation and robotics. In some cases, like moon exploration, we have no choice but to make machines which can see, because by the time a warning signal gets back to a human teleoperator the multimillion dollars robot has already walked over the precipice.

This book helps launch a new genre of vision: looking at people. But it is looking at people for a purpose – making the interface between human and computer better. Many of the techniques reported herein can be used to identify mug shots, to locate shop lifters or to automate immigration and passport control. I would not mind if ATM machines knew it was my face.

But those are not the new challenges. What is new in this book is the idea of a more sympathetic vision – looking to learn, looking to understand, looking to help. I hope many readers will be looking (too) at these examples, because we need to make up for lost time. Surely you don't want to sit in front of a screen all your life!

Preface

Present day Human–Computer Interaction (HCI) revolves around typing at a keyboard, moving and pointing with a mouse, selecting from menus and searching through manuals. These interfaces are far from ideal, especially when dealing with graphical input and trying to visualise and manipulate three-dimensional data and structures. For many, interacting with a computer is a cumbersome and frustrating experience. Most people would prefer more natural ways of dealing with computers, closer to face-to-face, human-to-human conversation, where talking, gesturing, hearing and seeing are part of the interaction. They would prefer computer systems that understand their verbal and non-verbal languages.

Since its inception in the 1960s, the emphasis of HCI design has been on improving the "look and feel" of a computer by incremental changes, to produce keyboards that are easier to use, and graphical input devices with bigger screens and better sounds. The advent of low-cost computing and memory, and computers equipped with tele-conferencing hardware (including cameras mounted above the display) means that video input and audio input is available with little additional cost. It is now possible to conceive of more radical changes in the way we interact with machines: of computers that are listening to and looking at their users.

Progress has already been achieved in computer speech synthesis and recognition [326]. Promising commercial products already exist that allow natural speech to be digitised and processed by computer (32 kilobytes per second) for use in dictation systems. Vision – the process of discovering from images what is present in a scene and where it is – is a more powerful but more complicated sense. The computer analysis and interpretation of video images – Computer Vision – also offers exciting and natural ways of communicating with computers and machines. From its amibitious inception, also in the early 1960s, computer vision researchers have aimed to understand the principles underlying visual competences in both natural and artificial systems by analysing vision as an information-processing task. The technical challenges are formidable. The complexity of the task is enormous and involves the processing of gigabytes of visual data per second. How should this information be processed to recover the positions and shapes of visible surfaces and to recognise familiar objects in a scene?

The principal motivation for this area of research used to be the applications in making autonomous robots, especially in space or for military uses. Only recently have computer scientists been able to apply these new technologies to developing novel ways of interacting with computers and machines. A combination of ingenious new algorithms and powerful computers has led to breakthroughs in computer vision. In structured environments, it is now possible to enable a computer that is linked to a video camera to detect the presence of a face, compute its gaze and analyse its expression. It is also possible to track the face, arm, hands and fingers in real-time, as well as to recognise and distinguish gestures. All these techniques are passive and wireless, with no need for the user to wear special gloves or markers. The information required is provided by a video camera or stereo pair of cameras looking at the user, and is processed automatically by the computer.

In 1996, the Fourth European Conference on Computer Vision was held at the University of Cambridge. Following the main meeting, an international workshop on computer vision for human–machine interaction took place. The speakers were selected from the leading academic and industrial research laboratories in the US, Asia and Europe. This book is a development of some of the presentations made at that workshop. It offers a snapshot of the state-of-the-art and a glimpse at the radical changes that are around the corner which will be an integral part of the way we will interact with computers in the next century.

The book consists primarily of accounts of research projects and descriptions of systems which use computer vision for looking at humans. It is divided into three parts. Part 1 looks at novel ways of interacting with computers and their application in building intelligent interfaces. Part 2 presents some of the algorithms for tracking human actions, the real-time tracking of faces and gaze, hands and bodies. Part 3 looks at techniques for recognising human gestures and analysing human behaviour. The book concludes with an extensive and integrated bibliography.

The HCI community has a strong tradition of analytical and empirical evaluation. Members of that community may be interested in reading this book. The projects described here, though, are in too raw a state and their description may not be sufficiently detailed for direct incorporation into end-user applications. The projects described here are all at the research stage but have enormous potential for future development. These are still early, exploratory days, but there is no question that the techniques presented here will be part of the revolutionary changes to come in the way humans will interact with machines and computers.

Roberto Cipolla and Alex Pentland

Part one

New Interfaces and Novel Applications

1

Smart Rooms: Machine Understanding of Human Behavior

A.P. Pentland

Abstract

This chapter describes progress in building computer systems that understand people, and can work with them in the manner of an attentive human-like assistant. To accomplish this, I have built a series of real-time experimental testbeds, called *Smart Rooms*. These testbeds are instrumented with cameras and microphones, and perform audio-visual interpretation of human users. Real-time capabilities include 3D tracking of head, hands, and feet, and recognition of hand/body gestures. The system can also support face recognition and interpretation of face expression.

1.1 Introduction

My goal is to make it possible for computers to function like attentive, human-like assistants. I believe that the most important step toward achieving this goal is to give computers an ability that I call *perceptual intelligence*. They have to be able to characterize their current situation by answering questions such as who, what, when, where, and why, just as writers are taught to do.

In the language of cognitive science, perceptual intelligence is the ability to solve the frame problem: it is being able to classify the current situation, so that you know what variables are important, and thus can act appropriately. Once a computer has the perceptual intelligence to know who, what, when, where, and why, then simple statistical learning methods have been shown to be sufficient for the computer to determine which aspects of the situation are significant, and to choose a helpful course of action [205].

3

In order to interact with people, the most important answers to "who, what, when, where, and why" are those concerned with human behavior. Consequently, I have focused my work on the perception of human behavior. I have concentrated on giving computers the ability to recognize people, to understand our expressions and gestures, and hear the tone and emphasis of the human voice [235]. If I can give computers the ability to perceive and categorize human interactions in a human-like manner, I expect that the computer will be able to work with people in a natural and common sense manner.

1.1.1 Experimental Testbeds

To carry out this plan of research I have created a series of experimental testbeds that are instrumented with cameras and microphones, thus allowing the computer to see, hear, and interpret users' actions. These testbeds are "smart rooms" that help users navigate the World Wide Web, to teleconference in virtual worlds, to find multimedia information, and to interact with artifical life agents [235]. The key idea is to develop perceptual intelligence: because the environment knows something about what is going on, it can act and react appropriately.

The idea of a smart room is a little like having a butler; i.e., a passive observer who usually stands quietly in the corner but who is constantly looking for opportunities to help. Imagine a house that always knows where your kids are, and tells you when they might be getting in trouble. Or a car that knows when you are sleepy and should stop for coffee (the interior of a car is a particularly important type of smart room).

The first prototype of a smart room was developed in 1991 by Pattie Maes, Trevor Darrell, Bruce Blumberg and me as part of the ALIVE (Artifical Life Interactive Video Environment) project; now there are smart rooms in Japan, France, England, and several places in the US. They are linked together by ISDN telephone lines to allow shared virtual environment and cooperative work experiments.

1.1.2 The Modeling and Estimation Framework

The general theoretical approach I have taken in these "smart environment" testbeds is to perform a maximum *a posteriori* (MAP) interpretation on very low-level, 2D representations of regions of the image data. The appearance of a target class Ω, e.g., the probability distribution function $P(\mathbf{x}|\Omega)$ of its image-level features $\mathbf{x}$, can be characterized by use of a low-dimensional parametric appearance model. Once such a probability distribution function (PDF) has been learned, it is straightforward to use it in a MAP estimator in order to detect and recognize target classes. Behavior recognition is accomplished in a similar manner; these parametric appearance models are tracked over time, and their time evolution $P(\mathbf{x}(t)|\Omega)$ characterized probabilistically to obtain a *spatio-temporal behavior model*. Incoming spatio-temporal data can then be compared to the spatio-temporal PDF of each of the various behavior models using elastic matching methods such as dynamic time warping [102] or Hidden Markov Modeling [278].

The use of parametric appearance models to characterize the PDF of an object's appearance in the image is related to the idea of view-based representation, as advocated by Ullman [295] and Poggio [243]. As originally developed, the idea of view-based recognition was to accurately describe the spatial structure of the target object by interpolating between various views. However, in order to describe natural objects such as faces or hands, I have found it necessary to extend the notion of "view" to include characterizing the range of geometric and feature variation, as well as the likelihood associated with such variation.

This approach is typified by my face recognition research [291, 222], which uses linear combinations of eigenvectors to describe a *space* of target appearances, and then characterize the PDF of the targets appearance within that space. This method has been shown to be very powerful for detection and recognition of human faces, hands, and facial expressions [222]. Other researchers have used extensions of this basic method to recognize industrial objects and household items [226]. Another variation on this approach is to use linear combinations of examples rather than eigenvectors; this type of appearance modeling has demonstrated a power similar to that of the eigenvector-based methods [102, 160], although it necessarily has a lower efficiency.

1.1.3 The Computer Architecture

Sensing and interpretation of human movement is accomplished by a modular computer architecture, which can be configured in a variety of ways, as more or less interpretation capability is required. The basic element is an SGI Indy computer; these computers are connected by video, audio, ISDN, and ethernet networks. This allows each computer to independently access whatever portion of the audiovisual input it needs, to share control information among the other computers, and to connect with other, distant, installations over ISDN phone lines. Normally each computer is dedicated to performing only one type of interpretation. For instance, if video tracking, audio input, and gesture interpretation capabilities were desired, then three computers would be used, one for each task.

1.2 Building Blocks of Perceptual Intelligence

The following sections will briefly describe each of a set of programs that can find, track, and interpret human behavior [235]. The final section will illustrate how these programs have been assembled into a real-time "virtual dog" that interacts with people in an interesting and lifelike manner. In order of description, the modules are:

- Pfinder, a real-time program that tracks the user, and recognizes a basic set of hand gestures and body postures;
- the face processor, an interactive-time program that recognizes human faces;
- the expression processor, an interactive-time program that uses motion-energy templates to classify people's facial expressions;
- vision-directed audio, a real-time system that uses the head position information provided by Pfinder to steer a phase-array microphone;
- behavior recognition, real-time systems that examine users' movements in order to determine what they are doing.

For additional detail the reader should examine the numerous papers, technical reports, interactive demos, and computer code available at our web site at http://www-white.media.mit.edu/vismod or by anonymous FTP from whitechapel.media.mit.edu.

1.2.1 Pfinder

Pfinder ("person finder") is a real-time system for tracking and interpretation of people. It runs at 10Hz on a standard SGI Indy computer, and has performed reliably on thousands of people in many different physical locations [15, 320, 235]. The system uses a multi-class statistical model of color and shape to segment a person from a background scene, and then to find and track people's head and hands in a wide range of viewing conditions. Pfinder produces a real-time representation of a user useful for applications such as wireless interfaces, video databases, and low-bandwidth coding, without cumbersome wires or attached sensors.

Fig. 1.1 Analysis of a user in the ALIVE environment. The frame on the left is the video input (n.b. color image shown here in black and white for printing purposes), the center frame shows the support map $s(x, y)$ which segments the user into blobs, and the frame on the right showing a person model reconstructed from blob statistics alone (with contour shape ignored).

Pfinder employs a maximum *a posteriori* (MAP) approach by using simple 2D models to perform detection and tracking of the human body. It incorporates *a priori* knowledge about people primarily to bootstrap itself and to recover from errors.

In order to present a concise description of Pfinder, I will only describe its representations and operation in the "steady state" case, where it is tracking a person moving around an office environment, neglecting the problems of initially learning a person's description.

Modeling the Person

Pfinder models the human as a connected set of 2D *blobs*, an old concept, but one to which in recent years little serious attention has been paid in favor of stronger local features like points, lines, and contours. The blob representation that we use was originally developed by me in 1976 [236] for application to multi-spectral satellite (MSS) imagery. The PDF of each blob is characterized by the *joint* distribution of spatial (x, y) and color features. Color is expressed in the YUV space, which is a simple approximation to human color sensitivity.

We define $\mathbf{m}_k$ to be the mean (x, y, Y, U, V) of blob k, and $\mathbf{K}_k$ to be the covariance of that blob's distribution. The mean of a blob expresses the concept "color a at location b," while the covariance expresses how the color and brightness of the blob changes across its surface. For instance, the blob statistics can express that one side is brighter than the other (perhaps due illumination from the side), or that the color changes from top to bottom (perhaps due to light reflected from the floor).

Each blob also has associated with it a *support map* that indicates exactly which image pixels are members of a particular blob. Since the individual support maps indicate which image pixels are members of that particular blob, the aggregate support map $s(x, y)$ over all the blobs represents the segmentation of the image into spatial/color classes.

The statistics of each blob are recursively updated to combine information contained in the most recent measurements with knowledge contained in the current class statistics and the priors. Because the detailed dynamics of each blob are unknown, we use approximate models derived from experience with a wide range of users. For instance, blobs that are near the center of mass have substantial inertia, whereas blobs toward the extremities can move much faster.

Modeling the Scene

It is assumed that for most of the time Pfinder will be processing a scene that consists of a relatively static situation, such as an office, and a single moving person. Consequently, it is appropriate to use different types of model for the scene and for the person.

The surrounding scene is modeled as a texture surface; each point on the texture surface is associated with a mean color value and a distribution about that mean. The color distribution of each pixel is modeled with the Gaussian described by a full covariance matrix. Thus, for instance, a fluttering white curtain in front of a black wall will have a color covariance that is very elongated in the luminance direction, but narrow in the chrominance directions.

In each frame visible pixels have their statistics recursively updated using a simple adaptive filter. This allows us to compensate for changes in lighting and even for object movement. For instance, if a person moves a book it causes the texture map to change in both the locations where the book was, and where it now is. By tracking the person we can know that these areas, although changed, are still part of the texture model and thus update their statistics to the new value. The updating process is done recursively, and even large changes in illumination can be substantially compensated within two or three seconds.

The Analysis Loop

Given a person model and a scene model, Pfinder then acquires a new image, interprets it, and updates the scene and person models. To accomplish this there are several steps:

(i) First, the appearance of the users is predicted in the new image using the current state of our model. This is accomplished using a set of Kalman filters with simple Newtonian dynamics that operate on each blob's spatial statistics.

(ii) Next, for each image pixel the likelihood that it is a member of each of the blob models and the scene model is measured. Self-shadowing and cast shadows are a particular difficulty in measuring this likelihood; this is addressed by normalizing the hue and saturation by the overall brightness.

(iii) Resolve these pixel-by-pixel likelihoods into a support map, indicating for each pixel whether it is part of one of the blobs or of the background scene. Spatial priors and connectivity constraints are used to accomplish this resolution.

(iv) Update the statistical models for each blob and for the background scene; also update the dynamic models of the blobs.

For some applications, Pfinder's 2D information must be processed to recover 3D geometry. For a single calibrated camera this can be accomplished by backprojecting the 2D image information to produce 3D position estimates using the assumption that the user is standing on a planar floor. When two or more cameras are available, the hand, head, etc., blobs can be matched to obtain 3D estimates via triangulation.

Fig. 1.1 illustrates Pfinder's functioning. At the left is the original video frame (shown in black and white rather than the original color). In the middle is the resulting segmentation into head, hands, feet, shirt, and pants. At the right are one-standard-deviation ellipses illustrating the statistical blob descriptions formed for the head, hands, feet, shirt, and pants. Note that despite having the hands either in front of the face or the body a correct description is still obtained. For additional detail see references [15, 320, 235].

1.2.2 Face Recognition

Once the rough location of the person's head is known, one can attempt to recognize their face. As with Pfinder, a maximum *a posteriori* (MAP) approach is applied to this problem. This has been accomplished by developing a method for determining the probability distribution function for face images within a low-dimensional eigenspace. Knowledge of this distribution then allows the face and face features to be precisely located, and compared along meaningful dimensions.

I am proud to note that this face recognition system was recently certified by the U.S. Army as being the most accurate in the world.

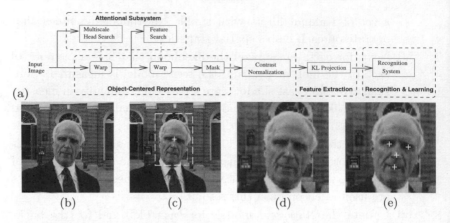

(a)

(b)   (c)   (d)   (e)

Fig. 1.2 (a) The face processing system, (b) original image, (c) position and scale estimate, (d) normalized head image, (e) position of facial features.

The following gives a brief description of workings of the system; for additional detail see [222].

Face and Feature Detection

The standard detection paradigm in image processing is that of normalized correlation or template matching. However this approach is only optimal in the simplistic case of a *deterministic* signal embedded in white Gaussian noise. When we begin to consider a target *class* detection problem — *e.g.*, finding a generic human face or a human hand in a scene — we must incorporate the underlying probability distribution of the object of interest. Subspace or eigenspace methods, such as the KLT and PCA, are particularly well-suited to such a task since they provide a compact and *parametric* description of the object's appearance and also automatically identify the essential components of the underlying statistical variability.

In particular, the eigenspace formulation leads to a powerful alternative to standard detection techniques such as template matching or normalized correlation. The reconstruction error (or residual) of the KLT expansion is an effective indicator of a match. The residual error is easily computed using the projection coefficients and the original signal energy. This detection strategy is equivalent to matching with a linear combination of *eigentemplates* and allows for a greater range of distortions in the input signal (including lighting, and moderate rotation. and scale). Some of the low-order eigentemplates for a human face are shown

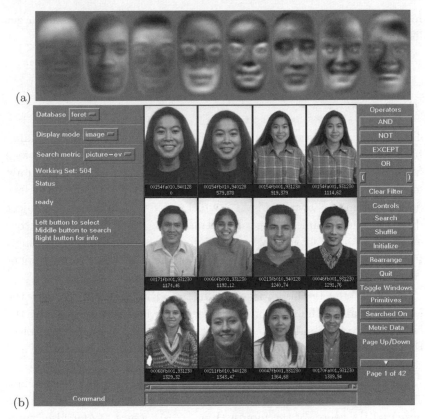

Fig. 1.3 (a) The first eight eigenfaces, (b) searching for similar faces in a database, using the Photobook image database tool [240].

in Figure 1.3(a). In a statistical signal detection framework, the use of eigentemplates has been shown to be orders of magnitude better than standard matched filtering [222].

Using this approach the target detection problem can be reformulated from the point of view of a MAP estimation problem. In particular, given the visual field, estimate the position (and scale) of the subimage which is most representative of a specific target class Ω. Computationally, this is achieved by sliding an m-by-n observation window throughout the image and at each location computing the *likelihood* that the given observation $\mathbf{x}$ is an instance of the target class Ω — i.e. $P(\mathbf{x}|\Omega)$. After this probability map is computed, the location corresponding to the highest likelihood can be selected as the MAP estimate of the target location.

The Face Processor

This MAP-based face finder has been employed as the basic building block of an automatic face recognition system. The function of the face finder is to locate very precisely the face, since Pfinder produces only low-resolution estimates of head location. The block diagram of the face finder system is shown in Fig. 1.2 which consists of a two-stage object detection and alignment stage, a contrast normalization stage, a feature extraction stage, followed by recognition (and, optionally, facial coding.) Fig. 1.2(b)-(e) illustrates the operation of the detection and alignment stage on a natural image containing a human face.

The first step in this process is illustrated in Fig. 1.2(c) where the MAP estimate of the position and scale of the face are indicated by the cross-hairs and bounding box. Once these regions have been identified, the estimated scale and position are used to normalize for translation and scale, yielding a standard "head-in-the-box" format image (Fig. 1.2(d)). A second feature detection stage operates at this fixed scale to estimate the position of 4 facial features: the left and right eyes, the tip of the nose and the center of the mouth (Fig. 1.2(e)). Once the facial features have been detected, the face image is warped to align the geometry and shape of the face with that of a canonical model. Then the facial region is extracted (by applying a fixed mask) and subsequently normalized for contrast. This geometrically aligned and normalized image is then projected onto the set of eigenfaces shown in Figure 1.3(a).

The projection coefficients obtained by comparison of the normalized face and the eigenfaces form a feature vector which accurately describes the appearance of the face. This feature vector can therefore be used for facial recognition, as well as for facial image coding. Fig. 1.3(b) shows a typical result when using the eigenface feature vector for face recognition. The image in the upper left is the one to be recognized and the remainder are the most similar faces in the database (ranked by facial similarity, left to right, top to bottom). The top three matches in this case are images of the same person taken a month apart and at different scales. The recognition accuracy of this system (defined as the percent correct rank-one matches) is 99% [222].

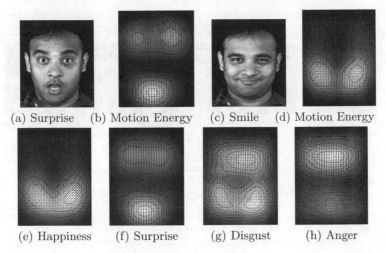

(a) Surprise   (b) Motion Energy   (c) Smile   (d) Motion Energy

(e) Happiness   (f) Surprise   (g) Disgust   (h) Anger

Fig. 1.4 Determining expressions from video sequences. (a) and (c) show expressions of smile and surprise, and (b) and (d) show the corresponding spatio-temporal motion energy pattern. (e) - (h) show spatio-temporal motion-energy templates for various expressions.

1.2.3 Expression Recognition

Once the face and its features have been accurately located, one can begin to analyze its motion to determine the facial expression. This can be done by using spatio-temporal motion-energy templates of the whole face [119, 120]. For each facial expression, the corresponding template expresses the *peak amount* and *direction* of motion that one would expect to see at each point on the face. Figures 1.4(a) - (d) show Irfan Essa making two expressions (surprise and smile) and the corresponding motion-energy template descriptions.

These simple, biologically-plausible motion energy "templates" can be used for expression recognition by comparing the motion-energy observed for a particular face to the "average" template for each expression. Figures 1.4(e) - (h) show the motion-energy templates for several expressions. To classify an expression one compares the observed facial motion energy with each of these motion energy templates, and then picks the expression with the most similar pattern of motion.

This method of expression recognition has been applied to a database of 52 image sequences of 8 subjects making various expressions. In each image sequence the motion energy was measured, compared to each of the templates, and the expression classified, generating the confusion

Expressions	Smile	Surprise	Anger	Disgust
Template				
Smile	**12**	0	0	0
Surprise	0	**10**	0	0
Anger	0	0	**9**	0
Disgust	0	0	1	**10**
Success	100%	100%	90%	100%

Table 1.1 *Results of facial expression recognition using spatio-temporal motion energy templates. This result is based on 12 image sequences of smile, 10 image sequences of surprise, anger, disgust, and raise eyebrow. Success rate for each expression is shown in the bottom row. The overall recognition rate is 98.0%.*

matrix shown in Table 1.1. This table shows just one incorrect classification, giving an overall recognition rate of 98.0%. For additional details see [119, 120].

1.2.4 Vision-Driven Audio

Audio interpretation of people is as important as visual interpretation. Although much work as been done on speech understanding, virtually all of this work assumes a closely-placed microphone for input and a fixed listening position. Speech recognition applications, for instance, typically require near-field ($< 1.5m$) microphone placement for acceptable performance. Beyond this distance, the signal-to-noise ratio of the incoming speech effects the performance significantly; most commercial speech-recognition packages typically break down over a 4 to 6 DB range.

The constraint of near-field microphone placement makes audio difficult to integrate into normal human life, so it is necessary to find a solution that allows the user to move around with no noticeable degradation in performance. The solution to this problem is to use the head-tracking

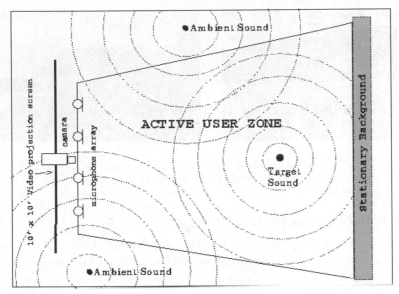

Fig. 1.5. Geometry of the vision-directed phased-array microphone system

ability of Pfinder to steer the audio input so that it focuses on the user's head.

There are several potential ways to steer audio input. One is to use a highly directional microphone, that can be panned using a motorized control unit, to track the user's location. However, this requires a significant amount of mounting and control hardware, is limited by the speed and accuracy of the drive motors, and can only track one user at a time.

It is therefore preferable to have a directional response that can be steered electronically. This can be done with the well-known technique of beam forming with an array of microphone elements, as illustrated in Fig. 1.5(a). Though several microphones need to be used for this method, they need not be very directional and they can be permanently mounted in the environment. In addition, the signals from the microphones in the array can be combined in as many ways as the available computational power is capable of, allowing for the tracking of multiple moving sound sources from a single microphone array. For additional detail, see references [15, 21].

(a)   (b)

Fig. 1.6 (a) Real-time reading of American Sign Language (with Thad Starner doing the signing), and (b) real-time classification of driver's actions in a driving simulator.

1.2.5 Recognizing Human Behaviors

Work on recognizing body position, face, expression, and sound are only the first steps toward perceptual intelligence. To make computers really useful, these basic perceptual functions need to be integrated with higher-level models of human behavior, so that we can begin to understand what the person is *doing*.

A general approach to interpreting human behavior is to directly extend the MAP techniques used for recognition of face, expression, and body pose. That is, to track the 2D parametric appearance models over time, and then probabilistically characterize the time evolution of their parameters. This approach produces the PDF of the behavior as both a function of time and 2D appearance. Behaviors can then be recognized by comparing them to these learned models using MAP methods. To obtain high accuracy behavior recognition, one must use an elastic spatio-temporal matching technique such as dynamic time warping [102] or Hidden Markov Modeling [278].

To recognize particular gestures or behaviors, for instance, the person is modeled as a Markov device, with internal mental states that have their own particular distribution of appearance and inter-state transition probabilities. Because the internal states of a human are not directly observable, they must be determined through an indirect estimation process, using the person's movement and vocalizations as measurements. One efficient and robust method of accomplishing this is to use the Viterbi recognition methods developed for use with Hidden Markov Models (HMM).

This general approach is similar to that taken by the speech recognition community. The difference is that here internal state is not thought of as being just words or sentences; the internal states can also be actions or intentions. Moreover, the input is not just audio filter banks but also facial appearance, body movement, and vocal characteristics, such as pitch, as inputs to infer the user's internal state. Two good examples of that employ this approach to behavior recognition are reading American Sign Language (ASL) [278], and interpreting automobile driver's behavior [239].

The ASL reader is a real-time system that performs high-quality classification of a forty-word subset of ASL using only the hand measurements provided by Pfinder (e.g., hand position, orientation, and width/height ratio). Thad Starner is shown using this system in Fig. 1.6(a). The accurate classification performance of this system is particularly impressive because in ASL the hand movements are rapid and continuous, and exhibit large coarticulation effect.

The second system interprets people's actions while driving a car [239]. In this system the driver's hand and leg motions were observed while driving in the Nissan Cambridge Basic Research Lab's driving simulator (see Fig. 1.6(b)). These observations are used to classify the driver's action as quickly as possible. The goal is to develop safer cars by having the automobile "observe" the driver, continuously estimate the driver's internal state (what action they are taking), and respond appropriately.

I found that the system was surprisingly accurate at identifying which driving maneuver the driver was beginning to execute (e.g., passing, turning, stopping, or changing lane). A recognition accuracy of 95.24%± 3.1% was obtained at 0.5 seconds after the beginning each maneuver, long before the major, functional parts of the maneuver were executed. This experiment shows that drivers execute *preparatory* movements that are reliable indicators of which maneuver they are beginning to execute.

1.3 Putting It All Together

Given these building blocks of perceptual intelligence, it is possible to try to "put it all together" and actually build autonomous creatures ("agents") that interact with people in a natural, life-like manner without use of goggles, position sensors, or wires. The ALIVE experiment, which stands for "Artificial Life Interactive Video Environment," has accomplished this goal [206]. Rather than try to model human-like agents immediately, however, the creatures in ALIVE are (mostly) animals. The hope was that in this manner we could focus on the basics of achieving natural, life-like behavior, without being distracted by the difficulties of modeling natural language or complex application domains.

ALIVE uses a single video camera to obtain a color image of a person, which is then placed (with correct depth and occlusion) within a 3D graphical world. The resulting image is projected onto a large screen that faces the user and acts as a type of "magic mirror" (Figure 1.7): the user sees herself surrounded by objects and agents. No goggles, gloves, or wires are needed for interaction with the virtual world. The creatures in this virtual world are autonomous, behaving entities that use the camera and microphones to sense the actions of the participant, interpret them, and react to them in real time. The perceptual intelligence of these agents is truly active and purposive [16, 9]

The creatures in ALIVE are modeled as autonomous semi-intelligent agents using principles drawn from the ethology literature [201]. They have a set of internal needs and motivations, a set of sensors to perceive their environment, a repertoire of activities that they can perform, and a physically-based motor system that allows them to move in and act on the virtual environment. A behavior system decides in real-time which activity to engage in to meet the internal needs of the agent and to take advantage of opportunities presented by the current state of the environment. The agent's kinematic state is updated according to the motor activities associated with the chosen behaviors, and the agent rendered on the graphics display. The user's location and hand and body gestures affect the behavior of the agents, and the user receives visual as well as auditory feedback about the agents' internal state and reactions.

The ALIVE system is built using Blumberg's and Maes's behavior modeling tools for developing semi-intelligent autonomous agents [43, 205]; its goal is to produce agents that select an optimal activity on every time step given their internal needs and motivations, past history, and the perceived environment with its attendant opportunities, challenges, and changes. The activities are chosen such that the agents neither dither among multiple activities, nor persist too long in a single activity. The behavior system is capable of interrupting a given activity if a more pressing need or an unforeseen opportunity arises.

When using the behavior toolkit to build an agent, the designer specifies:

- *The motivations or internal needs of the agent.* Internal needs are modeled as variables which may vary over time. For example, the "dog" agent in ALIVE has the internal need to receive attention from the user. Whenever the user pats the dog, this variable will temporar-

ily decrease in value and as a result the dog will be less motivated to
seek human attention.

- *The activities and actions of the agent.* An agent's set of activities
  is organized as a loose hierarchy with the top of the hierarchy representing more general activities and the leaves representing more
  specific activities. For example, the dog agent has several top-level
  activities such as Playing, Feeding, Drinking, etc. A top-level activity
  such as Feeding has several children: Chewing, Preparing-to-Eat, and
  Searching-for-Food. Searching-for-Food in turn has three children:
  Wander, Avoid-Obstacles, Move-to-Food, and so on. The lowest-level
  activities control the motor system, for example, making the dog move
  a little to the left or right, or making it bark in a certain way.

- *The virtual sensors of the agent.* The sensors of the agent are uniform
  between the real world and the virtual world. For instance, a distance
  sensing action aimed at the user will use the camera to estimate distance, whereas the same action aimed at another virtual creature will
  fire a ray in the direction of other creature and measure the distance
  to intersection with the other creature's bounding box.

Given the above information, the behavior system selects the activities most relevant to the agent at a particular moment in time given
the state of the agent, the situation it finds itself in, and its recent behavior history. One of the design goals of the behavior system, and the
modeling system in general, was that it be compatible with a physically-
based simulated motor system such as those proposed by Raibert [249]
or Zeltzer [331]. Consequently, the ALIVE agents use a combination of
physically-based and kinematic modeling to implement the motor system; Featherstone's spatial algebra [123] and an adaptive-step-size RKF
numerical integrator are used to model the movement of the agent in
response to forces applied by its driving motor. Details of the behavior
and modeling systems are reported upon in [43] and [42].

The ALIVE system represents the user as a "special" sort of 3D agent.
The position and state of the user-agent are based on the information
computed by the vision system (e.g., position, gesture) and the auditory
system (e.g., speech recognition, pitch recognition [21]). This allows the
artificial agents to sense the user using the same virtual sensors that
they use to detect virtual objects and other virtual agents. The person
agent is rendered in the final image using the live video image of the
actual user mapped to the correct place in the 3D virtual world.

In the most recent version of ALIVE the user interacts with a vir-

Fig. 1.7 (a) Image of user is composited in 3D with computer graphics; here the dog responds to pointing gesture by sitting. (b) Another example of a recognized gesture; the dog walks in direction indicated by user. (c) The dog shakes hands with user; note that this behavior depends on knowing the stance of the user. (d) The dog standing on hind legs to mimic user's gesture.

tual dog, as shown in Fig. 1.7. The dog has a repertoire of behaviors that include playing, feeding, drinking, receiving attention, and sleeping. The dog also uses auditory input, consisting of simple verbal commands that are recognized using a commercial speech recognition system, and produces auditory output, consisting of a wide variety of prerecorded samples which are played at appropriate times. The dog has both interactive behaviors and autonomous action; while its primary goal is to play with the user, internal motivations (e.g., thirst) will occasionally override.

This system has been installed in several public exhibitions, which has allowed us to gather experience with thousands of users in the system. The overwhelming majority report that they enjoy interacting with the system and consider the actions and reactions of objects and agents believable. I consider people's reactions to these systems to be a sort of informal Turing test; for instance, people attribute all sorts of intentions, goals, and reasoning ability to the dog, that is, they treat it as if it were an intelligent creature.

1.4 Conclusion

I have described my progress toward building computer systems that understand people, and can work with them in the manner of an attentive human-like assistant. To accomplish this I have built a series of experimental testbeds, called *Smart Rooms*, that are able to answer some of the who, what, where, when, and why questions with respect to human behavior.

These Smart Rooms have used cameras and microphones to accomplish real-time 3D tracking of head, hands, and feet, as well as recognition of hand and body gestures. The system can also support face recognition and interpretation of facial expression. By developing the perceptual intelligence needed to interpret human behaviors, and coupling them to a simple set of motor reactions, we have been able to build autonomous creatures that interact with people in an interesting and even lifelike manner. My hope is that this is the first step toward the development of truly useful computer assistants.

2
GestureComputer – History, Design and Applications

C. Maggioni and B. Kämmerer

Abstract

We describe a video-based system, called GestureComputer, for contact-less man-machine interaction. The system is able to detect human hand gestures and head movement in real-time. The software runs on state-of-the-art workstations without the need for special hardware and requires only a moderate amount of the available computational power, thus leaving room for the "real" application. We discuss the motivation, design ideas, underlying algorithms, applications, and product ideas of the GestureComputer system. Usability tests show the benefits obtained. The present chapter describes the system set-up and different approaches to gray-value and color segmentation. The segmentation of the human head as well as the recognition of the hand and different gestures are outlined. Supporting approaches for system calibration, definition of tracking regions, and data filtering are considered. Realisations on different platforms are the basis for applications that find their way to future products. Included are areas in medicine, virtual reality, communication, and unstructured environments. The chapter closes with results of a usability study and an outlook to further improvements for extended functionality.

2.1 Introduction

2.1.1 It all Started in the Bathtub

In autumn 1991 Christoph was lying in his bathtub and relaxing when his girlfriend came in. She asked how many chocolate bars he would like to eat. For some reasons he did not want to talk and just showed her the hand gesture for the number two. Suddenly the idea came to him - why

23

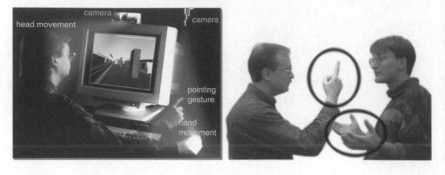

Fig. 2.1. (a) GestureComputer Set up. (b) Human-human interaction

not building a vision-based computer system that is able to recognise human hand gestures. Christoph searched the literature. Recognising that he was not the first person with this idea, he convinced his colleagues at Siemens, built a prototype system, and finally got approval for a research project. The rest of the story to date will be told on the remaining pages.

2.1.2 Motivation

Many existing and potential domains of computer applications suffer from input and output devices that are not well suited for the task at hand. For example visualisations of three-dimensional structures are difficult to manipulate and control with keyboard or mouse commands. Careful investigation of human interactions soon reveals the important role of hand gestures for communicating with other people and for manipulating three-imensional objects (Fig. 2.1b).

Hauptman [144] stated that there are intuitive, common principles for gesture communication forming a communication channel equally accessible to all computer users. The human hand is a very skilled input device able to coordinate many degrees of freedom at the same time. Thus it is naturally suited to control complex applications, which otherwise would have to be adjusted by a variety of control panels. As a consequence, three dimensional hand gesture recognition will form a very natural and easy to use computer interface [126, 318].

Besides the control of applications, the visualisation of 3D data becomes a more and more urgent challenge. Conventionally, stereo images are used to give a three-dimensional perception of an object rendered

Fig. 2.2. (a) Manipulation. (b) Holographic display

onto a two-dimensional screen. To supply the different images head-mounted displays with two screens, or special glasses (red-green or by shutter) allowing a time-sequential presentation with just one display, are used. Both techniques require the user to wear something in addition, to care for expensive and sensitive equipment and to cope with difficulties if he/she already needs glasses. A new approach to improve depth perception is called *virtual holography* [14]. The position of the human head is tracked and the image on the computer screen is updated accordingly to the changes in line of sight. This creates the illusion of the screen being a window into a three-dimensional world where the user may "look behind" objects or "look around the corner".

Those findings led us to focus research on novel input devices that utilise head and hands to control complex computer applications (Fig. 2.2). Now this is not a unique idea since systems for hand-gesture recognition using the DataGlove [334] or the determination of the 3D-position employing Polhemus sensors are well known. In contrast to those solutions we emphasised non-immersive and non-obstructive devices that do not hinder users and therefore increase the acceptance for their deployment in everyday tasks. Consequently, the decision was to use video cameras that observe head and hand movements thereby relieving users from cables, gloves, helmets, or even whole suits. Previous approaches to using a computer vision system as an input device for computer applications include the Videodesk [185], the Mandala system [301], the DigitalDesk [310] and GEST [270, 251]. All these systems have the limitations of dealing with only two-dimensional gestures, requiring a controlled uni-

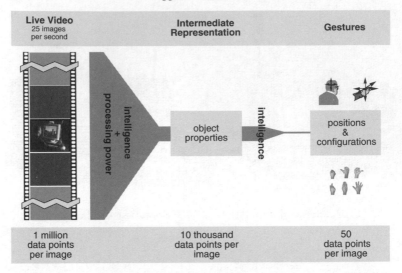

Fig. 2.3. Required data reduction

form image background, and using a lot of computational power and special hardware.

A comprehensive and more recent overview on video-based gesture recognition systems can be found in [151]. A collection of relevant articles on the topic is available in [31]. Further reading on the Gesture-Computer project was published in [317, 209, 210, 3, 208, 165].

We use the video based system as an additional input device to new or existing computer systems. From an industrial viewpoint any new input device has to be cheap, since it has to compete with existing low-cost solutions that have already found their way into products. In addition, performance, functionality, and robustness have to show claer advantages that persuade the company to spend money for costly developments. With the advent of powerful multimedia workstations, video input is available with no additional cost. This focuses our task on design and realisation of smart algorithms that reduce the enormous amount of video data to handsome numbers that can be processed in real-time, even leaving the possibility to run applications on the same machine (Fig. 2.3).

Taking all requirements into consideration we developed a computer system that is able to work in real-time on a standard workstation under

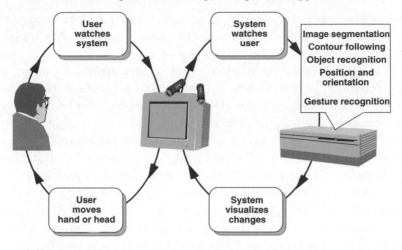

Fig. 2.4. GestureComputer overview

noisy and changing environmental conditions, and that detects the three-dimensional position and orientation of the human hand as well as the position of the head.

2.1.3 An Overview on the System Set up

Fig. 2.4 shows our proposed system structure that involves a classical feedback loop. Images of the user and his/her hand are acquired by CCD-cameras. The human hand is segmented using image processing techniques. Its position and orientation in 3D space are computed. Gestures are recognised and the interaction of the user's hand with the application is determined. Finally a three-dimensional model of the virtual hand is rendered on the screen.

When moving the real hand, the user sees the corresponding movement of the virtual hand on the screen. Human hand-eye co-ordination allows the user to control the system even if the image processing is somewhat inaccurate. Since our system operates in a feedback loop, timing is a crucial issue. If the total time needed for the whole loop is longer than 1/10 of a second the user will likely be confused and over-compensate, bringing the system to an unstable state [302]. The image processing system has to satisfy conflicting demands. On one hand it has to be reliable, stable and insensitive to changes in the image background and lighting conditions. On the other hand it has to be sufficiently fast. Since the CCD camera provides an enormous amount of data we have to use some ingenuity to arrive at a real-time system. The physical layout of the system and the position of the camera depend highly on the application. A natural place to put the camera is on top of the monitor facing the user, where it can also be used for video-conference applications. However, for applications requiring extensive use this is not a very good set-up. Without support for the elbow, raising the hand continually tires the arm (similar problems are encountered in DataGlove applications). The system configuration we use most frequently is to fix the camera above the monitor looking down onto the desk. The user can accomplish 2D operations by moving the hand on the desktop surface, whereas 3D gestures can be done by raising the hand. Thus we combine the benefits of the 2D mouse with those of 3D manipulation. Other possible set-ups include placing the camera on the ceiling, on a wall or even inside the keyboard looking upwards (see Section 3). For co-operative work a set-up where the monitor is mounted horizontally and the camera is looking down observing the hand movement and gestures of multiple users may be useful.

2.2 Approaches

We have chosen two different approaches for detecting the position and gestures of the human hand and head. Both share common building blocks that will be described in detail in the following sections.

The first one works on gray-level images and uses a cotton glove with an attached marker to speed up and simplify the image processing task (Fig. 2.5a). The marker simplifies the image processing by providing a well-constrained object to be recognised and tracked for continuous hand position determination. The second approach takes a color image as input. The image is segmented to find patches of human skin color by using a very fast color classifier (Fig. 2.5b).

Fig. 2.6 shows the building blocks of the GestureComputer system. They are used in different combinations and will be described in the next sections. Using these blocks we are able to detect the marker in gray-level images as well as human hand and head in color images.

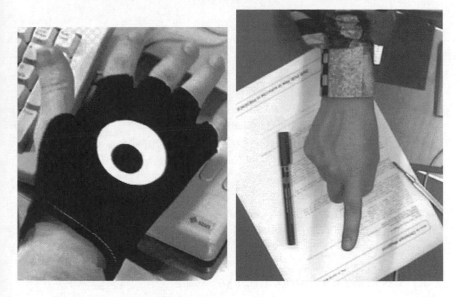

Fig. 2.5. (a) Gray-value image with marker. (b) Color hand image

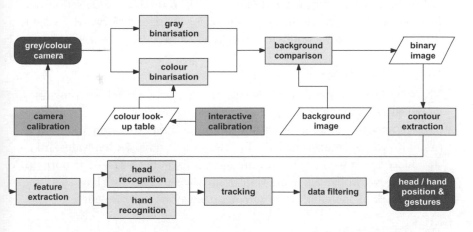

Fig. 2.6. Building Blocks

2.2.1 Image Calibration

The image is transferred into computer memory by using standard computer frame-grabber hardware. The image acquisition system has to be calibrated for the geometric set-up, the lens distortion of the camera, and the lighting conditions. A special calibration pattern with black, white and colored patches is either shown to the camera or projected onto the workspace by using a video projector.

A feature extraction algorithm determines the position and color values of the different patches. Calibration of the geometric set-up and lens distortion is done by using Tsai's method [292]. Frame-grabber parameters, due to camera gain, shutter speed, white balance, and color saturation, are adjusted using the color values of specific patches for an incremental match to predefined values.

2.2.2 Creating a Binarised Image

To reduce the amount of data and to allow an efficient computation of image contours we first convert the image into a binary representation. In case of a gray-value image, binarisation is straightforward. When using color images we apply a color classifier to do the binarisation.

Gray-level Based System

The gray-level image of the glove with marker is binarised by applying a global threshold (Fig. 2.5, Fig. 2.7). Knowledge of the form of the marker pattern and positional information computed in a later step are used to calculate an updated threshold for the initial binarisation value from the observed gray-values of the image. This is necessary due both to changing overall lighting conditions and to local effects such as shadows on the back of the hand when moving it away from light sources.

Color-Based System

In case of color images we use a classifier that decides if an object has skin color, thus performing the binarisation step. To improve speed we generate a look-up table that is addressed with the RGB-values of an image pixel. The values stored in the table-cells are the result of the color classifier. We have built a tool that enables the user to interactively generate this table. In a real-time video window the user specifies positive and negative examples of image regions with skin and background color. A positive/negative classifier is fed with this information,

Fig. 2.7. (a) Binarised gray-level input. (b) Skin color classification (hand)

Fig. 2.8. Skin color classification (head)

identifies regions in color space that have skin color and constructs the look-up table. Experiments have shown that the system is insensitive to moderate changes in lighting. The color segmentation is valid for a wide range of human skin types without need for retraining the color look-up table (Fig. 2.7b, Fig. 2.8).

Improvements Using a Background Image

By using a background image the performance and quality of the above segmentation step can be greatly improved. When starting the system we copy the first image into a background store. Whenever the binarisation of a pixel has to be done the pixel is first compared to the corresponding background pixel. If they differ by a certain threshold the above binarisation is performed. Otherwise the pixel is regarded as belonging to the background and therefore non skin-colored. The update of the background store is done by using information from the object segmentation process. All objects that have been identified as skin-colored but do not belong to head or hand regions are copied into the background store. The regions that have been hidden by head or hand and become visible when the user moves are also copied into the background.

2.2.3 Finding Object Contours

The result of the processing described above is a binarised image. The contours of the image objects are detected using a contour following algorithm similar to that of Pavlidis [233]. The algorithm scans the image line by line to find a jump in the pixel value, follows the contour and stores the chain-code in a list. Since all contours are closed, the process will eventually reach the starting point and scanning of the image continues. By using prior knowledge about the minimum size of the hand or head in the image, we can greatly speed up the scanning process by only sampling a grid of lines that is small enough to touch the desired objects in all cases. Suppose the interesting objects have a minimum height being 1/10 of the image height. The number of necessary pixel operations is computed as 1/10 times the image height for scanning a line plus the number of contour points. This is far below the total number of image pixels and is one key to the excellent performance of the algorithm.

2.2.4 Computing Moments as Object Features

The recognition of objects independent of their position, size, and orientation is an important goal in image processing and methods have been developed that are based on moment invariants [150, 198]. The two-dimensional moments of order p, q of an area A computed in a discrete, binarised image with image coordinates x, y is defined as:

$$m_{p,q} = \sum_{(x,y) \in A} \sum x^p y^q. \tag{2.1}$$

In particular $m_{0,0}$ is the area of A and $(m_{1,0}/m_{0,0}, m_{1,0}/m_{0,0})$ is the center of mass. The number of operations needed to compute the moments directly is proportional to the number of points in A. However, Green's theorem allows us to reduce the amount of calculations by an order of magnitude just by following the border of the area [198]. Let A be a simple connected domain and B the boundary of A in the clockwise direction, the moment calculation is equivalent to:

$$m_{p,q} = \frac{1}{p+1} \sum_{(x_i,y_i) \in B}^{N} \sum x_i^{p+1} y_i^q \Delta y_i \tag{2.2}$$

where $\Delta y_i = 1$ for $y_{i+1} > y_i$; $\Delta y_i = 0$ for $y_{i+1} = y_i$ or $\Delta y_i = -1$ for $y_{i+1} < y_i$. We use the outline of each area computed in the contour following step to calculate the first three moments $(m_{0,0}, m_{1,0}, m_{0,1})$ as well as some other object features. Note that each moment calculation step can be done together with the contour-following thus improving the algorithm's speed.

2.2.5 Object Recognition

Marker-Based Approach

In case of a gray-level image we use a marker-based approach to detect the human hand wearing a marked glove. The contours and moments computed in the previous step are used to detect the marker that can be characterised by the following:

- There are two objects that are circular with approximately the same centers.
- The outer circle is white and the inner one is black.
- The circle size has to be within known upper and lower bounds.
- We know the ratio of circle sizes.
- We know the previous position of the marker in the image.

The previous constraints are strong and misclassifications are very unlikely. Having detected the marker, we compute the parameters of position and orientation in space. The position in x and y direction is given by the center of mass derived from the moment calculation.

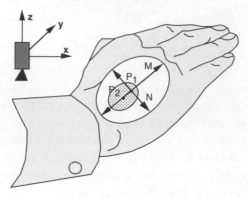

Fig. 2.9. Geometrical properties of the marker

The distance from the camera is a function of the known real marker size, camera parameters such as focal length, and the observed area of the marker in the image. The rotational parameters can be derived as follows: the line between the centers of the two circles P_1 and P_2 of the marker gives us the rotation of the hand along the z axes. Due to rotation around the x and y axes, a marker circle in general appears as an ellipse (Fig. 2.9). The major and minor axes M, N of an ellipse can be computed from the central moments and are used to determine the rotation around the x and y axes [332]. Note that we have ambiguities in the sign of the rotation around the x and y axes. In practice we can neglect this problem and constrain the hand rotations only to positive values.

Color-Based Approach: Detecting a Human Head

The head detection algorithm computes the position of the human head in the image plane (x, y, z). We use the contour and moment data computed in the previous step as input to the color-based head detector. First the contour data is searched for the object with the biggest area that fulfils certain size constrains and that matches the form of a human head (e.g. is elliptical). Sometimes it may happen that the head is split into several disconnected contour objects. This might happen in cases with spotlights on the skin, when the user wears glasses or has a beard. By using a connected components algorithm we merge the different parts belonging to the head object into one new object. The shape of the new head object is further analysed and the center of the forehead is determined by using a histogram approach that can deal with segmentation

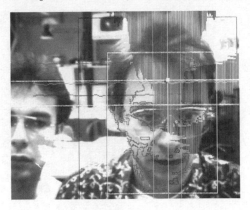

Fig. 2.10. Human head detection

errors (Fig. 2.10). The distance of the head from the camera is roughly estimated by calculating the width of the head area.

Colour-Based Approach: Detecting a Human Hand and its Gestures

The hand recognition system is able to detect the position of the palm in the image plane (x, y), the distance to the camera (z) and six static hand gestures based on finger configurations. The contour data computed in the previous steps form the input of the hand, fingertip, and gesture recognition process. The contour data is searched for a hand-shaped object that fulfils known size constrains. To remove jags, the contour data is smoothed by using a running average algorithm. The center of the hand contour is determined using the center of gravity and a region shrinking algorithm. Candidates for fingertips are defined as points that form a local maximum of distance from the center of the hand. To verify the fingertip points and to determine the correct position of the finger-tip we search for the longest T-like structure starting at the fingertip (Fig. 2.11a).

For each fingertip point F all pairs of points $(P1, P2)$ to the right and left side of the contour having the same distance to F are determined. The pair with the maximum value of d_1/d_2 where d_1 is bigger than a certain value is selected as the T-shape that best describes the finger. The value d_1 specifies the length of the finger and d_2 the width. To implement finger tracking over time all fingertip points are fed into a algorithm based on dynamic programming that tries to match the fin-gertips at time t to the fingertips at time $t - 1$. Because of the small

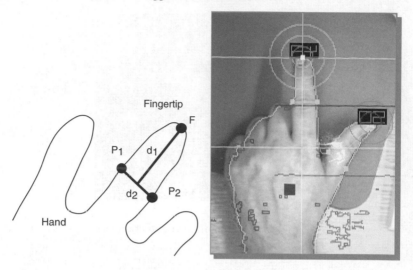

Fig. 2.11. Fingertip detection and tracking

number of fingertip points and the fact that the input is an ordered list, dynamic programming can be used efficiently (Fig. 2.11).

Finally, the fingertips are matched to a model of the human hand and static hand gestures are recognised. These gestures are defined by the number of visible fingers and their orientation relative to each other and to the palm. Fig. 2.12 shows an overview of some of the gestures we are able to recognise. The surrounding rectangle of the head or hand region is determined and all object pixel outside this region are regarded as new background pixels used to update the background store.

2.2.6 Tracking Regions

As we are processing real-time image sequences we can apply the knowledge from the current frame in order to predict features of consecutive frames. We use motion-estimation techniques to estimate the size and position of a region of interest to search for the marker, hand or head in the next image. In practical experiments this reduces the number of computations by a factor of five.

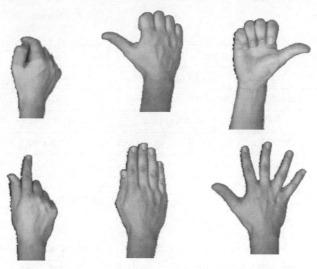

Fig. 2.12. Recognisable hand gestures

2.2.7 Data Filtering

In a final step the position data of the head, the palm, and the finger-tips are filtered using running average and hysteresis filters. We have developed a new directional hysteresis filter. In contrast to well known one-dimensional filters with a constant hysteresis threshold we use a threshold that is weighted with the angular difference of consecutive two or three-dimensional movement vectors. The main advantage of this filter is that small movements in similar directions are not suppressed. Sudden changes in direction that may occur in the case of light flickering or segmentation errors are eliminated. Knowledge about the movement characteristics of human heads and hands are used to eliminate sudden jumps in the position data.

2.3 System Aspects and Implementation

2.3.1 Structure of the Software

The GestureComputer system consists of three building blocks: a library to perform the hand and head segmentation; camera calibration; and the color classifier tools. The algorithms are implemented in C and can be easily configured to match the specific demand. The data abstraction of the frame-grabber interface makes it relatively easy to move

Computer	Image Size	MHz	Frames per sec
SGI Indy, Irix 5.3, built in grabber	640x480	150	20
Sun Sparc 10, SunOS 4.1, S2200 grabber	512x512	65	15
PC - Pentium, Win 3.1, Spea Showtime	320x240	90	16
PC - Pentium, Win 95, Matrox Meteor	320x240	120	25
Laptop 486DX2, Win 3.1, PCMCIA grabber	120x90	75	8
Mac Performa 630, MAC-OS 7.5.2, built in grabber	320x240	66	10

Table 2.1. *Performance of HeadTracking*

to a new platform. Currently a port to C++ that will speed up the development of new algorithms and portability is underway. An Application Programmers Interface exists that can be easily used. To get the head position, for example, the programmer has to call a function get-head-position(data). All the initialisation of the software is hidden and occurs when the function is called for the first time.

2.3.2 Implementation Platforms and Performance

We have ported the GestureComputer software to different computer platforms with different types of frame-grabbers. Platforms are SUN, Silicon Graphics Indy, Siemens RW 410, PC (Win 3.1 and Win 95) and Apple Macintosh. Table 2.1 shows the average performance of the head tracking algorithm integrated into the Virtual Cameraman application (see section 4.5) on different platforms.

2.4 Application Areas and Prototypes

2.4.1 User Interface

Virtual reality systems are one of the many application areas for video-based hand gesture recognition and head tracking. We avoid building an immersive virtual reality system that aims at the best possible simulation of an 3D world. Such systems use complex devices like head mounted displays and data gloves, but do not allow the user to interact with the real office world. In contrast our goal is to develop systems, sometimes called Desktop VR, that benefit from three-dimensional representations

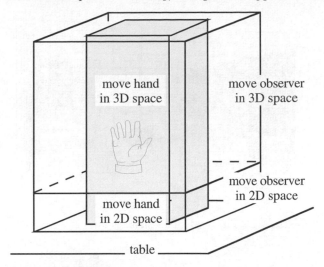

Fig. 2.13. Control volume for hand input

of virtual environments but use standard computer monitors and non-obstructive input devices.

Hand Control

Currently we use the hand recognition system to navigate through three-dimensional worlds and to manipulate three-dimensional objects. The observer is modeled by a virtual body whose position and rotation determines his/her point of view and a virtual hand that is used to manipulate objects.

The camera is mounted above the table monitoring a certain volume in space to the right, left or front of the computer screen. When the user is performing tasks requiring 2D input the hand can be moved on the tabletop like in a conventional mouse interface or in Krueger's system [184]. When the user raises a hand to make a complex gesture or to move objects in 3D space, the 3D mode is automatically entered. As long as the real hand is in the inner part of the control volume, it controls the movement of the virtual hand, but when the hand enters the border region, the observer's viewpoint moves in the corresponding direction.

We have designed several virtual worlds as examples of possible applications. Fig. 2.14 shows a simulation of our lab at Siemens, Munich, where one can fly around and move objects. The other example

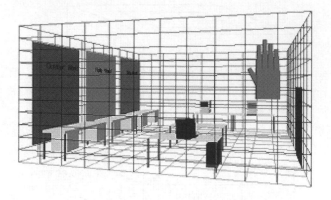

Fig. 2.14. The Siemens lab

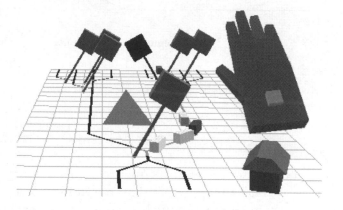

Fig. 2.15. Marshalling-Yard example

(Fig. 2.15) deals with a marshalling yard with animated trains. The user can fly around, touch objects like cars and switches and thus get information about them, or switch the points by touching them with a special gesture and thereby causes the trains to change tracks.

Head Control

The head tracking system is used to control the viewpoint to three-dimensional graphics on a screen forming a virtual holographic system. In this setup a second camera is mounted on top of the computer screen facing the user.

The virtual 3D object is situated in the center of the solid computer

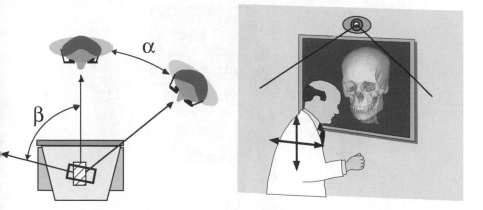

Fig. 2.16. Virtual holography - geometry (a) and CT display (b)

screen. Whenever the user changes the head position his/her line of sight is changed. This angle α is measured by the head tracking system and the 3D graphic is rerendered according to the new line of sight (Fig. 2.16). If the update rate of the system is fast enough (more than 10 frames/sec) the user has the impression of a real 3D object existing inside the volume of the monitor. The effect is similar to a well known experience in real life: Whenever an object cannot be moved we move ourselves around the object and our brain forms the 3D representation. In order to move around the object we introduce a scale factor between the head movement angle α and the virtual object rotation β.

2.4.2 Medicine

Suitable application areas for optical gesture recognition systems can also be found for diagnosis in medical treatment. Doctors will be able to observe three-dimensional computer tomographic scans of the human body, manipulate the viewpoint, perform virtual cuts or zoom in on specific organs by using simple to learn hand gestures. Interactive planning of surgeries (i.e. in minimal invasive surgery) might also benefit from a gesture recognition interface.

A potential application using the head tracking input device is a substitution for the backlit display used nowadays by doctors to view X-rays (Fig. 2.16). Three-dimensional data coming from various sources like computer tomographs, magnetic resonance or ultrasound devices are becoming more common in medicine. We plan to mount a high resolu-

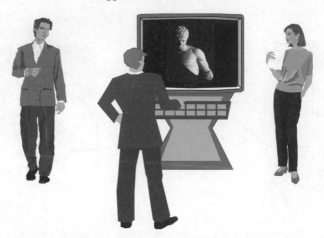

Fig. 2.17. Product placement terminal

tion computer screen on the wall to display this data. The viewpoint into
these 3D visualisations can be changed very easily by moving the head
left/right and up/and down. A few additional buttons on the display or
a speech recognition system will allow the doctor to stop head-tracking
and to proceed to the next data set.

2.4.3 Advertisement

A variation of the above virtual holographic system for medicine can be
used in product placement and advertisement (Fig. 2.17). New products
that only exist as computer graphics can be shown to the public in a
nice way. For use in a kind of virtual museum, pieces of art will be
photographed from all sides, compressed (JPEG) and stored on disk.
The visitor to the holographic museum is able to view the pieces from
many viewpoints by moving around the screen.

2.4.4 Harsh Environments

Another potential for gestural control can be found wherever an awkward
physical environment hampers the operation of complex systems. Gloves
or oily hands make using a keyboard or touch screen tricky. Being able to
select functions or parameters by pointing instead of touching or changing displayed information by moving the head could improve operations

Fig. 2.18. Virtual Cameraman

in industrial plants. During medical operations touchless video-based input devices can help to maintain a highly sterile environment.

2.4.5 Videoconferencing

Videoconferencing applications suffer from two problems: available network bandwidth and space on the computer screen. In a lot of desktop videoconferences the participants typically only want to see the faces of their partners. Thus a camera with a telephoto lens is often used and limits the mobility of the user. Using a wide angle lens allows the users to move in front of the screen but a lot of unnecessary image background is transferred and occupies screen space on the opposite monitor. This is especially true in the case of a video conference with more than two partners and shared applications. We have developed a system called "Virtual Cameraman" that is based on our head-tracking technique and overcomes the above problems. We are using a camera with a wide angle lens but transmit and display only the image area that is occupied by the users head. This frame smoothly follows the user's head movements thus forming a kind of virtual tele camera. Fig. 2.18 shows the geometrical relationship between screen size, full video size and the size of the head image. Using the Virtual Cameraman technique and a standard setup (camera on top of the screen) we can reduce the amount of data to be transferred up to a factor of ten without the need for compression.

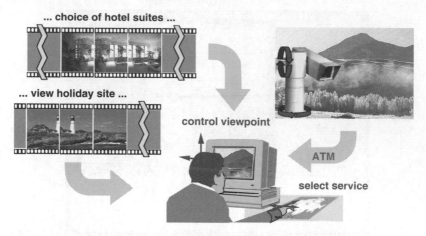

Fig. 2.19. Tele-Tourist application at Telecom 1995

2.4.6 The Tele Tourist - Looking Through the Telescope

For Telecom 1995 in Geneva, Switzerland, we realised an advanced combination of the GestureComputer and ATM telephone link. The GestureComputer served as the local viewing station with an intuitive user interface for the selection of different camera sites (Fig. 2.19). There were six video channels available, four from locally stored panoramic views, one from a video camera positioned at the fair and connected by a direct link, and one from a camera located on top of a building in Lugano, connected via an ATM link. The stored images showed famous places in Switzerland like the Matterhorn, Lac Leman, Uri, or Zurich.

Both live cameras could be adjusted by high speed servos whereas the view at stored images was a window moved electronically over the panorama. The GestureComputer system determined the position of the visitor's head and selected the viewing direction accordingly. Therefore the visitor had the illusion of looking through a telescope at landscapes far away. Because the position was determined quickly, movement was smooth and perception very natural. Selection of video inputs was even more advanced: simply pointing to one of six tiny plastic cameras mounted on a paper map of Switzerland switched the system to the respective video channel. The pointing gesture was actively recognised and other gestures like moving the flat or closed hand over the map were suppressed. This setup showed that a purely gesture based control is feasible, fast, and ergonomic, and people got used to it in short time.

2.4.7 Virtual Touchscreen

Interfaces to technical systems commonly rely on keyboards, switches, mice, or buttons. We propose as an extension to Wellner's [310] approach to use video projection and loudspeaker for the output of information together with speech and video-based gesture recognition for input. The projected display realises a Graphical User Interface on any useful physical surface. The GUI may be designed like a standard window-based display or may be tailored to the specific needs of the system to be controlled. In this way the projected display replaces conventional monitors (CRT, LCD). Commands, abstract information, or text may be input by speech recognition. Special noise reduction approaches help the system to be used even under difficult environmental conditions. By analogy with a touch screen, the input of analog values, positions, and selections is realised by pointing with the hand on the projected GUI. Through this approach any input hardware like keyboard, mouse, traditional touch screen or digitising tablet can be replaced. Pointing gestures and positioning within the GUI is recognised with the help of the GestureComputer system. The combination of the above-mentioned components realises a system that is visible only during operation, allocating working space with task-oriented assignment only during usage. Because the surface under the projection area has to meet minimal requirements regarding reflectivity and shape, any material may be chosen from a broad variety of possibilities. Therefore, completely new and innovative designs for control can be realised. The combination of projection display, speech input, and gesture recognition forms an advanced solution for future systems with applications e.g. for the "office at the sofa table", in medicine, or for Info Kiosks. Compared with physical interface modules positioned at the working areas the following benefits are obvious:

  (i) no permanent space requirements;

 (ii) display and font size easily adjustable by zoom (compares to very limited and expensive screen sizes);

(iii) sterile (e.g. if projection surface consists of high-grade steel);

(iv) safe against vandalism;

 (v) broad variety of suitable surfaces: (office: desktop with paper; household: kitchen table, sofa table; hospital: area besides operative field, production: conveyor belt, Info Kiosk: high-grade steel).

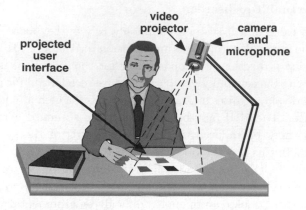

Fig. 2.20. Virtual Touchscreen in the office

VT – Office Application

Often desktops are crowded with electronic equipment like telephones, organisers, or computers. The Virtual Touchscreen offers the possibility of combining all those functionalities within just one system (Fig. 2.20). The user interface will be projected on the desktop only if requested, allowing other documents and equipment to be left where they are. Through a verbal command, an incoming phone call, or a special gesture the system is activated. The necessary modules may be attached to a lever system (or integrated in a desktop lamp) allowing a free choice in placing the GUI on the desktop. Because of the large projection area more complex but nevertheless usable interfaces can be realised.

VT - Public Information Terminals

Public terminals have to be protected against vandalism and environmental influences (dust, moisture, ...). This includes the protection of the monitor against dirt and damage as well as the protection of an input device like a mouse or keyboard against theft. Through the Virtual Touchscreen approach those influences can be minimised (2.21). Every part of the system may be mounted under the ceiling, unreachable for visitors and optimally protected. Only the projection surface has to be made from resistive material that can be easily cleaned.

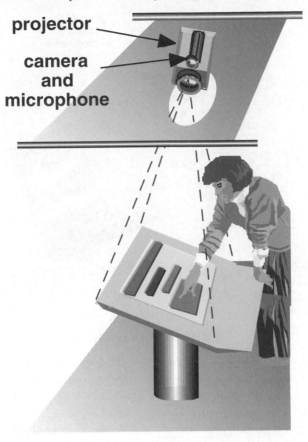

projector

**camera
and
microphone**

Fig. 2.21. Public information terminal

VT - Medicine

During diagnosis and treatment the control of technical equipment hinders doctors and raises problems because of sterility. Moreover, continual change of focus between the treatment area and the display reduces concentration. Both aspects are solved if the interaction area of the Virtual Touchscreen is projected besides the treatment area (Fig. 2.22). Suitable surfaces for projection may be the skin of the patient, a bright cloth, or a steel plate. Using his voice, the doctor activates different modes like system control or display options. A pointing gesture at projected sliders then enables e.g. the modification of contrast or radiation power or the selection of sub-areas for focusing.

Maggioni and Kämmerer

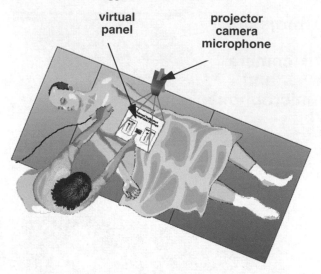

Fig. 2.22. Sterile display and input device

2.5 Usability Study

We performed a usability study on the Virtual Holography aspect of the system together with Professor Al Badre from Georgia Tech University, USA. The overall purpose of the study was to investigate the comparative effectiveness of manipulating objects in a non-immersive 3D space using various controls. In particular, our goal was to evaluate the use of the head to control rotation of 3D objects depicted on a computer display in comparison first with a direct manipulation control device ordinarily used with 2D surfaces (such as a mouse) and second with non-direct manipulation devices (such as wheels to affect rotation and viewpoint changing). The design for the experiment was a simple 3-way comparison between using the mouse only, the combination of mouse and head, or the combination of mouse and wheels to control movement and viewpoint changing. Participants were volunteers from Siemens Munich as well as students, ages 14 to 18 from an international school at Munich. A total of 58 participants were used.

2.5.1 Experiments

Participants were asked to perform a matching task in a 3D environment. Shaped toy-block like objects were presented to the user. These objects

Fig. 2.23. Task to accomplish

had to be fitted to matching holes of plate-shaped objects distributed in the environment. Thus the users had to make viewpoint changes in order to discover the matching plate. Finally, the users placed the object above the correct plate by using the mouse. Fig. 2.23 is a depiction of the 3D image that the participants had to rotate in order to match the object in the lower left corner of the picture. In both experiments, each participant was assigned to one of three main groups. All groups had to place the object by using a mouse as a pointing device. Group 1 was required to control the viewpoint changing of the 3D image with head movement; group 2 had to control viewpoint changing by using the mouse and thus had to toggle between viewpoint change mode and object placing mode by pressing a button; group 3 used the mouse to place objects and a set of wheels to control viewpoint changing (Fig. 2.24).

2.5.2 Usability Test Results

In terms of time to perform the task, the school data shows that the head tracking is the fastest input device for the task. The mouse comes next, while the wheel leads to the worst performance, being about twice as slow as the head tracking (Table 2.2). In the adults' study, the data shows that head tracking is the fastest input device for the task at hand. The mouse comes next, with about a 50%. The wheel leads to the worst performance, being about twice as slow as the head tracking.

The results clearly show that changing the viewpoint into a 3D scene

Fig. 2.24. Set-up of the usability study

Groups	Count	Average	Variance
School participants:			
Head	19	95	823
Mouse	18	141	4294
Wheel	18	137	4501
Siemens participants:			
Head	23	90	784
Mouse	18	133	1938
Wheel	6	176	4167

Table 2.2. *Time used to complete the task*

by using HeadTracking as an input device reduces the problem solving time compared to other input devices. These results are applicable in most domains of three-dimensional interaction.

2.6 Summary: GestureComputer – An Idea becomes Reality.

We have presented approaches for efficient image analysis to achieve real-time gesture recognition and head tracking. Binarisation of gray level or color images and contour extraction serve as basic modules for high level object identification. Knowledge about head and hand geometries is used for detailed examinations that lead to the determination of face areas even under difficult conditions, or to the extraction of fingertips for gesture recognition. The power and robustness of the realised algorithms allow a cost efficient implementation on state-of-the-art hardware, opening the way to real life applications. Head and hand movement, pointing, grabbing – the GestureComputer brings human interaction to technical systems. Applications have been identified that make use of new possibilities and benefit from intuitiveness, freedom, and improved usability through the GestureComputer. Extensive usability tests have scientifically proven the GestureComputer concept. The algorithms will be improved to deal better with changing lighting conditions and to ease the calibration process. New features like eye and mouth detection will be integrated to allow more accurate head position determination. Dynamic gesture and hand-gesture recognition will be added in the near future if requested by application domains. The current redesign phase will yield professional software for integration with products.

3

Human Reader: A Vision-Based Man-Machine Interface

K. Mase

Abstract

This chapter introduces the Human Reader project and some research results of human-machine interfaces based on image sequence analysis. Real-time responsive and multimodal gesture interaction, which is not an easily achieved capability, is investigated. Primary emphasis is placed on real-time responsive capability for head and hand gestural interaction as applied to the project's Headreader and Handreader. Their performances are demonstrated in experimental interactive applications, the CG Secretary Agent and the FingerPointer. Next, we focus on facial expression as a rich source of nonverbal message media. A preliminary experiment in facial expression research using an optical-flow algorithm is introduced to show what kind of information can be extracted from facial gestures. Real-time responsiveness is left to subsequent research work, some of which is introduced in other chapters of this book. Lastly, new directions in vision-based interface research are briefly addressed based on these experiences.

3.1 Introduction

Human body movement plays a very important role in our daily communications. Such communications do not merely include human-to-human interactions but also human-to-computer (and other inanimate objects) interactions. We can easily infer people's intentions from their gestures. I believe that a computer possessing "eyes" in addition to a mouse and keyboard, would be able to interact with humans in a smooth, enhanced and well-organized way by using visual input information. If a machine can sense and identify an approaching user, for example, it

53

can load his/her personal profile and prepare the necessary configuration before he/she starts to use it. If it senses the direction in which the user is looking, it could infer the user's attention and intention. The signals from a human are essentially multimodal because he/she may use every expressive physical function to compose a message in any kind of interaction. Therefore, the computer sensors and interface should be able to deal with the multimodality of human communications. Computers having a "face" and a "body" will also be a great help in facilitating human-computer interaction in various situations by providing the sensation of intimacy with the computer.

There have been many reported concepts of novel interfaces combining speech with nonverbal media such as facial expressions and gestures. Only a few attempts have been made, however, to actually build and test such systems. The author and his colleagues proposed a new interface concept in which the system uses both visual and audio media for human-computer interaction to provide multimodality to the interface [281]. We named this interface system the Human Reader (first described in [214]). It extracts and interprets human actions from vision and speech sensors, and, can accordingly, read the various bits of information emitted from users, such as commands, intentions, emotions, etc., and transfer it to computer application programs. We have developed several modules, called *"part-readers"*, in the first step and then integrated them to realize examples of systems with multimodal interfaces.

In this chapter, we will overview the results of the Human Reader project. First, we discuss the multimodal message interpretation process and describe the configuration of the Human Reader. Then we describe the methods to realize real-time two part-readers, Headreader and Handreader, and their real-time implementations as well as their applications in the context of a CG Secretary and a Finger-pointer. Next, we introduce a non-real-time part-reader, which we call the Facereader. Finally, new directions in interface research are addressed.

3.2 Multimodal Interface and Human Reader

3.2.1 Multimodal Interface

Multimodality does not merely mean using multimedia. Rather, it means that one or a set of elemental actions of a medium (e.g., part) can be interpreted differently by the context and/or the situation. For instance, a hand raising gesture with the index finger up could mean,

Table 3.1. *Human Gesture Media and Messages*

Gesture Media	Messages/ Functions	Example actions
Locator	Indicate location in space	Pointing, Head orientation
Selector	Select from a list	Hand spelling
Valuator	Indicate quantity	Dial manipulation
Imager	Indicate general images and concepts	Body language, facial expression

(i) counting, (ii) pointing, (iii) shaping, or (iv) emphasizing. The same action can mean different things. As humans are used to communicating in a multimodal manner, a multimodal interface is expected to provide natural interaction with the benefits of redundancy, unburdening and summation[46].

If we view human actions as message media it is helpful to categorize the kind of message we are extracting from the actions according to the "graphical input devices" used. Table 3.1 is a categorized list of human gestural media for conveying messages. These media are *selector, locator, valuator* and *imager*. *Selector* media include gestures that select between two or more states. *Locator* media contain pointing actions mainly used to indicate special location. *Valuator* media contain the gestures that indicate quantity, e.g., size of things. The last media, *Imager*, do not appear in the conventional graphical input device list and include gestures that visualize shapes, actions or sensitivities such as "round shape" or "difficult status". Most body language and facial expressions are categorized as belonging to an Imager medium, and thus it has strong expressive power; however, recognition of such sensitive states is quite difficult.

Psychological studies have categorized gestures differently. Ekman proposed five media, i.e., Emblem, Body manipulator, Illustrator, Emotional expression, and Regulator[115, 298]. McNeill categorized hand gestures with voice in more detail, i.e., Iconic, Metaphoric, Beat, and Deictic[68]. These categories cover most human gestures. However, the graphical input device metaphor makes it easy to understand the functionality of each category because we are already very familiar with those physical devices. Psychological categorization will become more impor-

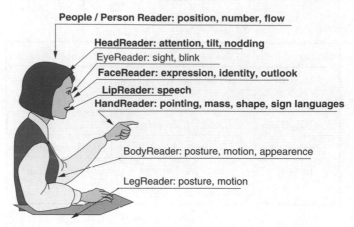

Fig. 3.1. Human Reader: Messages from the human body

tant as the interfaces evolve and distinctions within the imager media become necessary in the future.

3.2.2 Graceful Interaction and Human Reader

Humans emit various messages from their different body parts. Fig. 3.1 shows a few examples of messages, such as attention and nodding messages from head. We have designed an interface system that exploits human actions as media conveying the message of operation. The process starts with sensing of visual/auditory signals, continues with extraction of element actions, and finishes with integration and interpretation. Our approach is building *part-readers*, which correspond to each body part, and then integrating the part-readers to make an interface system.

For example, *Headreader* extracts head action, *Facereader* recognizes facial expressions, *Lipreader* recognizes spoken words from lip actions, and *Handreader* reads hand-pointing actions.

When exploiting computer vision technology for a human-machine interface, its design should have the following features.

   (i) Real-time interaction
  (ii) Evolutional potential
 (iii) Robust processing

The currently proposed algorithms and/or systems have achieved these requirements in the following ways:

(i) Real-time by Simplicity: complexity is minimized for real-time processing because latency is the least acceptable factor in interaction. Sensory devices should provide a high sampling rate, ideally over 100 pps. However, the more vision algorithms are integrated, the more time is consumed.

(ii) Evolutional by Portability: portable programming is necessary because the progress of hardware technology is vary rapid. Portable systems/programs make quick improvements possible.

(iii) Robust by Constraint: many usage conditions are often constrained to achieve quick interaction and robustness, e.g. user group and number, background, illumination and lighting, action, point of interest, resolution and accuracy, and scenario.

The following sections present examples of implementation. Real-time interaction has been realized for Headreader and Handreader. Facereader, however, has been realized as off-line processing in the Human Reader projects to pursue benefits of its functionality rather than the real-time feature. Recent progress in facial expression research for real-time interaction is covered in another chapter by Alex Pentland.

3.3 Headreader

Head action is the basis of upper body gestures along with hand gestures. For example, although facial expression and eye movements convey much information, their action is always relative to head movement. Headreader [214] extracts head action by using the contrast between the head and the face.

3.3.1 Detection of Head Movement

It is said that a human being has the ability to roughly perceive a person's face direction, even if the person is too distant to be recognised. This indicates that humans can perceive head orientation without identifying the eyes and mouth. Rather, we can assume that the contrast between hair and face and the appearance of hair style are sufficient for perceiving head orientation.

Head Projection Model and Motion Parameters

Headreader uses a simple elliptical head model that has a face and hair. Such a head model projected onto a view plane forms areas of the face

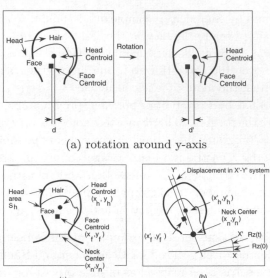

(a) rotation around y-axis

(b) rotation around z-axis

Fig. 3.2. Estimating rotational parameters

and of the whole head. If we consider the centroids of projected areas (the 1st-order momentum), the relative position changes as the head rotates. This is illustrated in Fig. 3.2. The changes are used to calculate the head motion parameters, mostly 3D rotational parameters. Translational parameters are clearly obtained from the position of the head centroid and the change in head area size. The rotational and translational parameters, (R_x, R_y) and (T_x, T_y, T_z), can be defined as follows:

$$R_x(t) = g_{rx}\left((\Delta y_h(t) - \Delta y_f(t))/\sqrt{S_h(t)}\right), \qquad (3.1)$$

$$R_y(t) = g_{ry}\left((\Delta x_h(t) - \Delta x_f(t))/\sqrt{S_h(t)}\right), \qquad (3.2)$$

$$T_x(t) = g_{tx}\left(\Delta x_h(t)/\sqrt{S_h(t)}\right), \qquad (3.3)$$

$$T_y(t) = g_{ty}\left(\Delta y_h(t)/\sqrt{S_h(t)}\right), \qquad (3.4)$$

$$T_z(t) = g_{tz}\left(\sqrt{\Delta S_h(t)/S_h(0)}\right), \qquad (3.5)$$

where $(x_h(t), y_h(t))$ and $(x_f(t), y_f(t))$ are the area centroid positions of head and face, respectively, at time t on the view plane coordinate system. The difference in a quantity from that a time $t = 0$ is given by Δ.

(For example, $\Delta x_h(t) = x_h(t) - x_h(0)\sqrt{S_h(t)/S_h(0)}$.) Similarly, $S_h(t)$ is the size of the head area. The $\{g\}$ are mapping functions, which can be represented by a linear function in the most simplified case, except that g_{rx} is a combination of two linear functions intersecting at $g(0) = 0$. The functions, g_{tx}, g_{ty}, g_{tz}, are also linear. Generally, the $\{g\}$ of (3.1) and (3.2) are represented by inverse trigonometric functions.

When the middle position of neck level is provided, we can compute the rotational parameter around the z-axis by the following equation:

$$R_z(t) = \tan^{-1}\frac{x_h(t) - x_n(t)}{y_h(t) - y_n(t)} - \tan^{-1}\frac{x_h(0) - x_n(0)}{y_h(0) - y_n(0)}, \tag{3.6}$$

where $(x_n(t), y_n(t))$ is the coordinate of the neck mid-point. This is illustrated in Fig. 3.2(b). In this case, we substitute $\Delta x_h(t)$, $\Delta x_f(t)$, $\Delta y_h(t)$, $\Delta y_f(t)$ in equations (3.1) and (3.2) for computing $R_x(t)$ and $R_y(t)$ with the ones in the rotated coordinate system. For example, $\Delta x'_h(t) = x'_h(t) - x_h(0)\sqrt{S_h(t)/S_h(0)}$.

3.3.2 Vision algorithm and implementation

This section discusses the vision algorithm that obtains parameters for the transformations described in the previous section. The algorithm is based on binary thresholding and region extraction. The following constraints are assumed:

(i) camera parameters are constant,
(ii) background scene is stable and illumination does not change,
(iii) head image above shoulder is always available,
(iv) contrast in brightnesses between hair and skin is high,
(v) hair style is similar to that of the head model used.

In addition to the general conditions (i) to (iii) for image sequence processing, conditions (iv) and (v) are limiting constraints of the user group that were necessary for the proposed method to achieve real-time interaction. As described below, however, this method is less affected by the use of eyeglasses or long hair covering the eyes.

Head Area Extraction

First, subtracting the background image $B(x, y)$ from the input image $F_t(x, y)$ produces the silhouette image $s_t(x, y)$:

$$s_t(x, y) = |f_t(x, y) - B(x, y)|, \tag{3.7}$$

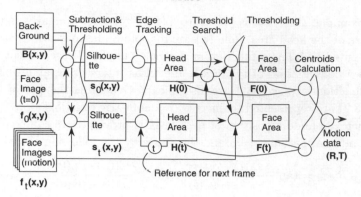

Fig. 3.3. Image processing diagram of headreader

Fig. 3.4. Result of head and facial area extraction

where t is time. Second, scanning and thresholding of the silhouette image extracts head area $H(t)$:

$$H(t) \equiv \{(x,y)|s_t(x,y) > T_h\}, \tag{3.8}$$

where T_h is a previously given threshold. From acquisition conditions (i) and (ii), $T_h = 0$ is sufficient. However, the acquisition conditions may vary because of camera variation, noise, unstable illumination, etc. Accordingly, we use a positive value for T_h. The silhouetting and head extraction proceed simultaneously line-by-line from the top of the image, and searching for edge pixels proceeds from both sides of the image to find the longest run. Fig. 3.4 shows an example result of area extraction.

The head area defined by the above algorithm, $\hat{H}(t)$, is a set of run segments. It is, therefore, different from the $H(t)$ defined by (3.8). The neck position is defined where the length of run segment is minimal or zero within the region far from the head top.

When acquiring a frontal image, $f_0(x, y)$ at time $t = 0$, the process computes the threshold (T_f) for facial area extraction and sets the reference parameters $S_h(0), x_h(0)$ and $y_h(0)$. Automatic threshold selection [230] is employed to chose T_f from the grey-level histogram of $\hat{H}(0)$.

Facial Area Extraction

Facial area extraction is also based on thresholding. The facial area $F(t)$ is defined by the following.

$$F(t) \equiv \{(x, y) | f_t(x, y) > T_f, \, (x, y) \in \hat{H}(t)\}. \qquad (3.9)$$

This is true if the hair is brighter than the face. Otherwise, the inequality is reversed.

Implementation

The feature extraction algorithm and the movement calculation algorithm were implemented on a workstation (SUN4/260) in the C language. Grey images are acquired with an image input system. The image size is 128×120 pixels with 8 bits per pixel. The system transfers input images to the main memory of the workstation, where the entire image processing operation is performed. Image processing takes $0.14--0.16$ seconds per frame. Image acquisition itself takes about 0.12 seconds of the total processing time. Thus, the actual image processing is considered to proceed at video rate.

It would seem at first glance that the accuracy of the processing result is independent of the processing speed. However, we can exploit the coherence between successive frames of an image sequence. For instance, we can reduce the processing time for head area search if we focus on the area around the area extracted in the previous frame; in this case, the coherence between the processing frames increases. Thus, we can obtain a good processing loop-back. This idea is incorporated in the program.

3.3.3 Experiment of Motion Detection and Discussion

Fig. 3.5 is the result of motion extraction from real images; (a) illustrates the input images and extracted centroid positions, and (b) plots variations of estimated rotation angles. The extraction results are quite good. Since this experiment did not measure the original rotation angles, the

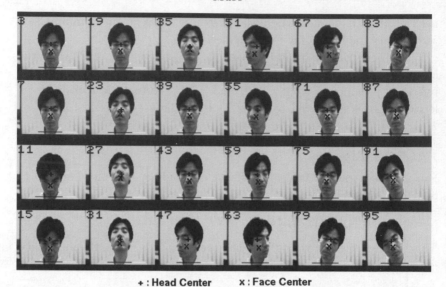

+ : Head Center   x : Face Center

(a) Samples of image sequence and centroids

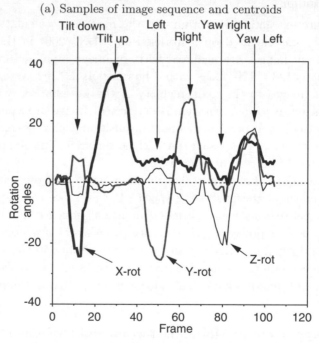

(b) Estimated rotational parameters

Fig. 3.5. Estimated rotational parameters from real human images

estimation accuracy is unknown. However, the graph shows that head movement was well tracked. Equation (3.10) is used in motion calculation to account for hair style compensation, which is obtained through a simulation with a CG head model motions.

$$R_x(t) = g_{rx}\left((\Delta y_h'(t) - \Delta y_f'(t))/\sqrt{S_h(t)}\right) + c_{ry}R_y(t), \qquad (3.10)$$

where c_{ry} is the compensating function which depends on hair style.

Real-time analysis and synthesis

The Headreader was connected to a graphics workstation (GWS) to complete the experiment on the analysis and synthesis of head motion. The system [215] takes face images with the TV camera of a low-cost picture phone and sends extracted motion information to the GWS, which duplicates the original motion with a CG head model. The 3D head model consists of about 600 trigonal patches and is displayed on the GWS in real-time. The system is a prototype of a future intelligent picture coding system, e.g., a model-based image coding scheme.

3.3.4 Interpretation of Head Action and Applications

An application of the Headreader to a human-machine interface is investigated in this section.

Command Interpretation

Head actions as nonverbal message media convey the "location" message by gazing and the "selection" message by nodding and shaking for "yes/no."

First, the head rotation angles are quantified to identify the gaze direction. For example, if we need a 2×2 selection window on screen, trinary quantification of angle θ is performed with thresholding parameters $\{th\}$s:

$$\theta > th^+, th^+ > \theta > th^-, th^- > \theta.$$

Next, changes in rotational angles around x- and y-axes are interpreted for the "yes/no" messages. For example, a DP matching scheme can be used. In this chapter, however, we introduce a method that uses local temporal statistics of rotational parameters to achieve real-time responses. The statistics used are the means m and variances var of angles and their temporal derivatives through the past several frames.

The following equations defines the mean values, m_{rx} and $m_{\Delta rx}$, and the variances, var_{rx} and $var_{\Delta rx}$.

$$m_{rx}(t) \;=\; \frac{1}{t_c} \sum_{T=t-t_c}^{t} R_x(T), \tag{3.11}$$

$$var_{rx}(t) \;=\; \frac{1}{t_c} \sum_{T=t-t_c}^{t} (m_x(t) - R_x(T))^2, \tag{3.12}$$

$$m_{\Delta rx}(t) \;=\; \frac{1}{t_c} \sum_{T=t-t_c}^{t} (R_x(T) - R_x(T-1)), \tag{3.13}$$

$$var_{\Delta rx}(t) \;=\; \frac{1}{t_c} \sum_{T=t-t_c}^{t} (m_{\Delta rx}(t) - R_x(T) + R_x(T-1))^2, \tag{3.14}$$

where t_c is the number of frames, which is set to 6 in the following experimental system to cover an approximately 1.0 second interval.

The following logical equations finally give the answer of "Yes" and "No". It checks the values of means and variances obtained by the equations above with pre-defined thresholding parameters, ths.

$$if(var_{rx} > th_1 \wedge var_{\Delta rx} > th_2 \wedge m_{rx} < th_{down} \wedge m_{rx} > th_{up}) \;\Rightarrow\; \text{Yes}$$

$$if(var_{ry} > th_3 \wedge var_{\Delta ry} > th_4 \wedge m_{ry} < th_{right} \wedge m_{ry} > th_{left}) \;\Rightarrow\; \text{No}$$

Headreader Interface of CG Secretary

The nodding and shaking head actions are used to express "yes/no" messages even by children and speech-impaired persons. Head shaking is the most basic action of interaction. A computer graphics secretary agent (CG Secretary) interacts with the user in front of a screen equipped with a TV camera. The tasks of the CG Secretary are:

  (i) to start a session when it detects a user within the view range,
 (ii) to check a video-mailbox and notify the user of its contents,
(iii) to ask the user his/her work menu choice and provide the program/workplace,
 (iv) to watch for interruptions by the user,
  (v) to close the session when the user leaves the view range.

In order to make the interaction possible based on this scenario, the Headreader was used as an eye of the CG Secretary in the following way:

  (i) user's presence: checking head area size,

Fig. 3.6 Interface of electronic CG Secretary : Recognition of "Yes/No" and menu selection from head actions (notification of a video-mail message)

(a) Snapshots of shaking head expressing 'NO'　　　　(b) Selecting upper-right sub-window

Fig. 3.7. Snapshot of head actions with CG Secretary

    (ii) user's choice of menu: checking head direction as representing gaze,

    (iii) user's command: interpreting "yes/no" actions.

Fig. 3.6 shows the setup of the CG Secretary application system, and Fig. 3.7 shows the selected scenes of user interaction with the CG Secretary: head shaking to stop the video program on screen and a menu selection. The video-mail and video programs are stored in a remote-controlled digital VTR. The previously recorded voice-messages of the CG Secretary are stored as sound files in the voice generator workstation. These are played by the control commands issued by the message integration and application server. Fig. 3.8 is an integrated illustration

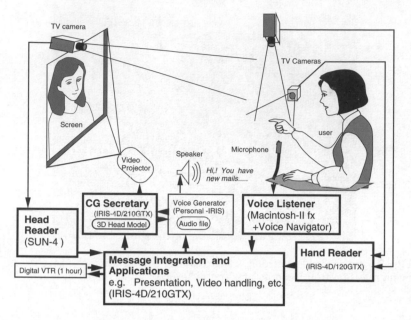

Fig. 3.8 System configuration of CG Secretary and FingerPointer prototypes

of the CG Secretary and FingerPointer prototypes. Note that the CG Secretary system did not employ the Voice Listener and the Handreader.

3.4 Handreader

Human hands are truly a multimodal message conveying device. They are used for such purposes as indication, counting, shaping, manipulation, gesturing, etc. Hand-gesture-based command interfaces have been proposed in many virtual reality systems and in computer aided design tools. In these systems, however, the user must wear special physical devices such as gloves and magnetic devices.

Handreader [130] involves computer image processing of hand and finger images. This system allows the user to input commands based on recognition of finger pointing and several hand gestures in a meeting space or living room. The user's pointing actions are captured by a pair of stereoscopic TV cameras: one mounted on the ceiling and the other on the side wall.

As a prototype of a gesture interface, Handreader is integrated with a Voice Listener and called "Finger-Pointer" (see Fig. 3.8). Gestures used in this system are classified as "locator", "selector", and to some extent "valuator", according to the categorization given in Table 3.1. Voice commands complement the gestural commands, and thus a multimodal interface is realized. This section first introduces the vision algorithms used for extracting gesture messages and then describes a novel method to determine pointing direction called "Virtual Projection Origin (VPO)". Next, the method of integrating voice and gesture media and examples of integrated commands are presented.

3.4.1 Hand Extraction with Stereo Vision

As shown in Fig. 3.8, Handreader uses two cameras to obtain the three-dimensional position of the hand and fingers. The camera on the wall is used to capture hand gestures as well as the position of the finger tip. The other camera on the ceiling captures the horizontal finger tip position. Infra-red (IR) LED array light sources are installed by the cameras in order to make the hand area extraction algorithm simple and robust against change in illumination. The light is unnoticable to users, but a video camera with an IR filter can detect hand position very easily.

Fig. 3.9(a) illustrates the method of determining finger tip location. First, it binarizes the two images captured by the cameras with a fixed threshold and extracts hand regions. Then, each image is scanned to find the tip that is closest to the screen. The candidate tip pixel is verified to determine 3D position, based on the length and thickness of the index fingers. Fig. 3.9(b) illustrates the method of determining thumb up/down action. The fan shaped scan area is constructed based on the finger tip and the center of wrist and scanned to search for the thumb tip pixel. This action is used to send a switcher message. Similarly, hand indication of numbers can be recognized by counting the number of outstretched fingers, as illustrated in Fig. 3.9(c) .

How do we draw a virtual line between the finger and a target in the distance? Often, we use a base reference point on or near the body and draw a line through the finger tip and the base reference point. The location of the base reference point, or the Virtual Projection Origin (VPO), depends on the person, pointing style, etc. However, since we can assume it is stable in a distinct session, a pre-session calibration to define the VPO is sufficient. Four corners of a target screen are used for such a calibration in which the user is instructed to point to each indicated corner for the system to find the VPO. An experimental

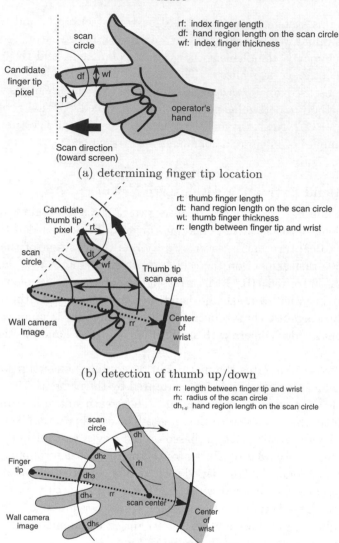

(a) determining finger tip location

(b) detection of thumb up/down

(c) detection of number of fingers

Fig. 3.9. Recognition of hand gestures

Table 3.2. *Command examples of combined hand gestures and voice*

Hand gesture	Voice example	Interface command
Locator (indication)	"This", "From", "To"	Point
Selector (thumb up/down)	none	Menu, Button
Valuator (finger number)	"Forward this many"	Dial

analysis with 20 subjects showed that the VPO is mostly distributed along the line of the eye on the pointing hand's side and the shoulder.

3.4.2 Finger-Pointer: multimedia and multimodal interface

Handreader provides multimodal information, i.e., valuator, locator, switcher. Voice information will give a clue for distinguishing the hand gestural commands. The Finger-Pointer provides integration of voice and pointing gestures by using a speech recognition unit. Table 3.2 lists examples of combinations of gesture and voice.

The Finger-Pointer realizes inter-channel synchronization between voice and image to avoid mismatch between the messages provided from the Handreader and the Voice-Listener. It introduces "time-tags" that use a common master clock. Each part-reader (here, one of the readers processes voice) applies a time-tag when it recognizes a message. The message integration server will use the time-tags when it integrates the output of the part-readers.

3.4.3 Application of Finger-Pointer

Three experimental application systems use the Finger-Pointer interface.

First, an electronic presentation system was constructed. The user can control page forwarding/backwarding, select commands in the listed menu, mark with a bullet on a slide, draw an underline and so on. In page controlling, a skip-page number can be specified by the finger numbering gesture. Fig. 3.10 is a snapshot of the system being used.

Next, a video browsing system was constructed. The system allows the user to use hand gestures to remote control a VCR; for example: Play, Stop and special search operations similar to those offered by a "Shuttle-Ring" of real VCRs. Fig. 3.11(a) is a snapshot of controlling the VCR.

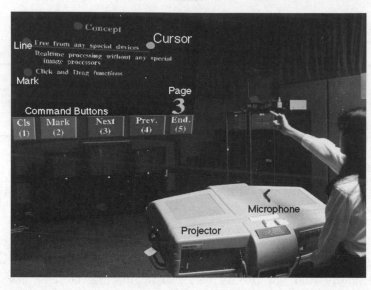

Fig. 3.10 Finger-Pointer: interface for presentation system using hand gestures and voice

Third, a user may want to write a character or draw simple graphics in space. A Space Sketchpad is the third application that can be realized with the Finger-Pointer. Fig. 3.11(b) is a snapshot of the system being used.

3.5 Facereader

Facial expression is a major medium for non-verbal communication. It complements verbal communication and can convey sufficient information by itself. Thus, the ability to understand expressions would make communication smoother and more accurate. Advanced research into man-machine interfaces must tackle this issue. For instance, future computers and household appliances should automatically respond to annoyed users by offering helpful information. This section presents a method that uses optical flow to estimate facial muscle movements [211] and then recognizes these movements as various facial expressions.

The human face has several distinctive features such as eyes, mouth and nose. We need to extract their movements and shape-deformations in order to recognize facial expressions. Many techniques have been developed for extracting facial features and finding fiducial points us-

(a) VCR Controlling (Play and Jog)

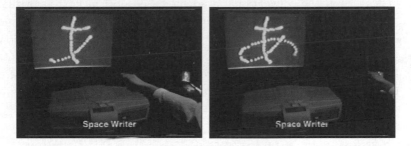

(b) Space writing

Fig. 3.11. Finger-Pointer: interface to VCR remote and Space Sketchpad

ing image processing and computer vision for automatic facial recognition [265]. We use optical flow to extract the muscle movement. It seems more straightforward to extract muscle movement from skin displacement than to estimate each muscle action from feature point movement. Optical flow information can be extracted easily, even at low contrast edges. Furthermore, the facial skin at the cheek and forehead has the texture of a fine-grained organ, which is a key factor for optical flow estimation.

We investigated the recognition of facial expressions in two ways: the top-down and bottom-up approaches. The top-down method is applied to estimate facial muscle movement, and we found that the obtained optical flow information was sufficient to extract information of facial muscle movements as a description of facial expressions. Furthermore, we constructed a bottom-up expression recognition system to categorize emotional expressions.

3.5.1 Facial Expression and Optical Flow

Considering that expressions are formed by the contraction of facial muscles, it is reasonable to assume that deformation of the skin provides valuable information on muscle action. That is, muscle contractions are triggered by the nerve impulses generated by emotions, and the skin is deformed by the contraction of those muscles under the skin. Because most muscles associated with expressions are attached to some facial feature, e.g., lips and eyes, the features are deformed. Simultaneously, the deformation can be seen on the cheeks and forehead as dimples or wrinkles. Even the conventional gradient based optical flow algorithm firstly introduced by Horn and Schunck can extract skin motion from the subtle texture of these regions. The advantage of the optical flow algorithm is that there is no need to extract and trace particular points in the image sequence. Mase and Pentland [213] exploited this concept to extract lip movements and for application to computer lip reading.

3.5.2 Extraction of Muscle Movement

Optical Flow Muscle Model

First, in order to see how well optical flow information can capture muscle movement, the amount of muscle contraction was computed from optical flow data. We used windows that define the major directions of muscle contraction (skin deformation). This allows the effect of each muscle to be determined. The average length of directional components in the major window axis is calculated from the optical flow vectors in each window.

$$m_{i,t} = \frac{1}{S_i} \int_{window_i} \mathbf{u_t}(\mathbf{x}) \cdot \mathbf{n}_i \; dx, \qquad (3.15)$$

where $\mathbf{u_t}(\mathbf{x}) \equiv (u_t(x,y), v_t(x,y))$ is the optical flow field computed from two successive frames at times t and $t+1$. Here, S_i and $\mathbf{n}_i$ are the area size and the normal vector of the ith window ($i = 0, ..., 11$), respectively. Fig. 3.12 (lower-right) uses arrows to indicate the direction of muscle contraction, which is equivalent to $-\mathbf{n}_i$. Windows are manually located using feature points as references. For example, window 0 is placed on the line connecting the lip's left extremity and the left eye's left extremity. We denote by m_i the estimated muscle movement in the ith window; it is a function of time (frames). Although the movement is a velocity, it is also regarded as an averaged displacement in a unit period.

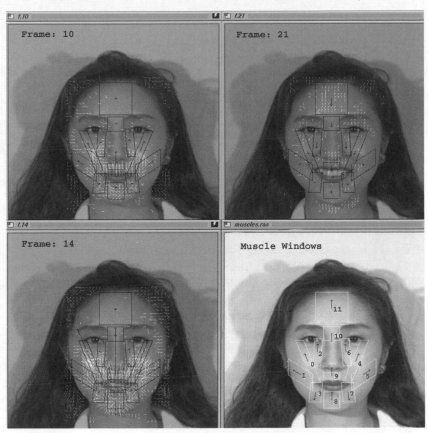

Fig. 3.12. Windows for measurement and estimated muscle motions

Fig. 3.12 shows a recorded image and estimated muscle velocities during one full cycle of a "happy" expression of a woman. The white and black arrows are computed optical flow and estimated velocities, respectively. The optical flow field is computed for each pixel and is shown for every three pixels. Image size is 256 by 256 pixels. The estimated motions are functions of time. From this preliminary experiment, it can be stated that the information of optical flow data sufficiently reflects the muscle movement invoked by expressions.

FACS-based Description of Expression from Muscle Model

In this section, we introduce an association table between our muscle-model and a subset of AU (Action Unit), and show an example of describing expression with AUs.

The major AUs for six fundamental expressions (happiness, anger, surprise, disgust, sadness and fear) are first extracted from the literature. They are AUs 1, 2, 4, 5, 6, 7, 9, 10, 12, 15, 17, 20 , 25 and 26. An association was then formed between our muscle model and the extracted AUs by referring to the FACS manual and to literature in anatomy. Because AU descriptions are mostly static and only partly dynamic, our dynamic muscle model cannot be directly associated with a particular AU. The relationship between action and its effect on shape must be considered to develop intuitively. Moreover, our muscle model does not cover the whole facial area, thus some AUs are not included.

The muscle action derived from our muscle model can be associated with several action units as listed in Table 3.3. Since lip-part (AU25) and jaw-drop (AU26) are not distinguishable from m_8 (lower part of mouth) of the muscle model, we score AU26 for positive m_8. It seems that m_9 is related mainly to the Orbicularis oris and partly to other muscles, and is often observed when the mouth opens. Therefore, AU25 (lip part) was associated with negative m_9. It may be better to assign AU25 only when negative m_9 and positive m_8 are observed, but we only consider *one* to N associations of muscle action and AUs in this discussion for simplicity.

Thus, for example, estimated muscle motions can be scored, for example, as AUs 6(0.6)+12(0.35)+17(0.28)+25(0.8)+26(0.20) if we consider only strong actions [211]. The figures in the parenthesis, e.g. 0.6, indicate the AU's strength, which is equated to the maximum absolute velocity between the frames containing neutral and maximum positions of expression. The scored AU combination is fairly close to the combinations of AUs 6+12+26 or AUs 6+12+17, which often appear with the happiness expression as shown in the FACS's AU photographs. Because the example score was computed from an image sequence, it is natural to include several "happy" expressions. Unfortunately, AU25(0.8) cannot be clearly interpreted in such expressions.

Table 3.3. *Relationship between Muscle Windows and Action Units*
(AUn^- occurs if $m_i < 0$, and AUn^+ occurs if $m_i > 0$.)

Window	Muscles	Actions and Results	Closest AUs
m_0(left) m_4(right)	Zygomaticus mj Orbicularis oculi	pull up lip extreme raise cheek	AU6$^-$(cheek raiser)
m_1(left) m_5(right)	Zygomaticus mj Buccinator	pull lip corners backward	AU12$^-$(lip corner puller)
m_2(left) m_6(right)	Levator labii	raise upper lip	AU10$^-$(upper lip raiser)
m_3(left) m_7(right)	Depressor Angli oris	depress lip corners	AU15$^-$ (lip corner depressor)
m_8	Mentalis Jaw action Dipressor labii	raise chin drop jaw and part lips	AU17$^-$(chin raiser) AU26$^+$(jaw drops), [AU25$^+$(lips part)]
m_9	Orbicularis oris (relaxed)	relax upper lip or part lips	AU25$^-$(lips part)
m_{10}	Depressor sup Levator labii	make wrinkle at root of nose	AU9$^-$(nose wrinkler)
m_{11}	Ventor frontalis Depressor sup	raise brow or lower brow	AU1$^-$(inner brow raiser) AU4$^+$(brow lowerer)

3.5.3 Recognition of Expression by k-Nearest-Neighbor Rule

The previous section presented a top-down method that describes facial expressions in terms of facial muscle movements, which could later be related to categorized expressions such as happy and anger. This section presents an expression recognition system based on the classical bottom-up pattern recognition approach.

The expression recognition system presented here directly categorizes facial expressions into emotional categories by deriving a feature vector from sample image sequences.

Feature Vector Selection

A non-parametric pattern recognition method, the k-nearest-neighbor rule [111], is used to classify the image sequences of various facial expressions. As is well known, the nearest-neighbor rule is a sub-optimal procedure for classification.

First, we define a K-dimensional feature vector whose elements are derived from optical flow data of sample image sequences. The time information is discarded by treating the flow data at each frame as independent. Consequently, the first and second degrees of moment (means and covariances) of flow data are calculated in each spatially and temporally local region. Suppose the image sequence is N(column) by M(row) pixels with a period of T(frames) for the k-th expression sample. The image is evenly divided into n by m regions by a ratio of $r = N/n = M/m$. The resulting basic feature data is the set of

$$\mu_{u,i,j} = \frac{1}{T}\frac{1}{r^2} \sum_{0<t\leq T} \sum_{(x,y)\in R(i,j)} u_t(x,y), \qquad (3.16)$$

$$\mu_{v,i,j} = \frac{1}{T}\frac{1}{r^2} \sum_{0<t\leq T} \sum_{(x,y)\in R(i,j)} v_t(x,y), \qquad (3.17)$$

$$\sigma_{uu,i,j} = \frac{1}{T}\frac{1}{r^2} \sum_{0<t\leq T} \sum_{R(i,j)} (u_t(x,y) - \mu_{u,i,j})^2, \qquad (3.18)$$

$$\sigma_{uv,i,j} = \frac{1}{T}\frac{1}{r^2} \sum_{0<t\leq T} \sum_{R(i,j)} (u_t(x,y) - \mu_{u,i,j})(v_t(x,y) - \mu_{v,i,j}) \qquad (3.19)$$

$$\sigma_{vv,i,j} = \frac{1}{T}\frac{1}{r^2} \sum_{0<t\leq T} \sum_{R(i,j)} (v_t(x,y) - \mu_{v,i,j})^2, \qquad (3.20)$$

where $\mu_{u,i,j}$ and $\mu_{v,i,j}$ are the means of optical flow of horizontal and vertical components, respectively, at the (i,j)-th divided region $R(i,j)$, and $\sigma_{uu,i,j}$, $\sigma_{uv,i,j}$ and $\sigma_{vv,i,j}$ are the covariances of optical flow. This results in a $K(=5mn)$-dimensional vector whose dimensionality should be reduced. As a convention, we denote the vector by

$$\mathbf{F} = \{f_1, f_2, ..., f_k, ..., f_K\}. \qquad (3.21)$$

To reduce the dimensionality of the vector, we introduce the following criterion function of separation goodness for the kth element of $\mathbf{F}$.

$$J(k) = \frac{var_B(k)}{var_W(k)}, \qquad (3.22)$$

where $var_B(k)$ is the between-class variance of f_k and $var_W(k)$ is the within-class variance of f_k as defined by the following equations. For the c-class problem,

$$var_W(k) = \sum_{i=1}^{c} \left(\frac{1}{n_i} \sum_{f_k \in \theta_i} (f_k - \bar{f}_{k,i})^2 \right) \qquad (3.23)$$

$$var_B(k) = \sum_{i=1}^{c} (\bar{f}_{k,i} - \bar{f}_k)^2 \qquad (3.24)$$

where θ_i is the set of class i, $\bar{f}_{k,i}$ is the mean of f_k within the class i and $\bar{f}_k$ is the total mean of f_k [111, sec. 4.11]. We choose $\hat{K}$ elements for the objective feature vector

$$\hat{\mathbf{F}} = \{f_1, ..., f_{\hat{K}}\}, \qquad (3.25)$$

which consists of elements that provide the $\hat{K}$ largest values of the criterion function $J(k)$.

This operation yields the feature vector that should most perfectly classify the sample pattern from the basic data. We can confirm its completeness by applying the nearest-neighbor rule to the sample data. This feature vector was constructed for each test data and was used in recognition tests. Experimental results from actual data are shown in the next section.

Experimental Results

Image sequences of various facial expressions of the author were collected; 20 as sample data and 30 as test data. The instructions described in [116] were followed to make expressions of various emotions. The sample data consisted of the four classes ($c = 4$) of expression, i.e. happiness, anger, disgust, and surprise. Each class has five image sequence samples. Parameters for the feature vector were developed from the sample data set as described in the previous section. The recognition test was then executed using the test data set. The recognition was based on the k-nearest neighbour rule for the feature vectors of the test data derived from optical flow fields.

The image sequences were acquired off-line with a digital video tape recorder and then stored as image files for further processing. The head of the subject was fixed to prevent global flotation, which would have significantly degraded optical flow calculation. Ordinary and constant illumination was applied to the facial area. Because the video signal is interlaced, the original image was sub-sampled at half the signal rate.

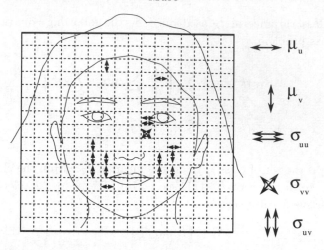

Fig. 3.13. Locations of selected feature vector

Finally, image sequences ($M = 256$ by $N = 240$ pixel size and $T = 30$ frames length) were extracted for each expression instance. Target expressions in the video sequences were manually spotted.

Feature Extraction from Sample Data

The optical flow of each image sequence was computed with Horn-Schunck's algorithm and the maximum number of iterations was set to 20. The optical flow field was divided into $m = 16$ by $n = 15$ rectangular regions and feature parameters were computed using equations (3.16)–(3.24). The dimension of the feature vector was set to ($\hat{K} = 15$), which was selected so as not to exceed the number of samples.

Fig. 3.13 illustrates the positions of elements chosen as the feature vector.

Since we use the three nearest samples for voting, the data is labeled *rejected* only if three different classes are simultaneously voted to it. Nineteen image sequences out of 20 were classified correctly in the experiment (i.e. 95% recognition accuracy for 20 sample data sets) and one sample was rejected. The minimum distance to the feature vectors of sample data $\{\hat{\mathbf{F}}_n\}$ from test data $\hat{\mathbf{F}}'_n$ is calculated by the following formula;

$$D(\hat{\mathbf{F}}') = \min_{\hat{\mathbf{F}}_n} \|\hat{\mathbf{F}}_n - \hat{\mathbf{F}}'_n\|^2, \tag{3.26}$$

where $\hat{\mathbf{F}}_n$ is the normalized feature vector of $\hat{\mathbf{F}}$ such that each element

Table 3.4. *Correlation matrix of recognition results*
Five classes (including unknown test data)

human \ computer	happiness	anger	surprise	disgust	total
happiness	7				7
anger		4		1	5
surprise		2	5		7
disgust				3	3
subtotals	7	6	5	4	22
unknown	1	1	5	1	8
total	8	7	10	5	30

of sample data $f_{\hat{k}}$ has the normal distribution, $p(f_{\hat{k}}) \sim N(0,1)$. When the k-nearest-neighbor rule is applied to the test data, the same means and variances are used for the normalization of test data.

Recognition of Test Data

Ten people categorized the 30 test image sequences into five classes, which were the original four plus the class of unknown expressions. The test data is categorized if more than six people choose the same class, otherwise it is categorized as unknown.

Accordingly, the data is not evenly distributed over the classes. Table 3.4 shows final recognition results illustrated by the correlation matrix between the computer-recognized result and human assessments. Table 3.4 lists corresponding results of the five-class categorization.

Table 3.4 shows that facial expression recognition performance is fairly good for the four categories tested. The overall recognition accuracy was 19/22, or 86%, by taking only known categories into consideration.

3.6 Other Part-Readers

Other Part-Readers were investigated in the Human Reader project, such as the People Image Reader and the Person Image Reader.

The People Image Reader is a locator system, which is derived to detect the position and motion of one or more human subjects. Capabilities include detection of human presence, counting subjects, and

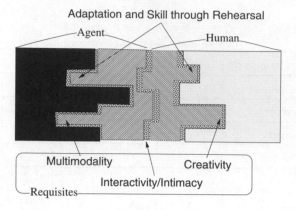

Fig. 3.14. MIC (multimodal, interactive/intimate and creative) interface

understanding the direction of crowd movement. One application of People Image Reader is pedestrian counting [267].

The Person Image Reader is similar in concept to face recognizers [291]. The face functions both as a selector that matches faces with names to identify individuals [6] and as an imager that sends messages about types of facial features and expressions (round, wrinkled, pleasant) [36]. This correlation of face, identity, and name is indispensable to the achievement of a secure yet convenient interface. Also, a person's facial expression contributes as much to establishing a basis for conversation as do clothing and posture. However, research on the development of such an imager has yet to appear.

3.7 MIC Interface Agent

We do want to have a "natural interface" that is comparable to human-to-human interactions. However, what in fact is a "natural interface"? We rely on the human capabilities of intelligence, adaptivity and autonomy to achieve such a natural interface to specific tasks in the real world. The most important point is that the interface should know about the task it is interfacing to the human. Without knowing the task, it loses the context, and thus cannot properly interpret messages. The Part-readers presented in the previous sections are not the interface yet in that sense, but simply visual sensors. When they are integrated with an application module, they can act as a real interface, such as the CG Secretary, the FingerPointer, etc.

"Interface Agent" is a solution to providing a natural interface because it implies the agent may include a part of the task, or at least it should act autonomously based on the situation. The naive but worthy expectations of the Interface Agent can be considered as the following:

(i) visual perceptibility,
(ii) translating machine interface,
(iii) social, intelligent and adaptive capability,
(iv) intimacy.

Thus, in Interface Agent research, I think much attention should be given to not only multimodality and interactivity but also creativity of human. The MIC (multimodal, interactive and creative) interface is the interface that we pursue in researching and developing the Interface Agent (Fig. 3.14).

3.8 Conclusion

If we can provide a warm and communicative environment, the other partner can read even subtle messages. The objective of the Human Reader project and the subsequent research of the MIC Interface is to provide such an environment in a human-computer interaction scheme. This chapter presents results of the Human Reader project, focusing on the multimodal and interactive aspects. Computer vision or image processing capability is not yet sufficient to provide such a naturally communicative atmosphere [235]. However, such intelligent vision sensors will inevitably be improved and used in human-computer interfaces in the future. Computer vision technology will be used as the "eyes" of the Interface Agent, which will be, I believe, the interface we are looking for.

4

Visual Sensing of Humans for Active Public Interfaces

K. Waters, J. Rehg, M. Loughlin, S.B. Kang
and D. Terzopoulos

Abstract

Computer vision-based sensing of people enables a new class of *public* multi-user computer interfaces. Computing resources in public spaces, such as automated, information-dispensing kiosks, represent a computing paradigm that differs from the conventional desktop environment and correspondingly, requires a user-interface metaphor quite unlike the traditional WIMP interface. This chapter describes a prototype public computer interface which employs color and stereo tracking to sense the users' activity and an animated speaking agent to attract attention and communicate through visual and audio modalities.

4.1 Introduction

An automated, information-dispensing Smart Kiosk, which is situated in a public space for use by a general clientele, poses a challenging human-computer interface problem. A *public* kiosk interface must be able to actively initiate and terminate interactions with users and divide its resources among multiple customers in an equitable manner. This interaction scenario represents a significant departure from the standard WIMP (windows, icons, mouse, pointer) paradigm, but will become increasingly important as computing resources migrate off the desktop and into public spaces. We are exploring a social interface paradigm for a Smart Kiosk, in which computer vision techniques are used to sense people and a graphical speaking agent is used to output information and communicate cues such as focus of attention.

Human sensing techniques from computer vision can play a significant role in *public user-interfaces* for kiosk-like appliances. Using unob-

83

trusive video cameras, they can provide a wealth of information about users, ranging from their three-dimensional location to their facial expressions and body language. Although vision-based human sensing has received increasing attention in the past five years (see the proceedings [237, 2, 31]) relatively little work has been done on integrating this technology into functioning user-interfaces. A few notable exceptions are the pioneering work of Krueger [185], the Mandala Group [299], the Alive system [206], and a small body of work on gesture-based control for desktop and set-top box environments (see [234] for a survey).

This chapter describes our prototype kiosk and some experiments with vision-based sensing. The kiosk prototype currently consists of a set of software modules that run on several workstations and communicate through message-passing. It includes modules for real-time visual sensing (including motion detection, colored object tracking, and stereo ranging), a synthetic agent called DECface [306], and behavior-based control.

We describe this architecture and its implementation in the following sections and present experimental results related to proximity-based interactions and active gaze control. Section 4.2 describes some characteristics of the user-interface problem for public kiosk-like devices. Section 4.3 discusses and describes how computer vision can be used in a public user-interface. Section 4.3.2 presents persistence behavior tracking for proximate, midrange and distant interactions as well as stereo tracking using color. Section 4.3.3 describes the feedback technology of DECface. Section 4.3.4 describes the behaviors we are interested in developing. Section 4.4 describes implementation details of our prototype kiosk. Section 4.5 reports on vision-directed behavior experiments performed with the prototype. Section 4.6 reviews previous work in vision-based human sensing. Section 4.7 describes future work and Section 4.8 concludes the paper.

4.2 Characteristics of Public User-Interfaces

The dynamic, unconstrained nature of a public space, such as a shopping mall, poses a challenging user-interface problem for a Smart Kiosk. We refer to this as the *public user-interface* problem, to differentiate it from interactions that take place in structured, single-user desktop [269] or virtual reality [206] environments. We have developed a prototype Smart Kiosk which we are using to explore the space of effective public interactions. Our prototype has three functional components: human sensing, behavior, and graphical/audio output. This section outlines some basic requirements for public interactions and their implications for the components of a Smart Kiosk.

The effectiveness of a Smart Kiosk in reaching its target audience can be measured by two quantities, *utilization* and *exposure*. Utilization refers to the percentage of time the kiosk is in use, while exposure refers to the number of different users that interact with the system during some unit of time. Maximizing utilization ensures the greatest return on the cost of kiosk technology, while maximizing exposure prevents a small number of users from monopolizing the kiosk's resources. We are exploring interaction models that are *human-centered, active*, and *multi-user*, as a way of maximizing kiosk utilization and exposure.

We are interested in human-centered interactions, in which communication occurs through speaking and gestures. Since a Smart Kiosk is situated in its users' physical environment, it is natural for it to follow rules of communication and behavior that users can interpret immediately and unambiguously. This is particularly important given the broad range of backgrounds of potential users for Smart Kiosks, and the lack of opportunity for user training. Human-centered output can be obtained through the use of a graphical, speaking agent, such as DECface. Human-centered input consists of visual and acoustical sensing of human motion, gesture, and speech. The behavior component plays a critical role in regulating the communication between the agent and the users, and setting the users' expectations for the interaction.

Active participation in initiating and regulating interactions with users is the second vital task for public interfaces. By enticing potential users, a Smart Kiosk can maximize its utilization, for example, by detecting the presence of a loiterer and calling out to him or her. This requires the ability to visually detect potential customers in the space around the kiosk and evaluate the appropriateness of beginning an interaction. Active interfaces must behave in socially acceptable way. A kiosk interface that is too aggressive could alienate rather than attract potential users. Thus an active interface requires both vision techniques for sensing potential users and behavioral models for interactions.

In addition to being active and human-centered, a kiosk situated in a public space must also be able to deal with the conflicting requests of multiple users. Two basic issues arise when the resources of the interface are shared by multiple users. First, the interface must be able to communicate its focus of attention to the user population, so the center of the interaction is known by all users at all times. The eye gaze of the

DECface agent provides a natural mechanism for communicating focus of attention. Effective gaze behavior requires a graphical display with compelling dynamics and a model of gaze behavior. Gaze behavior is designed both to indicate the focus of attention and to draw the audience into the interaction through eye contact.

Besides communicating a focus of attention, the interface must build and maintain a representation of its audience to support multi-user interactions. At the minimum, it must track and identify the position of its current users, so it can recognize arrivals and departures. This makes it possible to include new users into the interaction in an efficient manner and ensure a fair allocation of resources. In addition to visual sensing capabilities, a multi-user interface must have a behavioral model of the interaction process that allows it to monitor its allocation of resources to its community of users and make tradeoffs between conflicting demands.

4.3 The Smart Kiosk Interface

In order to explore the public interaction issues described above, we have developed a prototype Smart Kiosk interface based on visual sensing, a speaking DECface agent, and some simple behaviors. This section describes the components of the interface and their design.

4.3.1 Designing the Interaction Space

We currently assume that the kiosk display is the focal point of an interaction with multiple users which will take place in a space ranging from the front of the display out to a few tens of feet. Users walking into this space will be imaged by one or more cameras positioned around the kiosk display. Fig. 4.1 illustrates the sensor and display geometry for our kiosk prototype.

We can characterize the effect of camera and display positioning on the visual sensing tasks for the kiosk interface. The image resolution available for human sensing varies inversely with the square of the distance from the interface. As a result, it is possible to classify roughly the human behaviors, articulation, and features that can be measured from images into categories based on proximity to the interface. Table 4.1 defines a taxonomy in which proximity dictates the type of processing that can take place. These categories are nested, since a task that can be done at some distance can always be performed at a closer one. In

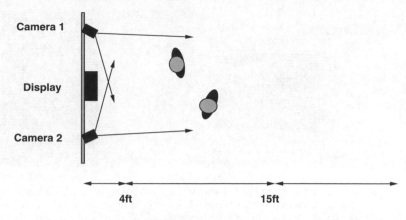

Fig. 4.1 Interaction space for a Smart Kiosk. Two cameras monitor the position of multiple users in front of the kiosk display.

our current system we define "proximate" as less than about 4 feet, "midrange" as from 4 to 15 feet, and "distant" as greater than 15 feet.

	Proximate	Midrange	Distant
Human features	Face/Hands	Head and torso	Whole body
Human articulation	Expression	Orientation/Pose	Walking
Human behaviors	Emotion	Attention	Locomotion

Table 4.1 *Taxonomy of visual sensing for public user-interfaces based on distance from the focal point of interaction.*

4.3.2 Person Tracking Using Motion and Color Stereo

Color and motion stereo tracking provide visual sensing for the Smart Kiosk prototype. We represent each user as a blob in the image plane, and triangulate on the blob centroids from two cameras to localize each user in the environment (see [13] for a related approach). Stereo tracking provides 3D localization of users relative to the kiosk display. This information can be used to initiate interactions based on distance from the kiosk and to provide DECface with cues for gaze behavior in a multi-user setting.

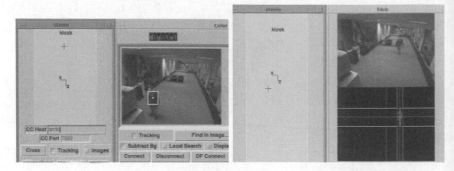

Fig. 4.2 Sample output from the color tracking (left) and motion blob tracking (right) modules. Images were obtained from the right camera of the stereo pair. The left-hand portion of each display shows a plan view of the scene with a cross marking the 3D location of the individual projected onto the ground plane.

We use motion-based blob detection to localize a single person at a long range from the kiosk. We assume that the user is the only moving object in the scene and employ standard image differencing to identify candidate blob pixels. A bounding box for blob pixels is computed by processing the difference image one scanline at a time and recording the first "on" pixel and the last "off" pixel value above a predefined threshold (see Fig. 4.2 for an example). This simple approach is very fast, and has proven useful in our current kiosk environment.

We use a modified version of the color histogram indexing and back-projection algorithm of Swain and Ballard [282] to track multiple people in real-time within approximately 15 feet of the kiosk. We obtain histogram models of each user through a manual segmentation stage. Like other researchers [320, 207, 299, 282], we have found normalized color to be a descriptive, inexpensive, and reasonably stable feature for human tracking. We use local search during tracking to improve robustness and speed. To avoid color matches with static objects in the environment, background subtraction is used to identify moving regions in the image before indexing. Sample output from the color tracker is illustrated in Fig. 4.2.

Given motion- or color-based tracking of a person in a pair of calibrated cameras, stereo triangulation is used to estimate the user's 3D location. We use motion stereo for proximity sensing at far distances, and color stereo for short range tracking of multiple users. In our kiosk prototype, we use a pair of verged cameras with a six-foot baseline. Ex-

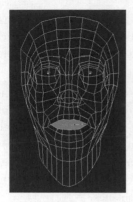  

Fig. 4.3 DECface rendered in wireframe (left), as a texture mapped anonymous face (middle) and a female face (right).

trinsic and intrinsic camera parameters are calibrated using a non-linear least-squares algorithm [283] and a planar target [168]. Given blob centroids in two images, triangulation proceeds through ray intersection. The 3D position is chosen as the point of closest approach in the scene to the rays from the two cameras that pass through the detected centroid positions.

4.3.3 Feedback: DECface

DECface, a talking synthetic face, is the visual complement of the speech synthesizer DECtalk [108]. Where DECtalk provides synthesized speech, DECface provides a synthetic face [306]. By combining the audio functionality of a speech synthesizer with the graphical functionality of a computer-generated face, it is possible to create a *real-time* agent as illustrated in Fig. 4.3.

DECface has been created with the following key attributes for our reactive agent: an ability to speak an arbitrary piece of text at a specific speech rate in one of eight voices from one of eight faces, the creation of simple facial expressions under control of a facial muscle model [305], and simple head and eye rotation.

4.3.4 Behavior

The behavior module dictates the actions that the Smart Kiosk carries out in response to internal and external events. The behavioral repertoire of the kiosk is coded as a collection of behavior routines. Individual behavior routines are executed by an action selection arbitrator which decides what to do next given the internal state of the kiosk and the external stimuli that it receives.

The behavior routines generally exercise control over the sensing and DECface modules. A behavior routine will, in general, direct the vision module to acquire perceptual information that is relevant to the particular behavior. It will also direct the DECface module to produce an audiovisual display to the outside world in accordance with the behavior. The behavior routines are organized in a loose hierarchy with the more complex invoking one or more primitive routines.

It is useful to distinguish two types of behavior: reflexive and motivational. Reflexive behaviors are predetermined responses to internal conditions or external stimuli. A simple reflexive behavior is the awakening triggered when a dormant kiosk senses movement in its territory. Another example is the eye blinking. Eye blinks are triggered periodically so that DECface's eyes exhibit some natural liveliness. A somewhat more complex reflexive behavior determines the detailed actions of the eyes and head when the gaze is redirected. Psychophysical studies of the human oculomotor system reveal that eye and head motions are coupled, with the relatively larger mass of the head resulting in longer transients compared to those of the eyes [66].

In contrast, a motivational behavior is determined by the internal "mental state" of the kiosk, which will in general encode the emotional condition of the kiosk and any task-directed plans that it may have. For example, when communicating with a user, DECface is motivated to look at the person. Thus, gaze punctuates the interaction [10]. This gaze behavior combines sensed information about the user's current location with predefined rules about the role of gaze in human interactions. As a more elaborate example, the kiosk may be programmed with a good sense of humor, and this would motivate it to attract a group of people and tell them jokes. The joke behavior routine would call upon more primitive behavior routines, including gaze control, to talk to different people in the group and keep everyone engaged in the discussion.

An effective strategy for implementing a behavioral repertoire is first to implement a substrate of simple reflexive behaviors before proceeding with the implementation of increasingly complex motivational behaviors. The behavioral repertoire of the kiosk determines its personality in public interaction. For example, smiling, receptive behaviors give

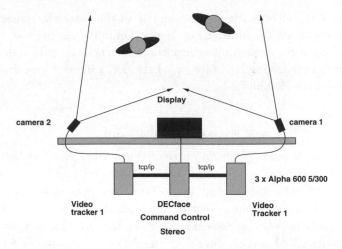

Fig. 4.4 Smart Kiosk prototype. A 24 bit color display is positioned on one side of a partition and three Digital Alpha workstations on the other.

the impression of a friendly kiosk. Alternatively, abrupt, challenging behaviors create the impression of a hostile kiosk.

4.4 Implementation

The kiosk prototype is implemented as a set of independent software modules (threads) running on a network of workstations and communicating by message-passing over TCP/IP sockets. We currently have five types of modules: motion blob detection, color tracking, stereo triangulation, DECface, and behavior. Fig. 4.4 illustrates the hardware configuration used in the kiosk prototype. All of the experiments in this paper used three Digital Alpha[1] workstations. Two of the workstations were used for the two color or blob tracking modules, and the third was used for the DECface, stereo, behavior, and routing modules. Images were acquired from two Sony DXC-107 color CCD cameras and digitized with two Digital Full Video Supreme digitizers.

The network architecture supports both direct socket connections between modules and communication via a central routing module. At initialization, all modules connect to the router, which maps module names to IP addresses and can log message transmissions for debugging

---

[1] The following are trademarks of Digital Equipment Corporation: Alpha, DEC, DECaudio, DECtalk, ULTRIX, XMedia, and the DIGITAL logo.

purposes. The router limits the complexity of the network connections and supports on-the-fly addition and removal of modules. In cases where maximum network throughput is important, as when the output of color stereo tracking is driving DECface gaze behavior, a direct connection between modules is established.

4.5 Experimental Results

We conducted three experiments in real-time vision-directed behavior on our prototype kiosk. The first experiment used proximity sensing in conjunction with some simple behavioral triggers to detect a single, distant user and entice him or her to approach the kiosk. The user was detected independently by two cameras, using the real-time motion blob algorithm described earlier. Stereo triangulation on the blob centroids provided estimates of the person's distance from the kiosk. This information was sent to the behavioral module. The range of 3D detection was fairly large, beginning at approximately seventy feet and ending a few feet away from the kiosk. For this experiment we implemented a simple trigger behavior which divides the workspace into near, middle, and far regions, and associates a set of sentences to the transitions between regions. As the user's distance from the kiosk changed, the behavior model detected the transitions between regions and caused DECface to speak an appropriate message.

The second experiment explored the use of close-range tracking to drive DECface gaze behavior. A single user was tracked, using the color stereo algorithm described earlier. The user's 3D position was converted into a gaze angle in DECface's coordinate system and used to control the x-axis orientation of the synthetic face display in real-time. We implemented a simple gaze behavior which enabled DECface to follow the user with its gaze as the user roamed about the workspace. Fig. 4.5 shows five frames of the display from the user's viewpoint as he walks past the kiosk from left to right.

The third experiment built upon the vision-directed gaze behavior above to show the kiosk's focus of attention when communicating with multiple users. For this example we implemented a very simple "story-telling" behavior for an audience of two persons. A six-sentence monologue is delivered by DECface to one user, and is interspersed with side comments that are directed at the second user. We used the direction of DECface's gaze to indicate the recipient of each sentence, and employed 3D color stereo tracking to update the gaze direction in real-time as the

Fig. 4.5 Five frames of a view through a Handicam while DECface tracks a user in 3D using color.

Fig. 4.6 3D color tracking of two individuals during the "storytelling" sequence. During the sequence the two individuals exchange locations.

users change positions. Fig. 4.6 shows two snapshots of the audience during the story-telling experiment.

4.6 Previous Work

There are two bodies of work that relate closely to the Smart Kiosk system. The first are investigations into vision-based interfaces for desktop computing [251], set-top boxes [128], and virtual environments [185, 299, 269, 207, 206, 234]. In particular, the Alive system [206], and the works that preceded it [185, 299], have explored the use of vision sensing to support interactions with autonomous agents in a virtual environment.

The second body of related work is on algorithms for tracking human motion using video images [238, 220, 252, 23, 253, 320, 13]. Our color and motion blob algorithms are most closely related to those of Wren *et al.* [320], which are employed in the Alive system. The color histogram representation for blobs [282] that we employ is more descriptive than their single color blob model and therefore more appropriate to our task of identifying multiple users based on color alone. We use stereo for depth recovery rather than the ground plane approach used in Alive because we do not want to segment the entire body or rely on the visibility of the user's feet (also see [13]).

4.7 Future Work

The key to an effective public interface is natural communication between kiosk and users within the framework of the users' world. There are many ways in which we can develop our kiosk to approach this goal. We will focus on two aspects: (1) improving the users' communication with the kiosk through vision and other modalities, and (2) developing more compelling kiosk behaviors.

Our visual sensing work has been focussed on detecting and tracking people in the distance and at midrange, to support the initiation and control of interactions. We plan to develop close-range sensing to identify users' facial expressions and gaze. This will allow the kiosk to become more aware of users' intentions and mental states.

Our prototype kiosk senses and tracks people in a simple, open environment. A fully developed kiosk may be situated in environments as diverse as airports, shopping malls, theme parks, hotels, and cinema lobbies. In these situations, the level of interaction between the user and the kiosk can be enhanced if the kiosk has at its disposal a model of its environment. By determining through stereo the current location of the user relative to itself, the kiosk can situate the user relative to the model of its environment and respond or react more intelligently to the user's actions.

To this end, we have developed an algorithm to reconstruct the scene using multiple panoramic (full 360° horizontal field of view) images of the scene (Fig. 4.7). The 3D model of the scene is recovered by applying stereo on the multiple panoramic views to create a 3D point distribution (Fig. 4.8(left)) [167]. This 3D point distribution is then used to create a 3D mesh that is texture-mapped with a color panoramic image to produce a 3D reconstructed scene model (Fig. 4.8(right)) [166]. We plan to incorporate models created using this method into the kiosk that we are developing.

We also plan to add alternate input modalities to our kiosk. Speech understanding will enable a user to interact with the kiosk in a direct way. The combination of speech and visual sensing will provide a rich and natural communication medium.

The second focus of our future work is development of more com-

Fig. 4.7. Three panoramic views of the kiosk space scene.

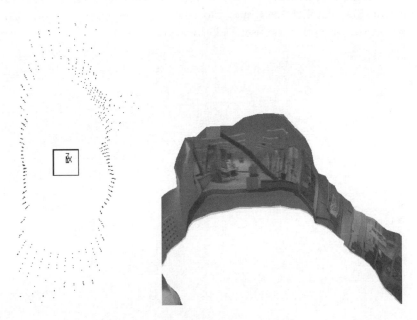

Fig. 4.8 Top view of recovered 3D point distribution (left) and portion of texture mapped reconstructed 3D scene model (right).

plex and more compelling kiosk behaviors. We can develop behavioral characteristics for DECface's voice, speech pattern, facial gestures, head movement and expressions that will cause users to attribute a personality to the kiosk. We would also like the kiosk to create goals dynamically, based on its charter, user input, and the direction of the current interaction. These goals drive the motivational actions of the kiosk. Management of competing goals and flexibility in response to a changing user population will be key.

4.8 Conclusion

We have demonstrated a significant role for visual sensing in public user-interfaces. Using simple vision and graphics technology, we have developed an engaging user-interface capable of reacting directly to an individual's actions. In addition, we have begun to explore the role of gaze in communicating intention and focus of attention through the use of a synthetic character with an articulate face.

Like other researchers, we have found that color is a valuable feature for tracking people in real-time, and that it can be used in conjunction with stereo to resolve the users' 3D location.

5

A Human–Robot Interface using Pointing with Uncalibrated Stereo Vision

R. Cipolla and N.J. Hollinghurst

Abstract

Computer vision provides many opportunities for novel man–machine interfaces. Pointing and face gestures can be used as a simple, passive means of interfacing with computers and robots. In this chapter we present the results of an investigation into the use of a gesture based interface for robot guidance. The system requires no physical contact with the operator, but uses uncalibrated stereo vision with active contours to track the position and pointing direction of a hand. With a ground plane constraint, it is then possible to find the indicated position in the robot's workspace, by considering only two-dimensional collineations. With feedback to the user, points can be indicated to an accuracy of about 1cm in a 40cm workspace, allowing simple pick-and-place operations to be specified by pointing with a finger.

5.1 Introduction

There has been a lot of interest lately in the use of hand gestures for human–computer interfacing: they are intuitive for the operator, and provide a rich source of information to the machine. This type of interface is particularly appropriate in applications such as virtual reality, multimedia and teleoperation [280, 130, 22].

Most current commercial implementations rely on sensors that are physically attached to the hand, such as the 'DataGlove' [127]. More recently, systems have been proposed using *vision* to observe the hand. Some require special gloves with attachments or markings to facilitate the localization and tracking of hand parts [317, 80], but others operate

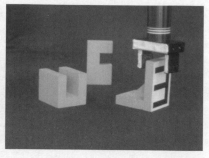

Fig. 5.1 The arrangement of the uncalibrated stereo cameras, table and robot. The cameras view the robot, workspace and operator's hand from a distance of about 1.6m. The operator points at an object, and the robot picks it up under visual control.

without intrusive hardware. This is attractive because it is convenient for the user and potentially cheaper to implement.

Here we present an experimental implementation of such a system, concentrating in particular on the case of *pointing* at a distant object. We have developed a simple vision-based pointing system as an input device for a robot manipulator, to provide a novel and convenient means for the operator to specify points for pick-and-place operations. We use *active contour* techniques to track a hand in a pointing gesture, with conventional monochrome cameras and fairly modest computing hardware (Fig. 5.1).

A single view of a pointing hand is ambiguous: its distance from the camera cannot be determined, and the 'slant' of its orientation cannot be measured with any accuracy. Stereo views are used to recover the hand's position and orientation, and yield the line along which the index finger is pointing. In our system, we assume that the user is pointing towards a 'target surface,' which is a horizontal plane. We show how a simple result from projective geometry can be applied to this case, allowing the system to be implemented with *uncalibrated* stereo, that requires no measurements or special assumptions about camera positions and parameters.

5.2 Geometrical Framework

5.2.1 Viewing the plane

Consider a pinhole camera viewing a plane. The viewing transformation is a plane collineation between some world coordinate system (X, Y),

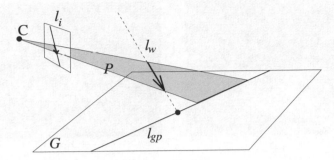

Fig. 5.2 Relation between lines in the world, image and ground planes. Projection of the finger's image line l_i onto the ground plane yields a constraint line l_{gp} on which the indicated point must lie.

and image plane coordinates (u, v), thus:

$$
\begin{bmatrix} su \\ sv \\ s \end{bmatrix} = \mathbf{T} \begin{bmatrix} X \\ Y \\ 1 \end{bmatrix},
\tag{5.1}
$$

where s is a scale factor that varies for each point; and $\mathbf{T}$ is a 3×3 transformation matrix. The system is homogeneous, so we can fix $t_{33} = 1$ without loss of generality, leaving 8 degrees of freedom. To solve for $\mathbf{T}$ we must observe at least four points. By assigning arbitrary world coordinates to these points (e.g. $(0, 0)$, $(0, 1)$, $(1, 1)$, $(1, 0)$), we define a new coordinate system on the plane, which we call *working plane coordinates*.

Now, given the image coordinates of a point anywhere on the plane, along with the image coordinates of the four reference points, it is possible to invert the relation and recover the point's working plane coordinates, which are invariant to the choice of camera location [225]. We use the same set of reference points for a stereo pair of views, and compute two transformations $\mathbf{T}$ and $\mathbf{T}'$, one for each camera.

5.2.2 Recovering the indicated point in stereo

With natural human pointing behavior, the hand is used to define a line in space, passing through the base and tip of the index finger. This line will not generally be in the target plane but intersects the plane at some point. It is this point (the *'piercing point'* or *'indicated point'*) that we aim to recover. Let the pointing finger lie along the line l_w in space (see

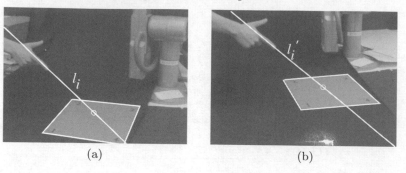

(a)   (b)

Fig. 5.3 Pointing at the plane. Uncalibrated stereo pair of pointing hand showing the image constraints and four coplanar points of the ground plane.

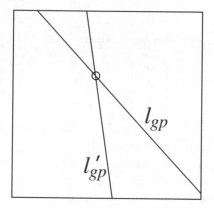

Fig. 5.4 Combining constraints from two views. By taking the lines of pointing in left and right views (see above), transforming them into the canonical frame defined by the four corners of the grey rectangle, and finding the intersection of the lines, the indicated point can be determined; this is then projected back into the images.

Fig. 5.2). Viewed by a camera, it appears on line l_i in the image, which is also the projection of a *plane*, $\mathcal{P}$, passing through the image line and the optical centre of the camera. This plane intersects the ground plane $\mathcal{G}$ along line l_{gp}. We know that l_w lies in $\mathcal{P}$, and the indicated point in l_{gp}, but from one view we cannot see exactly where.

Note that the line l_i is an image of line l_{gp}; that is, $l_i = \mathbf{T}(l_{gp})$, where $\mathbf{T}$ is the projective transformation from equation (1). If the four reference points are visible, this transformation can be inverted to find l_{gp} in terms of the working plane coordinates. The indicated point is constrained to lie upon this line on the target surface.

Repeating the above procedure with the second camera C' gives us another view l'_i of the finger, and another line of constraint l'_{gp}. The two constraint lines will intersect at a point on the target plane, which is the indicated point. Its position can now be found relative to the four reference points. Fig. 5.3 shows the lines of pointing in a pair of images, and the intersecting constraint lines in a 'canonical' view of the working plane (in which the reference point quadrilateral is transformed to a square). This is a variation of a method employed by Quan and Mohr [248], who present an analysis based on cross-ratios.

By transforming this point with projections T and T', the indicated point can be projected back into image coordinates. Although the working plane coordinates of the indicated point depend on the configuration of the reference points, its back-projections into the images do not. Because all calculations are restricted to the image and ground planes, explicit 3D reconstruction is avoided and no camera calibration is necessary. By tracking at least four points on the target plane, the system can be made insensitive to camera motions.

5.3 Tracking a pointing hand

5.3.1 Background

A large number of systems have been proposed for visual tracking and interpretation of hand and finger movements. These systems can broadly be divided into:

- those concerned with gesture identification (e.g. for sign language), which compare the image sequence with a set of standard gestures using correlation and warping of the templates [102], or classify them with neural networks;
- those which try to reconstruct the pose and shape of the hand (e.g. for teleoperation) by fitting a deformable, articulated model of the palm and finger surfaces to the incoming image sequence [186].

Common to many of these systems is the requirement to calibrate the templates or hand model to suit each individual user. They also tend to have high computational requirements, taking several seconds per frame on a conventional workstation, or expensive multiprocessor hardware for real-time implementation.

Our approach differs from these general systems in an important respect: we wish only to recover the line along which the hand is pointing, to be able to specify points on a ground plane. This considerably reduces

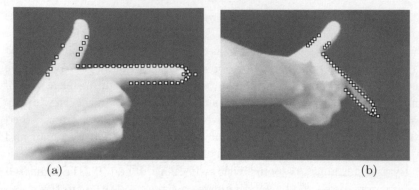

(a)   (b)

Fig. 5.5 The finger-tracking active contour, (a) in its canonical frame (b) after an affine transformation in the image plane (to track a rigid motion of the hand in 3D). It is the index finger which defines the direction of pointing; the thumb is observed to facilitate the tracking of longitudinal translations which would otherwise be difficult to detect.

the degrees of freedom which we need to track. Furthermore, because the hand must be free to move about as it points to distant objects, it will occupy only a relatively small fraction of the pixel area in each image, reducing the number of features that can be distinguished.

In this case it is not unreasonable to insist that the user adopt a rigid gesture. For simplicity, the familiar 'pistol' pointing gesture was chosen. The pointing direction can now be recovered from the image of the index finger, although the thumb is also prominent and can be usefully tracked. The rest of the hand, which has a complicated and rather variable shape, is ignored. This does away with the need to calibrate the system to each user's hand.

5.3.2 Tracking mechanism

We use a type of active contour model [169, 77, 143] to track the image of a hand in the familiar 'pointing' gesture, in real-time. Our tracking mechanism was chosen mainly for its speed, simplicity, and modest demand for computer resources. A pair of trackers operate independently on two stereo views.

Anatomy

Each tracker is based on a template, representing the shape of the occluding contours of an extended index finger and thumb (see Fig. 5.5). At about 50 sites around the contour (represented in the figure by dots) are *local edgefinders* which continuously measure the normal offsets between the predicted contour and actual features in the image; these offsets are used to update the image position and orientation of the tracker.

The tracker's motion is restricted to 2D affine transformations in the image plane, which ensures that it keeps its shape whilst tracking the fingers in a variety of poses [39]. This approach is suitable for tracking planar objects under weak perspective; however it also works well with fingers, which are approximately cylindrical.

The positions of these sampling points are expressed in affine coordinates, and their image positions depend on the tracker's *local origin* and two *basis vectors*. These are described by six parameters, which change over time as the hand is tracked.

Dynamics

At each time-step, the tracker searches for the maximum image gradient along each sampling interval, which is a short line segment, normal to and centred about a point on the active contour. This yields the *normal offsets* between points on the active contour and their corresponding edge segments in the image.

The offsets are used to estimate the affine transformation (translation, rotation, scale and shear) of the active contour model, which minimises the errors in a least-squares sense. A first-order temporal filter is used to predict the future position of the contour, to improve its real-time tracking performance. The filter is biased to favour rigid motions in the image, and limits the rate at which the tracker can change scale — these constraints represent prior knowledge of how the hand's image is likely to change, and increase the reliability with which it can be tracked.

To extract the hand's direction of pointing, we estimate the orientation of the index finger; the base of the thumb is tracked merely to resolve an *aperture problem* [294] induced by the finger's long thin shape.

5.4 Implementation

5.4.1 Equipment

The system is implemented on a Sun SPARCstation 10 with a Data Cell S2200 frame grabber. Images are provided by two monochrome CCD cameras, which view the operator's hand and the working area from a distance of about 1.6 metres. The angle between the cameras is about 30°. A Scorbot ER-7 robot arm is also controlled by the Sun (Fig. 5.1).

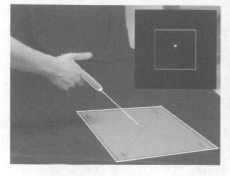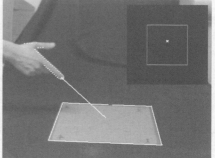

Fig. 5.6 Stereo views of a pointing hand. The two views are shown side by side. In each view an active contour is tracking the hand. The inlaid square is a representation of the indicated point in working plane coordinates.

5.4.2 Experiment

Setup

In this experiment, the corners of a coloured rectangle on the table-top are used to define the working coordinate system. A pair of finger-trackers (one for each camera) is initialised, one after the other, by the operator holding his hand up to a template in the image and waiting a few seconds while it 'moulds' itself to the contours of the finger and thumb. Once both trackers are running, the hand can be used as an input device by pointing to places on the table-top. In our implementation, the position and orientation of the finger, and the indicated point on the plane, are updated about 10 times per second.

Performance

Fig. 5.6 shows the system in operation. The corners of the white rectangle are the four reference points, and the overlaid square shows the position of the indicated point. Movements of the operator's hand cause corresponding movements of this point in real-time.

Visual tracking can follow the hand successfully for several minutes at a time; however, abrupt or non-rigid hand movements can cause one or both of the trackers to fail. Because it samples the image only locally, a failed tracker will not correct itself unless the user makes a special effort to recapture it.

Users report that the recovered point does not always correspond to their subjective pointing direction, which is related to the line of sight from *eye* to fingertip as well as the orientation of the finger itself. Initial

Left Image   Canonical View   Right Image

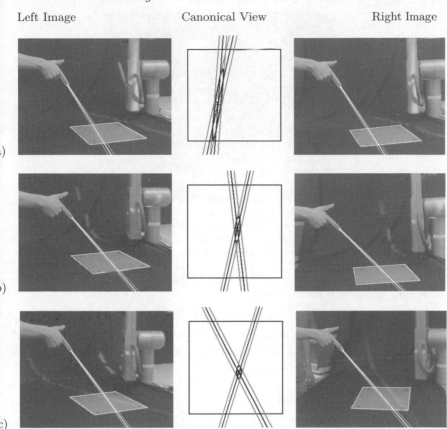

Fig. 5.7 Indicated point uncertainty for 3 different camera configurations. 2σ bounds for the pointing lines, their projections into working plane coordinates, and error ellipses for the indicated point, when the angle between stereo views is (a) $7°$ (b) $16°$ (c) $34°$. The uncertainty is greatest when the camera angle is small and the constraint lines nearly parallel.

subjective estimates of accuracy are in the order of 20–40mm. If the user receives feedback by viewing the system's behavior on a monitor screen, a resolution within 10mm can be achieved. It is a natural human skill to servo the motion of one's hand to control a cursor or other visual indication.

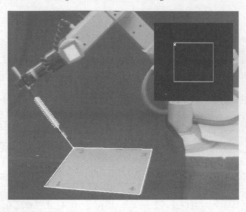

Fig. 5.8 Mechanical pointing device used to test the accuracy of our system. We aligned the rod with known points on the workspace, and recorded its coordinates as recovered by the vision system.

5.4.3 Accuracy evaluation

To evaluate our system, we calculate the uncertainty of the images of the hand and reference points in our experimental setup. Using Monte Carlo methods, these are propagated into working plane coordinates, to assess the accuracy of the indicated point.

Finger tracker uncertainty

We can obtain a measure of uncertainty for the finger's position and orientation in the image by considering the *residual offsets* between modelled and observed image edges. These are the components of the normal offsets that remain after fitting a pair of parallel lines to model the index finger's occluding edges, with least-squares perpendicular error. They take into account the effects of image noise and occlusion, as well as pixel quantisation effects, and mismatches between the model and the actual shape of the index finger.

These offsets indicate that the image position of the finger's midline can be determined to sub-pixel accuracy (standard deviation typically $\sigma = 0.3$ pixels), and the orientation to an accuracy of $0.6°$.

From this uncertainty measure we calculate $\pm 2\sigma$ bounds on lines l_i and l'_i; and, by projecting these onto the ground plane, estimate the uncertainty in the indicated point.

Fig. 5.7 shows the results for three different configurations of the cameras, with a 95% confidence ellipse drawn around the indicated point. The constraint line uncertainties are much the same in each trial, but the uncertainty on the indicated point varies according to the separation between the stereo views: when the cameras are close together, the constraint lines are nearly parallel and tracker uncertainty is very significant (figure 5.7a); as the baseline is increased and the stereo views become more distinct, the constraint lines meet at a greater angle and accuracy is improved (Fig. 5.7c).

Experimental accuracy

Ground truth about the position and orientation of a human finger is, of course, very difficult to measure without intrusive equipment that could interfere with our stereo vision system. We therefore tested the accuracy of the pointing system using an artificial pointing device (Fig. 5.8). The test pointer was a white cylinder, about 15cm long, bounded by black end stops and wrapped around a rod which could be positioned by the robot arm to an accuracy of about 1mm. Whilst not identical to a human hand, it had approximately the same dimensions and was tracked in a similar manner.

A number of trials were carried out with the vision system tracking the rod as it was aligned with points on a grid on the target surface. The RMS error was 2.3% of the working plane coordinates, or 9mm in a 40cm workspace. The maximum reported error was 3.7% (15mm).

5.4.4 Robot control application

The proposed application for this stereo pointing system is to control a robot manipulator as it grasps and places small objects on a flat table-top. The reference points are defined by observing the robot gripper itself as it visits four points in a plane (using active contours similar to those which track the pointing hand [148]). This not only defines the working coordinate system but relates it to the robot's own world coordinate system. Finger-trackers are then initialised as before.

The robot is now instructed to move repeatedly to where the hand is pointing, in a horizontal working plane raised 50mm above the table-top. By watching the robot's motion, the operator is provided with a source of direct feedback of the system's output, allowing him or her to correct for systematic errors between subjective and observed pointing direction, and align the gripper over objects in the robot's workspace.

When the distance between hand and workspace is large, the system is sensitive to small changes in index finger orientation (as one would expect). To reduce this sensitivity, the operator maintains a steep angle

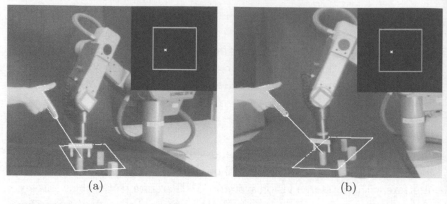

(a)   (b)

Fig. 5.9 Gestural control of robot position for grasping, seen in stereo. The robot gripper servos to the position indicated by the pointing hand; here it is being instructed to align itself with the small wooded block to be grasped. The four reference points (white rectangle) were defined by the robot's gripper in a plane 50mm above the table.

to the horizontal, and points from a distance of less than 50cm from the plane, whilst still keeping his or her hand clear of the robot. One can then comfortably position the gripper with sufficient accuracy to pick up small objects (Fig. 5.9).

A complete system [79] has been implemented which integrates the pointing interface with a grasp planner and stereo hand-eye coordination. The system comprises three distinct stages. In the first stage, an operator indicates the object to be grasped by simply pointing at it. Next, the stereo vision system segments the identified object from the background (by grouping edges into planes) and plans a suitable grasp strategy. Finally, the robotic arm reaches out towards the object and executes the grasp under visual feedback [79].

5.5 Conclusion

Pointing can be used successfully to specify positions on a two-dimensional workspace for a robot manipulator. The system is simple and intuitive for an operator to use, and requires practically no training.

This method for computing the indicated point proves to be robust in the presence of tracker uncertainties and noise. Its accuracy depends on the geometry of the stereo cameras, and is best when they are at least an angle of 30° apart. The system does not require camera calibration because all calculation takes place in the image and ground planes. By

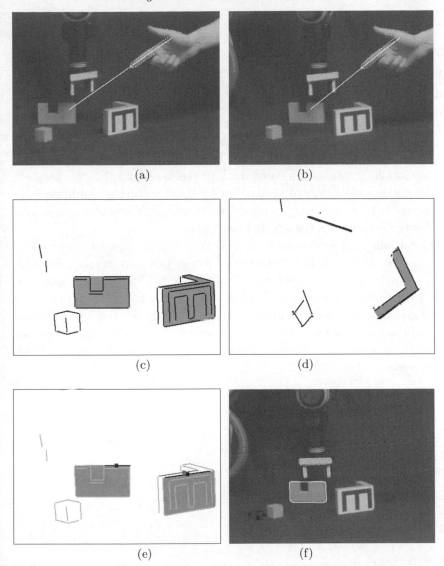

Fig. 5.10 Visually guided grasping of an object: (a,b) stereo views of a pointing hand indicating the object to be grasped; (c,d) reconstruction of the scene; (e) permissible grasp sites; (f) alignment of gripper with target using visual feedback.

tracking at least 4 points on the plane it could be made invariant to camera movement.

The main problem for this system is tracking a pointing hand reliably in stereo. At present, this is only possible in an environment where there is a strong contrast between the hand and the background. Our current system requires the index finger and thumb to be kept rigid throughout operation. Tracking speed is limited by our hardware (a single Sun SPARCstation) and could be improved by adding faster computing or image processing equipment. Improvements to hardware performance would allow more sophisticated tracking mechanisms to be incorporated, permitting more degrees of freedom for hand gesturing. Additional robustness to clutter can be provided by enforcing epipolar constraints between trackers in the left and right images.

Although subjective pointing direction depends upon eye as well as hand position, it is not necessary to model this phenomenon. Instead, by providing the operator with feedback about the *objective* pointing direction (e.g. having a robot follow the pointing hand in real-time), the hand can be aligned with any desired object on the working plane. Points can then be indicated with sufficient accuracy to guide simple pick-and-place operations that might otherwise have been specified using a teach pendant.

Part two
Tracking Human Action

6

Tracking Faces

A.H. Gee and R. Cipolla

Abstract

The ability to track a face in a video stream opens up new possibilities for human computer interaction. Applications range from head gesture-based interfaces for physically handicapped people, to image-driven animated models for low bandwidth video conferencing. Here we present a novel face tracking algorithm which is robust to partial occlusion of the face. Since the tracker is tolerant of noisy, computationally cheap feature detectors, frame-rate operation is comfortably achieved on standard hardware.

6.1 Introduction

The ability to detect and track a person's face is potentially very powerful for human-computer interaction. For example, a person's gaze can be used to indicate something, in much the same manner as pointing. One can envisage a window manager which automatically shuffles to the foreground whichever window the user is looking at [153, 152]. Gaze aside, the head position and orientation can be used for virtual holography [14]: as the viewer moves around the screen, the computer displays a different projection of a scene, giving the illusion of holography. Another application lies in low-bandwidth video conferencing: live images of participant's face can be used to guide a remote, synthesised "clone" face which is viewed by other participants [180, 197]. A head tracker could also provide a very useful computer interface for physically handicapped people, some of whom can only communicate using head gestures. With an increasing number of desktop computers being supplied with video cameras and framegrabbers as standard (ostensibly for video mail applications), it is becoming both useful and feasible to track the computer user's face. We have developed techniques for inferring the gaze direction of arbitrary faces in static images [132], but here we focus on a novel model-based visual tracking algorithm [133] which has proved to be very effective at tracking faces as they move at high speed in image sequences.

6.2 Model-based visual tracking

A visual tracking algorithm can be found at the heart of many real-time computer vision systems. The most robust class of tracking algorithms are the so-called "model-based" trackers, which exploit prior knowledge of the target's shape to enhance resilience to occlusion and noise. For a face tracking application, where there are few stable features to detect and track, the resilience offered by a model-based approach is highly desirable. It is a straightforward matter to acquire an adequate model of a new face [133].

Almost all model-based trackers work on the same basic principle:

Measurement: A number of key features, usually corners or edges, are detected in each frame of the image sequence. These features are known to correspond to features in a 3D model of the target.

Pose estimation: The image positions of the detected features are used to calculate the target's *pose* relative to the camera: that is, its relative position and orientation.

Filter: The result of this pose calculation is often filtered to reduce the effects of noise in the feature detectors, usually drawing on some sort of smooth motion assumption (which is reasonable, given that the motion of rigid objects is governed by inertia).

Predict: The position of the target is predicted in the next frame, again using the smooth motion assumption, and the key features are searched for in small windows around their expected image positions. This *local* search allows the tracker to run quickly, and overcomes any problems establishing correspondence between model and image features.

In this chapter we examine each of these stages in the context of the face tracking application, arriving at a novel model-based tracking algorithm.

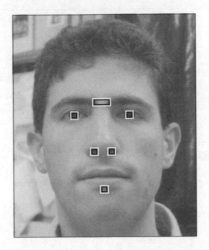

Fig. 6.1. Features and search windows for face tracking.

6.2.1 Detecting facial features

The visual features used in the face tracking algorithm are shown in Fig. 6.1. Dark-pixel finders (which simply return the location of the darkest pixel within their local search windows) are used to locate the eyes, nostrils and the shadow below the lower lip. A coarse correlation-based detector is used to detect the centre of the eyebrows using a dark-light-dark correlation template. While this set of features has proved adequate for our own trials, it is possible that other features, coupled with suitable feature detectors, could be used to great advantage on other faces.

The advantage of such simple feature detectors is their speed: more conventional feature detectors, which typically require some sort of convolution operation, are much slower. In real-time tracking applications speed is of the essence, even if this means sacrificing some accuracy. Subsequent stages of the tracking algorithm must be sufficiently robust to cope with noisy feature detection.

6.2.2 Estimating the face's pose

Given the detected image features, and the corresponding points in the 3D model of the face, the next stage is to calculate the pose of the face relative to the camera. Assuming a full perspective camera model

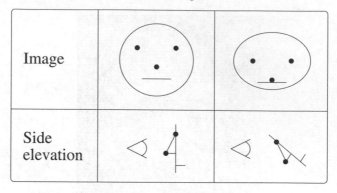

Fig. 6.2. Three points admit two poses under weak-perspective.

(the pinhole camera model), a closed-form technique exists to calculate the pose, up to a four-fold ambiguity, from three of the features [125]. However, the calculation requires significant camera calibration, and is also fairly complicated. Simplification is possible if we assume a weak-perspective (or scaled orthographic) camera model [257, 287], valid when the viewing distance is large compared with the depth variation across the face. The weak-perspective projection from a point (X, Y, Z) on the face (in model-centered coordinates) to an image point (x, y) is described mathematically as follows:

$$\begin{bmatrix} x \\ y \end{bmatrix} = s \begin{bmatrix} R_{11} & R_{12} & R_{13} & t_x \\ R_{21} & R_{22} & R_{23} & t_y \end{bmatrix} \begin{bmatrix} X \\ Y \\ Z \\ 1 \end{bmatrix} \tag{6.1}$$

The projection describes a rigid body rotation by the rotation matrix $\mathbf{R}$, a translation parallel to the image plane (t_x, t_y), orthographic projection onto the image plane and an isotropic scaling s in the plane. Under these viewing conditions, three points admit only two possible poses, which can be found using the "alignment" algorithm [154]. The calculation is reliable, simple, stable and closed-form. It takes as input three image points (x_i, y_i) with corresponding model points (X_i, Y_i, Z_i), and returns the rotation matrix $\mathbf{R}$, the translation vector (t_x, t_y) and the scale factor s for the two possible solutions. The inevitable two-fold ambiguity in the pose solution is illustrated in Fig. 6.2, which shows a stylized face in two different poses being viewed through a weak-perspective camera. In both images the eye and nose points appear in identical relative position.

In fact the pose estimation problem is over-constrained, since there are more points available (six) than are required (three). Assuming the measurements are corrupted by zero-mean Gaussian noise, the optimal pose can be found using least-squares regression. For this reason, many tracking algorithms [134, 143, 203] employ all the measurements and some sort of least-squares pose fitting criterion. Least-squares techniques do not, however, perform well in the presence of occlusion. Under such conditions, the Gaussian noise assumption breaks down and the detectors attempting to localise occluded features produce spurious measurements. Consider, for example, Fig. 6.3, which shows the tracking error of one of the nostril detectors. The detector performs well when the nostril is visible, finding the nostril position to within, typically, three pixels. When the head is turned so that the nostril is less prominent, between cycles 500 and 1100, the feature detector starts to show a bias as it finds instead the shadow around the outline of the nose. This sort of behavior is typical of simple visual feature detectors, and demonstrates that it is unwise to assume zero-mean Gaussian noise on the detector outputs. A standard least-squares fit to the six measurements is therefore inappropriate.

Instead we use RANSAC [125], a robust regression scheme, to accurately estimate the face's pose. All combinations of three measurements out of the six available are considered in each frame. For each set of three measurements, the two solutions proposed by the alignment algorithm are assessed on the basis of consensus: if the pose is also consistent with some of the other measurements, this constitutes an extended consensus which lends support to that pose hypothesis.

The notion of consensus is illustrated in Fig. 6.4, which shows a frame from a typical image sequence. A set of facial features is detected in the image using imperfect feature detectors whose outputs are displayed as crosses. All measurements are good except at the left nostril (measurement 5). If measurements 1, 2 and 3 are used to estimate the pose, the model back-projects into the image as shown on the left (back-projected model points are displayed as squares). Five of the measurements are consistent with this pose (by *consistent*, we mean that they lie within some predetermined tolerance, say r pixels, of the back-projected model points). If measurements 1, 3 and 5 are used to estimate the pose, then the size of the consensus set is only three, as shown on the right. Thus consensus can be used to select the best pose from the $2 \times {}^6C_3$ candidate solutions, reliably rejecting outlying measurements.

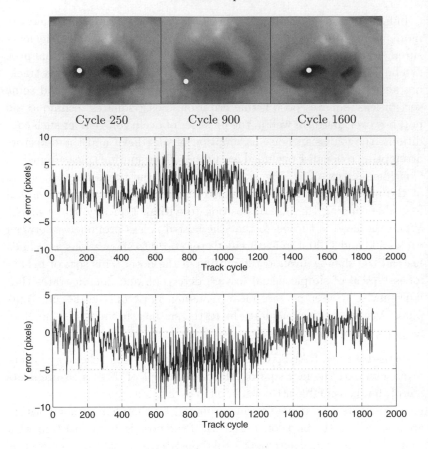

Fig. 6.3. Tracking error of a typical feature detector.

6.2.3 Filtering

The effects of inaccurate pose estimates can be reduced using a motion model: the face is expected to move smoothly from frame to frame. The Kalman filter paradigm describes how to optimally weigh the prediction of the motion model and the measured pose, assuming zero-mean Gaussian distributions for the measurement and process noise. However, computer vision researchers have reported problems using this sort of approach: while optimal for zero-mean Gaussian noise, the Kalman filter fails to cope with the sort of measurement and process noise often encountered in visual tracking [156, 203].

The use of the RANSAC regression scheme provides an opportunity

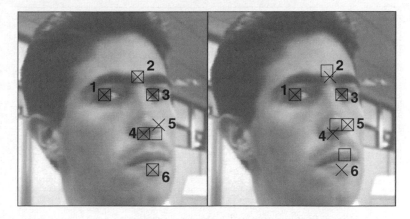

Fig. 6.4. Using consensus to select the best pose.

to perform the pose estimation and filtering simultaneously. First it is necessary to assign a probability distribution to the size of the consensus set. Assuming each of the n feature detectors can localise its feature to within r pixels of its true location with probability p, and the size of the consensus set for a particular pose $\mathcal{H}$ is k, then the conditional probability of obtaining the measurements m is given by the binomial distribution:

$$P(m \mid \mathcal{H}) = {}^{n}C_{k} \ p^{k}(1-p)^{n-k} \qquad (6.2)$$

While it is possible to select a pose solution based solely on the evidence term (6.2), it would be advantageous also to consider any motion prior at this point, so avoiding a separate and costly filtering stage. If the tracking rate is fast so that the face moves only a small amount from frame to frame, then a suitable prior would be

$$P(\mathcal{H}) \propto \exp\left(-\frac{\|\mathbf{v}\|^2}{2\sigma_l^2} - \frac{\|\boldsymbol{\omega}\|^2}{2\sigma_a^2}\right) \qquad (6.3)$$

where $\mathbf{v}$ and $\boldsymbol{\omega}$ are the linear and angular velocities implied by the pose hypothesis $\mathcal{H}$ (calculated using the pose estimate in the previous frame), and σ_l and σ_a are the assumed standard deviations of these quantities (which can be estimated with some knowledge of the expected motion). It is not necessary to attempt to model the individual components of velocity and their covariances: any assumed covariance matrices would, in any case, be somewhat arbitrary for the sort of motion often encountered in visual tracking tasks [203]. In (6.3) $P(\mathcal{H})$ expresses the belief

---

1. Choose three image points and calculate the two solutions for the face's pose using the alignment algorithm.

2. For each calculated pose, back-project the face model into the image using (6.1). Calculate the size of the consensus set (k) and the linear and angular velocities ($\mathbf{v}$ and ω) using the pose in the previous frame.

3. Repeat 1 and 2 for all combinations of three points. Choose the pose that maximises $P(\mathcal{H} \mid m)$ in (6.4).

Fig. 6.5. The temporal consensus tracking algorithm.

that little inter-frame motion is more likely than large inter-frame motion, regardless of any available measurements. The best pose estimate for each frame can then be selected from the $2 \times^n C_3$ possible solutions as the one which maximizes the a posteriori probability

$$P(\mathcal{H} \mid m) \propto^n C_k \; p^k (1-p)^{n-k} \times \exp\left(-\frac{\|\mathbf{v}\|^2}{2\sigma_l^2} - \frac{\|\omega\|^2}{2\sigma_a^2}\right) \qquad (6.4)$$

The resulting algorithm, which we have dubbed the "temporal consensus" tracker, is summarised in Fig. 6.5. The algorithm elegantly combines robust pose estimation with motion filtering: there is no need for a separate Kalman filtering stage. The performance of the tracker is fairly insensitive to the four parameters r, p, σ_a and σ_l, and compares favorably with other face trackers described in the literature. The temporal consensus tracker runs at frame rate on standard hardware, and can track faces at angular velocities up to 80 deg/s, and angular accelerations up to 800 deg/s^2 [133]. No make-up is required to enhance the facial features, and the tracker is tolerant of mild occlusion and changes in facial expression. In our experiments the tracker is initialized by hand in the first frame, though techniques do exist for the automatic location of facial features, using either parameterized models (eg. [95]) or grey-level templates (eg. [62]).

6.3 Head gesture interfaces

A prime application of the head tracking algorithm lies at the front-end of a head gesture computer interface. Such interfaces are of particular

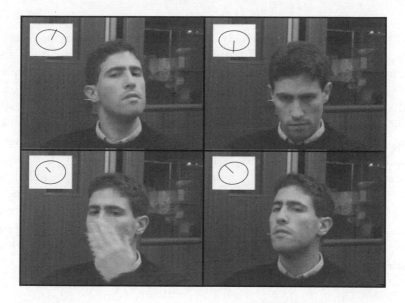

Fig. 6.6. Some frames from a head tracking sequence.

value to physically handicapped people, who might have considerable difficulty using conventional input devices. For example, the JESTER system [241], currently under commercial development, uses head gestures to replace the mouse in generic PC-based Windows applications. In its standard configuration, JESTER senses head pose using a commercially available magnetic transducer, such as the Polhemus 3Space Isotrak. Unfortunately, magnetic pose transducers cost many times more than the PC equipment they are connected to. Far more desirable would be a vision-based transducer, especially now that many computer systems are being supplied with video cameras and framegrabbers as standard.

We have integrated the visual face tracker into the JESTER system, and found that its output is good enough to enable successful recognition of a variety of head gestures. Some typical frames from a head gesture sequence, along with the tracker's orientation estimates (illustrated as drawing pins in the top left hand corner of each frame) can be found in Fig. 6.6. Note the tracker's tolerance of mild occlusion of the face. It remains to be seen whether the tracker is sufficiently robust to cope with the unpredictable head movements of severely handicapped people.

6.4 Conclusions

With computer users increasingly likely to find themselves facing a camera as well as a screen, applications for face tracking algorithms are bound to emerge. There is already interest in face tracking for hands-off gesture-based HCI, gaze detection, "virtual holography" and actor-driven animation. With these applications in mind, a new model-based tracking algorithm has been described, eschewing least-squares pose fitting in favour of a more robust approach. The well-established "alignment" algorithm has been embedded within the RANSAC regression paradigm to form the heart of the tracker. By elegantly combining intra-frame observations with inter-frame motion constraints, it is possible to avoid a separate and costly filtering stage. The resulting tracker works very well when applied to the difficult task of tracking a human face under adverse conditions, and should be equally successful with a variety of other targets.

7

Towards Automated, Real-time, Facial Animation

B. Bascle, A. Blake and J. Morris

Abstract

With the rapid growth of new technologies, in particular the graphics industry and teleconferencing technology, has come the need for more realistic animation of human characters. The most accurate way of achieving this seems to be actually to measure human motion. An area of particular interest is facial motion. This chapter presents a real-time approach based on active contours, developed to track facial deformations and rigid movements. The level of performance achieved in following agile movements in real-time relies on powerful statistical tools for measuring and modeling non-rigid dynamics.

7.1 Introduction

There has been a good deal of recent interest in measuring facial motion for animation. This has a wide range of applications, such as teleconferencing, video-games, aids for the deaf and human-computer interaction. Currently a popular approach to this task uses reflective markers to estimate the three-dimensional position of key features of the face and drive corresponding key control points on mesh-based graphical face models. The main drawbacks of this approach are the discomfort of wearing markers, and the need to use images captured specially for the purpose. Natural images, in which subjects wear no markers, cannot be used, preventing the opportunistic use of prerecorded sequences.

In this chapter we describe the approach developed to track facial deformations, designed for an interface currently being developed to drive facial animation. Facial deformations are tracked reliably from camera images, in conditions close to normal; only light make-up is required to

123

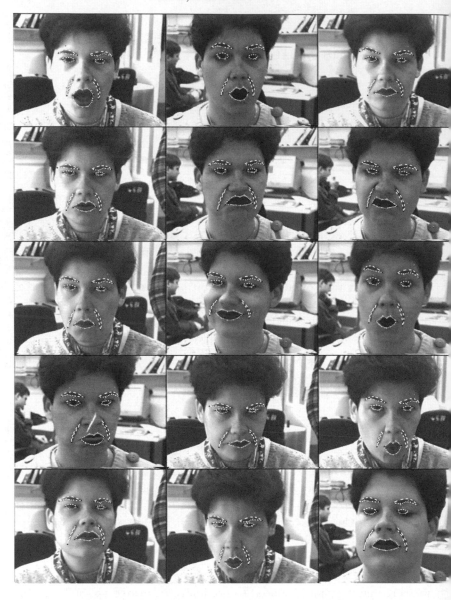

Fig. 7.1. **Tracking facial expressions in real-time.**

highlight a few facial features. Furthermore, work [172] in progress is expected to help progressively to get rid of any requirement for make-up at all. Real-time performance from an Indy 4400 SC 200MHz workstation is illustrated by the results shown in Fig. 7.1 and further details are available at web-site http://www.robots.ox.ac.uk/~ab.

7.2 Tracking facial expressions

The ability to track the human face has many applications. It can be used to determine head orientation, as in holography [14] or for guiding a "clone" face in teleconferencing [180, 197]. Sometimes the gaze direction is the information of interest [132] but more and more often, tracking the entire face is the goal [133]. Some applications are specifically concerned with particular facial features, such as the mouth in speech recognition [172] while others require a face to be located in an image [88]. Face tracking is also useful for recognition purposes [120, 38, 191].

7.2.1 Face templates

Techniques for sketching faces [93] suggest that the most important features to convey facial expression are the eyes, eyebrows, mouth and "wrinkles" that frame the mouth and that the outlines of those features are often sufficient to capture an expression. Additional features that could be used are the wrinkles that appear and vanish on the forehead depending on the subject's expression, but they are transient. Our template is formed by the contours of the following four features: eyes, eyebrows, mouth and wrinkles. Finn *et al* (1995) have reported success using similar features obtained through tracking dots on the face. Studies by several authors have demonstrated that in grey level images, mouth and wrinkles show poor contrast. Currently therefore black make-up is used to underline these features. However, work in progress suggests that this constraint can be removed [172], by using colour information.

A face template can be built as a B-spline curve [20] incorporating multiple knots wherever necessary, so that discontinuities of the curve or its first derivative can be obtained. In our system, splines are quadratic and are customised to fit a given person. The curve can be written as a parametric B-spline with N spans and N_c control points:

$$\mathbf{r}(s,t) = \begin{pmatrix} \mathbf{B}(s) & \mathbf{0} \\ \mathbf{0} & \mathbf{B}(s) \end{pmatrix} \mathbf{Q}(t), \ 0 \leq s \leq N$$

where the elements of $\mathbf{Q} = (X_1, \ldots, X_{N_c}, Y_1, \ldots, Y_{N_c})^T$ are simply the x and y coordinates of the set of control points for the B-spline. The number of control points is equal to the number of spans ($N_c = N$) for closed curves, whereas $N_c = N + d$ for open curves (with appropriate variations in both cases if necessary to account for multiple knots). The vector $\mathbf{B}(s)$ consists of:

$$\mathbf{B}(s) = (B_1(s), \ldots, B_{N_c}(s))$$

where the $B_m(s)$ arc the values at arc-length s of the B-spline basis functions appropriate to the order of the curve and its set of knots [20]. Tracking B-spline curves such as these can be accomplished by generating estimates of the curve control points.

7.2.2 Shape space

As studies have shown [39], unconstrained deformable models have limited tracking capabilities due to their instability. They normally have too many degrees of freedom and are thus sensitive to noise and background clutter. To solve this problem, suitable configuration spaces can be used such as the affine space [39] for rigid, planar motion. Simple motion models are unsuitable however for the complex non-rigid deformations that occur in facial motion. Therefore, for tracking purposes, one has to build a deformation space that allow only specific non-rigid distortions [87, 101]. Constructing such a space linearly is possible using a number (10–20) of key-frames, hand-drawn over frozen frames. It is sometimes desirable also to add some affine degrees of freedom, to the key-frame set. The resulting set is sufficient to span the configuration space.

From this, a basis of minimum size can be constructed by Principal Component Analysis (PCA) to form the "shape-space" for the tracking task. The relationship $\mathbf{Q} \leftrightarrow \mathbf{X}$ between the B-spline parameterisation and the shape-space parameterisation is expressed in terms of two matrices W and W^+:

$$\mathbf{Q} = W\mathbf{X} + \bar{\mathbf{Q}} \text{ and } \mathbf{X} = W^+ [\mathbf{Q} - \bar{\mathbf{Q}}]$$

The W matrix contains as its columns the vectors of the basis obtained above by PCA and W^+ is its pseudo-inverse. The details of the way in which these basis vectors were determined for the face-tracking task are described below.

7.2.3 Key-frames

Key-frames are chosen as typical non-rigid deformations of the template corresponding to possible expressions of the face. As many as possible of the different expressions to be tracked must be included in the training set for PCA in order that as many expressions as possible should be contained in the possible shape space. In the results shown here, no distinguished treatment is given to deformations due to rigid head motion (we did not use the affine space) so that facial expressions during rigid rotation head must be included along with expressions in the "canonical" position (facing the camera).

Fig. 7.2 shows several of those key-frames. Several basic expressions (neutral, smile, unhappiness, sneer, surprise, talking) have been considered as studies have shown that a few well chosen representatives can be used to classify most of human facial expressions [116]. Each representative has been collected for each of three possible orientations of the head with respect to the camera (facing "straight", "right" and "left"). It should be noted that these expressions seem to be fairly person-dependent, and that idiosyncratic mannerisms, such as lifting one eyebrow, must also be added to the key-frame pool if an individual is to be tracked accurately over a full range of expressions.

7.2.4 Principal Component Analysis

Principal Component Analysis (PCA) is performed on the key-frame set by finding the eigenvectors and eigenvalues of

$$\sum_n \mathbf{Q}_n \mathbf{Q}_n^T \mathcal{H}$$

where

$$\mathcal{H} = \int_0^N \begin{pmatrix} 1 & 0 \\ 0 & 1 \end{pmatrix} \otimes (\mathbf{B}(s)\mathbf{B}(s)^T) \, ds,$$

in which $\otimes$ denotes the "Kronecker product". Note that $\mathcal{H}$ is the "metric" matrix that arises from the "normal equations" [246] for the problem of least-squares approximation with B-splines. Examples of such matrices are given in [39].

Only the main components of the Principal Component Analysis are retained — those eigenvectors corresponding to the largest eigenvalues. They form the basis for shape-space. In practice 8 degrees of freedom are enough to capture most of the possible deformations (e.g. 95.5 % of the

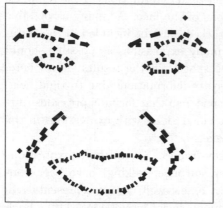
Smile facing the camera

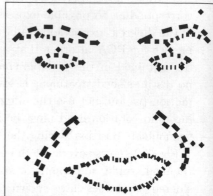
Smile facing to the side

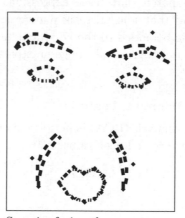
Surprise facing the camera

Fig. 7.2 Key-frames. Here are shown a few of the key-frames that are used to define the space of possible face configurations/expressions.

system variance) we wish to describe. To these 8 are added two degrees of freedom of two dimensional translation (which were not present in our group of key-frames), to give a basis of 10 shapes in total. The facial displacement represented by the first few principal components is illustrated in figure 7.3.

7.3 Learning dynamics

It is well known that tracking is more effective when a Kalman filter is used to predict where to look in successive frames [39]. However, for this prediction to be accurate, a suitable motion model must be provided for the deformable curve. The Kalman filter requires that the model be specified as a stochastic difference equation — a difference equation driven by multi-dimensional Gaussian noise. A second order model, as used in our system, is the simplest model that can be used to represent both constant velocity motion and oscillation and has proved sufficiently powerful for our purposes. The improvement of trained over untrained behaviour of the system is illustrated by figures 7.4 and 7.5.

7.3.1 Second order model

Discrete-time, second-order, stochastic dynamics are defined by the following second-order stochastic differential equation in shape-space:

$$\mathbf{X}_{n+2} = A_0\mathbf{X}_n + A_1\mathbf{X}_{n+1} + (I - A_0 - A_1)\overline{\mathbf{X}} + B\mathbf{w}_n, \tag{7.1}$$

where matrices A_0, A_1 represent the deterministic component of the model and B is a coefficient for the stochastic input.

Training is performed by tracking a training sequence in shape-space using a default dynamical model. Tracking with default dynamics may not have outstanding stability, lacking the ability to follow agile deformations, but is sufficient for a training-set of representative expressions, moving at modest speeds. Dynamics learned from this tracked set can be installed in a new Kalman filter and will in turn improve tracker stability and performance. A few successive cycles of training with training sets of increasing agility lead to enhanced tracking capabilities. It is to be noted that the trained dynamics shown in figure 7.4 have been obtained after two cycles of training.

First component

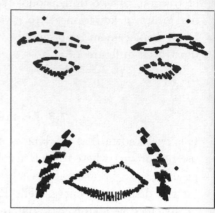

Second component

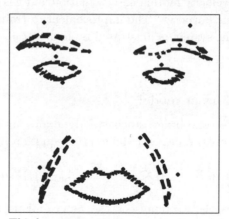

Third component

Fig. 7.3 **Principal Component Analysis.** The first 3 components of PCA performed on our base of key-frames of facial expressions are shown. The first component corresponds to a vertical compression/dilatation of the face such as occurring when surprised or talking. The second component contains mainly mouth deformations such as during a smile. The third component shows a narrowing of eyes and mouth.

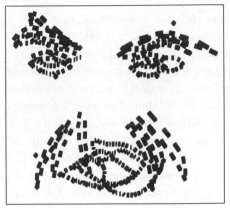 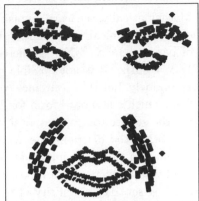

(a) Simulation of untrained dynamics   (b) Simulation of trained dynamics

Fig. 7.4 **Trained dynamics.** The dynamical evolution of the active contour according to untrained/trained dynamical models. Pure noise driven dynamics are shown — no data is involved. It is clear that the evolution predicted by the trained model is more consistent with expected facial motions.

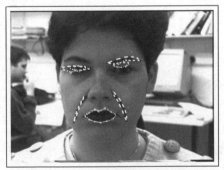 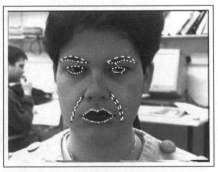

(a) Untrained tracking   (b) Trained tracking

Fig. 7.5 **Utility of trained dynamics.** (a) Tracking on the image sequence of Fig. 7.1. (a) With untrained dynamics, tracking is not very stable and can "unlock" after a sequence of rapid deformations. (b) In contrast, with trained dynamics tracking is more accurate and more stable.

7.3.2 Learning algorithm

Mathematically, the learning task is to estimate the coefficients A_0, A_1, B of the dynamical equations of the system from a training sequence of parameters $\mathbf{X}_1, ..\mathbf{X}_m$, gathered at the image sampling frequency of $1/\Delta = 50\text{Hz}$. It is not possible in principle, nor necessary, to estimate B uniquely, but the covariance coefficient $C = BB^T$ can be determined, from which a standard form for B can be computed as $B = \sqrt{C}$ applying the square root operation for a positive definite square matrix [19]. To obtain the discrete-time system parameters, Maximum Likelihood Estimation (MLE) is implemented via least-squares minimisation. The result is a tracker tuned to those facial deformations that occurred in the training-set. For simplicity of notation here we assume that the mean $\overline{\mathbf{X}}$ has been subtracted off

$$\mathbf{X}_n \rightarrow \mathbf{X}_n - \overline{\mathbf{X}},$$

though in practice the mean must be estimated too [254]. Matrices A_0, A_1, C are estimated by maximising the log-likelihood function L of the observed system states given the values of A_0, A_1 and C. The estimated parameters $\hat{A}_0, \hat{A}_1$ are the solution of the simultaneous equations [41]:

$$S_{20} - \hat{A}_0 S_{00} - \hat{A}_1 S_{10} = 0 \qquad (7.2)$$
$$S_{21} - \hat{A}_0 S_{01} - \hat{A}_1 S_{11} = 0.$$

where moments S_{ij} of the time-sequence are defined as

$$S_{ij} = \sum_{n=1}^{m-2} \mathbf{X}_{n+i}\mathbf{X}_{n+j}^T, \quad i,j = 0,1,2. \qquad (7.3)$$

Then C can be obtained from:

$$\hat{C} = \frac{1}{m-2}Z(\hat{A}_0, \hat{A}_1), \qquad (7.4)$$

where

$$\begin{aligned} Z &= S_{22} + A_1 S_{11} A_1^T + A_0 S_{00} A_0^T - S_{21} A_1 - S_{20} A_0^T \qquad (7.5) \\ &\quad + A_1 S_{10} A_0^T - A_1 S_{12} - A_0 S_{02} + A_0 S_{01} A_1^T \end{aligned}$$

7.4 Conclusion

Tracking facial expressions has been achieved very successfully using our approach based on active contours with dynamical learning. Tracking is performed in real-time on live camera images, and can handle complex natural-life facial deformations. Our current research is progressing towards analysing the tracking output to separate the contributions of head motion and facial deformations due to changes of expression. This is a necessary precursor to automated control of graphical animation.

8

Interfacing through Visual Pointers

C. Colombo, A. Del Bimbo and S. De Magistris

Abstract

A key issue in advanced interface design is the development of friendly tools for natural interaction between user and machine. In this chapter, we propose an approach to non-intrusive human-computer interfacing in which the user's head and pupils are monitored by computer vision for interaction control within on-screen environments. Two different *visual pointers* are defined, allowing simultaneous and decoupled navigation and selection in 3D and 2D graphic scenarios. The pointers intercept user actions, whose geometry is then remapped onto the environment by a *drag and click metaphor* providing dialogue with a natural semantics.

8.1 Introduction

In the last few years, a huge effort has been made towards building advanced environments for human-machine interaction and human-human communication mediated by computers. Such environments can improve both the activity and satisfaction of individual users and computer supported cooperative work. Apart from some obvious implementation and design differences, virtual reality [255], augmented reality [309] and smart room [235] environments share the very same principle of providing users with a more natural dialogue with (and through) the computer with respect to the past. This is obtained through a careful interface design involving interface languages mimicking everyday experience and advanced interaction techniques.

Recently, the simultaneous growth of computing power and decrease of hardware costs, together with the development of specific algorithms and techniques, has encouraged the use of computer vision as a non intrusive technology for advanced human-machine interaction. Experiments using computer vision for gesture interpretation tasks such as lip-reading, recognition of facial expressions, and head motion understanding [172, 119, 14] have been carried out. Vision-based interfaces allow user gestures and actions to be intercepted and used to support interaction in a wide semantic range. For example, in [278] a vision-based hand gesture interpretation technique is used to develop an interface based on sign language, where each sign is related to a specific hand configuration pattern which must be known *a priori* to the user. Such a rich interaction semantics at the user level is not always desirable, as it may limit the naturality of the dialogue.

In this chapter, we propose a vision-based technique to communicate with a computer through pupil shifts and head motion. A friendly interface is obtained by stressing the continuous-geometric aspects of interaction and supporting natural languages based on visual inspection and selection. Interaction via head and eyes can be effective for both disabled users affected by severe limb motor pathologies and general users requiring non-intrusive interaction tools. The technique, which is presented in the context of a virtual reality environment provided with hypertextual access, can be easily adapted to other tasks and scenarios, and support interaction in multimedia, videoconferencing, telepresence, usability monitoring, and augmented reality environments.

In our approach, a set of image features encoding head and eye position is continuously tracked via computer vision. The features are then remapped onto the interaction environment, as the result of a geometric and semantic interpretation of user action. The location currently observed and the user's interest are inferred by monitoring head and pupil displacement and geometric persistency. This allows us to replicate the two basic functions of dragging and clicking in 2D and 3D with a pair of *visual pointers*, according to a paradigm which allows pointing and navigation (geometric), and selection (semantic) actions.

8.2 Visual Pointers

As shown in Fig. 8.1, our operating context is composed by a camera and an on-screen multi-window environment. User actions are the result of a change of interest, due either to the low-level visual content of the environment (color, texture, etc.) or to some purposive, high-level user task (context-switching while browsing a hypertext, ameliorating interaction through a viewpoint change, exploring the scene, etc.).

Fig. 8.1 The basic elements of vision-based interaction: environment, user, and camera.

8.2.1 Geometry

To intercept shifts of interest, which involve the user's visuo-motor system, a vision-based interaction tool is designed to track and process simultaneously the displacements of both the head — rigid body in space, six degrees of freedom (DOF) — and the eyeball — two DOF, orientation of the visual axis in space† — subsystems with respect to some fixed reference frame. Such a tool is equivalent to the combination of a 3D pointing device and a 2D pointer, respectively. As the two subsystems are kinematically independent, the associated pointers can also be made independent one from the other by decoupling the measurement of head and eyeball displacements through computer vision.

From the geometric viewpoint, the basic elements of the interaction (camera's image plane, screen and user's face) can be modeled as planar surfaces in space. We also model the visible portions of the user's eyeballs, actually pseudo-spheres, as planar surfaces, and *regard any gaze shift related to an eyeball rotation as a translation of the pupil in the face plane.* Let A, B and Γ denote the screen, user and camera planes respectively, and fix the local frames α, β and γ as in Fig. 8.2.

A first geometric aspect of the interaction concerns the head's relative geometry (position and orientation) with respect to a given reference frame ρ. This is encoded in the linear transformation between

† As for the eyeball DOF, we will actually refer to the intersection of the visual axis giving the direction of gaze, with the screen plane providing the location actually observed.

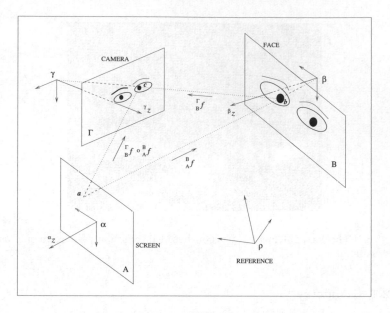

Fig. 8.2. Visual interaction: geometric aspects.

the coordinate representations of a generic point in space $\boldsymbol{p}$ in the β- and ρ-frames. Using homogeneous coordinates for $\boldsymbol{p}$, such a transformation can be compactly expressed by a 4×4 matrix $_{\rho}^{\beta}\mathrm{T}$ such that $[^{\beta}\boldsymbol{p}^{\mathrm{T}}\ 1]^{\mathrm{T}} = _{\rho}^{\beta}\mathrm{T}\ [^{\rho}\boldsymbol{p}^{\mathrm{T}}\ 1]^{\mathrm{T}}$. As changes of frame can be composed linearly, the $\rho \mapsto \beta$ transformation can be reconstructed from the $\rho \mapsto \gamma$ and $\gamma \mapsto \beta$ transformations:

$$_{\rho}^{\beta}\mathrm{T} = _{\gamma}^{\beta}\mathrm{T}\, _{\rho}^{\gamma}\mathrm{T} \quad , \tag{8.1}$$

thus letting the camera come into play as an element of the interaction. The $_{\rho}^{\gamma}\mathrm{T}$ transformation is time-independent, as long as the camera is fixed, while the $_{\gamma}^{\beta}\mathrm{T}$ transformation does depend on the current position of the user's head.

A second aspect of the interaction involves user's eyeball movements and screen inspection. As the result of an eyeball shift, a specific location of the screen is pointed, and its visible content is projected through the pupil onto the highest-resolution area of the retina, the fovea. Thus, geometrically speaking, we can *regard at each instant the pupil's position in the face plane*, $\boldsymbol{b}$, *as the perspective image of the observed screen point* $\boldsymbol{a}$, i.e. $\boldsymbol{b} = _{A}^{B}f(\boldsymbol{a})$, with $_{A}^{B}f : A \to B$ a nonlinear projection map depending, among other parameters, on the entries of $_{\alpha}^{\beta}\mathrm{T}$. The relative distance between the user and the camera is such that, in our context, conditions are met to approximate the perspective camera with an affine camera model [225]. This allows us to say that a linear backprojection map $_A^Bh^{-1} = _B^Ah : B \rightarrow A$ (with $_A^Bh \approx _A^Bf$) exists which brings pupil positions to screen locations. The same reasoning can be applied to define the camera-to-face backprojection $_\Gamma^Bh : \Gamma \rightarrow B$, and write the map $_\Gamma^Ag$ between camera-projected pupil positions c and screen locations a as a composition of linear maps:

$$_\Gamma^Ag = _B^Ah \circ _\Gamma^Bh : \Gamma \rightarrow A \quad . \tag{8.2}$$

Such a camera-to-screen backprojection map is a linear approximation to a perspectivity (the "picture of a picture" [225]) and, as the product of two maps which involve the user frame β, it is time-dependent.

The transformations of eqs. (8.1) and (8.2) embed the information used by our 3D and 2D pointers, respectively. In Section 8.3 we show how to compute and update such information based on image data.

8.2.2 Semantics

The dialog semantics currently implemented in our visual interface is based on a *drag and click metaphor*, which lets the user interact with the environment with his head and eyeballs to perform navigational, pointing and selection actions as with conventional pointing devices.

Explicitly, eyeball and head displacements with respect to a fixed reference are interpreted as pointer drags, or *navigational actions*. Pointers can also trigger a *selection action* (click) as they persist in the neighborhood of a geometric configuration for a convenient time interval. Since the production of discrete events is reduced here to the on-off mechanism of time thresholding for selection, pointers have basically the same semantic expressivity of a 1-button mouse. This design choice virtually demands the whole burden of expressivity from the interaction environment.

The semantics implemented attempts to assign a natural meaning to the user's head and eye movements (basically head translations and rotations and pupil shifts of fixation) so that even a naive user can feel comfortable interacting with the system. The head can be used to navigate or to displace objects (drag) in the environment and also to select, or "freeze," a 3D scene of interest (click). Eyeball drags, which take into account a displacement within the scene, can be used e.g., for on-screen drawing or exploration, and eyeball clicks to select relevant 2D information.

8.3 Implementation

This section discusses the modeling and measurement aspects of our drag and click approach to vision-based interaction.

8.3.1 Projection and user modeling

Affine projection model. The relative geometry between any two frames is described by six DOF. For example, the transformation between the user and camera frames can be expressed as

$$\begin{matrix}{}^{\gamma}_{\beta}\mathrm{T} = \begin{bmatrix} \mathrm{R}(\tau,\sigma,\phi) & & \boldsymbol{t} \\ 0 & 0 & 0 & 1 \end{bmatrix} \end{matrix}, \tag{8.3}$$

where $\boldsymbol{t} = [t_1\, t_2\, t_3]^{\mathrm{T}}$ is a translation 3-vector, and $\mathrm{R}(\tau,\sigma,\phi)$ is a 3×3 rotation matrix, completely defined by the three angles τ (tilt), σ (slant) and ϕ (orientation). Specifically, if each of the interaction frames is chosen with its third axis normal to the associated plane (see again Fig. 8.2), then $\sigma \in [0, \pi/2]$ is the angle between the face and the image planes, vanishing identically if the two planes are parallel.

Affine perspective projection† of a face point onto the camera plane, ${}^{\Gamma}_{B}h$, can be described in terms of a translation 2-vector $\boldsymbol{h}$, and a 2×2 projection matrix

$$\mathrm{H} = \kappa \begin{bmatrix} \cos\tau & -\sin\tau \\ \sin\tau & \cos\tau \end{bmatrix} \begin{bmatrix} -\cos\sigma & 0 \\ 0 & 1 \end{bmatrix} \begin{bmatrix} \sin\phi & -\cos\phi \\ \cos\phi & \sin\phi \end{bmatrix}, \tag{8.4}$$

which is the composition of two planar rotations by τ and $\phi - \pi/2$, of an anisotropic scaling by $\cos\sigma$ along a specific image direction, and an isotropic scaling of the imaged pattern by a factor κ proportional to the camera's focal length [85].

User features being tracked. Head displacements and pupil positions can be estimated at one time by tracking the visual appearance of the users' eyes. Indeed, the *external contour* of the eye, which is fixed

---

† We assume here that all intrinsic parameters of the projection, and especially the pixel size ratio, have their ideal values. In such a case, the affine projection is a weak perspective [225].

to the head‡, can be related to head displacements, while the internal *iris* contour, which is concentric with the pupil, moves according to user pointing actions (eyeball shifts). Analyzing separately the pupil point- ing and head displacement characteristics of user actions allows us to adopt a two-step eye tracking approach:

(i) *Track the external eye contour.* This determines a search bound for the pupil's position in the image.

(ii) *Track the pupil inside the search bound.* This is motivated by the physiological constraint that the pupil must always lie inside the external eye contour.

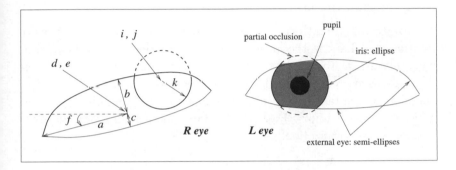

Fig. 8.3. Modeling the left and right eyes.

Image measurements for head tracking and pupil detection are ob- tained by deforming a reference elastic template so as to adapt it to current image data. Let us assume that the reference frame ρ is the β-frame at initialization time $(t = 0)$, i.e. $\rho = \beta(0)$. Let's also assume that ρ and γ have mutually parallel third axes, i.e. $\sigma(0) = 0$. Then, by eq. (8.4), the reference template models a fronto-parallel view of the eyes, possibly translated by $h(0)$, and scaled and mirrored with respect to the face plane content by

$$H(0) = \kappa(0) \begin{bmatrix} 1 & 0 \\ 0 & -1 \end{bmatrix} . \tag{8.5}$$

‡ Our rigidity constraint assumes that any change of the visual appearance of the eye contour is related to a head displacement. At a very short time scale, even a non-rigid change of facial expression — say, passing from normality to utmost stupor — influences the external eye appearance. However, at longer time scales only geometric-driven changes are significant.

The template is composed of two sub-templates, which capture the characteristics of the user's external eye and iris, respectively (Fig. 8.3).

The external eye sub-template features two semi-ellipses sharing their major axis, thus depending on six parameters, namely the common major axis (a), the two minor axes (b, c), the ocular center image coordinates (d, e), and the common orientation (f). A circle, parameterized through the coordinates of its center (i, j) and its radius (k), is used for the iris sub-template. Notice that part of the iris is usually occluded by the eyelids: this fact has to be explicitly taken into account in the tracking strategy.

8.3.2 Sensing the user

Template initialization. At system startup, a raw estimate of the eye location and shape in the image is derived, and the template is accordingly initialized. To speed up processing, the two image regions containing the eyes are first roughly located by means of *edge dominance maps*, i.e., maps which take into account the dominance of brightness gradient in a given direction [62]. Fig. 8.4 illustrates the two-step procedure for automatic eye localization.

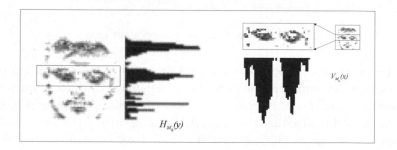

Fig. 8.4. Eye localization using dominance maps.

Once the regions including the eyes are found, the template is adjusted against image data by an energy-minimization criterion (see e.g., [329]). A quadratic energy term, including the $9 = 6 + 3$ template parameters per eye, is minimized, so that the template is relaxed inside the eye regions by gradient descent. After relaxation, the deformable template is used to initialize the run-time tracker, a lightweight process which allows for faster tracking behavior than template relaxation.

Tracking the external eye. The tracker is modeled after the external eyes only. Its image shape is controlled by a discrete set of points, which are initialized soon after template relaxation, by uniformly sampling the external eye contours. At run-time, the tracker parameters are refined and updated by means of a simple tracker-to-image fitting approach, based on least squares and the extraction of brightness edge points (Fig. 8.5). Thanks to our affine projection model, the tracker can be made quite robust by allowing it to deform only in an affine fashion.

Explicitly, let the tracker instance at a generic time $t > 0$ be $\{x_i(t)\}$, $i = 1 \ldots N$, let its centroid be $x_B(t)$ and let the reference tracker be $\{x_i(0)\}$ with centroid $x_B(0)$. Template tracking proceeds as follows:

(i) *Prediction.* In an image neighborhood of the previous tracker instance (time $t - 1$), a local search of edge points (brightness gradient maxima) takes place at each of the N tracker points and along normal directions to the tracker itself. The set $\{\widetilde{x}_i(t)\}$ of edge points (predicted set) is computed by means of a 5-point, recursive coarse-to-fine algorithm based on finite differences [100]. Search intervals along each direction are adaptively adjusted based on the previous tracking results.

(ii) *Least squares fit.* The LS approximation of the new tracker centroid is simply the centroid (average point) of the predicted set evaluated in the previous step, i.e. $\widetilde{x}_B(t) = \frac{1}{N}\sum_i \widetilde{x}_i(t)$. A 2×2 matrix $\widetilde{L}(t)$ is also evaluated via LS as the best approximation of the affine transformation about the origin between the predicted set and the reference template. This is done by minimizing the quadratic cost $\sum_i \|(\widetilde{x}_i(t) - \widetilde{x}_B(t)) - \widetilde{L}(t)(x_i(0) - x_B(0))\|^2$ by solving the linear homogeneous system obtained by partial differentiation w.r.t. the unknown four parameters.

(iii) *Filtering.* The six parameters of the affine image transformation $(\widetilde{L}(t), \widetilde{x}_B(t))$ are smoothed using a recursive filter. For the generic parameter p, the filtered value is $\widehat{p}(t) = w_p\, p(t) + (1 - w_p)\, \widehat{p}(t-1)$. To achieve a better control of the tracking process, a different filter gain $w_p \in [0, 1]$ can be assigned to each parameter.

(iv) *Affine projection.* Once the affine transformation $(\widehat{L}(t), \widehat{x}_B(t))$ is obtained, the new tracker instance is finally computed as $x_i(t) = x_B(t) + \widehat{L}(t)(x_i(0) - x_B(0))$ for all i, with $x_B(t) = \widehat{x}_B(t)$. This last step ensures that at each time $t > 0$ the tracker is an affine-transformed instance of the reference tracker, initialized at $t = 0$. Moreover, such a tracking approach is independent of the specific tracker being used: different eye shapes can be tracked by simply changing the shape of the reference template — say, using parabolic arcs instead of elliptic arcs.

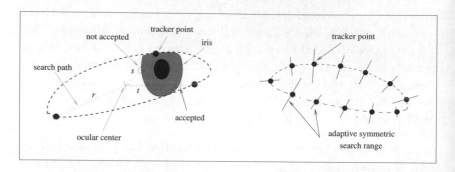

Fig. 8.5. Affine-deformable eye tracker and search of iris candidate points.

Locating the pupil. Once the new external eye position is found, it is necessary to search for the current iris shape and position inside the new tracker contour. This is done according to a technique akin to the one used before, but also different from that in some significant points:

- *Affine model.* To deal with generic face views with nonzero slant angles† which would produce an elliptic-shaped iris, an elliptic iris tracker is considered. This is initialized with the reference circular iris obtained after template relaxation.

- *Occlusions.* To avoid erroneous results due to possible partial iris occlusions, the edge points belonging to the external eye tracker are automatically excluded from LS fitting with the iris tracker; in this way, an external contour point is not taken into account as a predicted iris point $\widetilde{\boldsymbol{y}} = [\widetilde{x}\ \widetilde{y}]^{\mathrm{T}}$. To avoid occlusions, we use edge search lines which are radial paths connecting external eye tracker points with the tracker's centroid: the search proceeds inwards and, as shown in Fig. 8.5, only negative gradient points are taken into account.

- *Matching.* The steps of fitting and affine projection are simultaneous. This is obtained by explicitly using the elliptic tracker analytic expression into the objective function. Specifically, the new raw ellipse parameters are extracted by fitting predicted points with a generic

---

† This proves useful when the intrinsic camera parameters such as the pixel size ratio are not perfectly compensated.

conic via Least Squares, and then constraining the conic to be an ellipse. That is, find the generic five conic parameters c_l which minimize the squared error $\sum_i \left[\tilde{x}_i^2 + c_1 \, \tilde{x}_i \tilde{y}_i + c_2 \, \tilde{y}_i^2 + c_3 \, \tilde{x}_i + c_4 \, \tilde{y}_i + c_5 \right]^2$, these are expressed in terms of ellipse center, major and minor axes, and orientation [84].

After the filtering step, the current center of the iris is taken as the new location of the pupil and used to update the 2D pointer.

8.3.3 Controlling the environment

Using the 3D pointer. Head displacements relative to the reference frame can be estimated from a comparison between the current and reference trackers. At any time $t \geq 0$, the tracker is obtained by a camera projection of the face plane when the face frame is $\beta(t)$; following the notation of Subsection 8.3.2, we denote this projection as $(\mathrm{H}(t), \boldsymbol{h}(t))$, where the generic tracker is related to the reference tracker through the affine transformation $(\mathrm{L}(t), \boldsymbol{x}_\mathrm{B}(t))$ s.t. $\boldsymbol{x}_\mathrm{B}(t) = \boldsymbol{h}(t)$ and $\mathrm{L}(t) = \mathrm{H}(t) \, \mathrm{H}^{-1}(0)$.

If we can assume fronto-parallel interaction, i.e., that the user's face remains almost parallel to the screen during the whole interaction time†, then $\sigma(t) \approx 0 \; \forall t > 0$,

$$\mathrm{H} = \kappa \begin{bmatrix} -\sin \phi & \cos \phi \\ \cos \phi & \sin \phi \end{bmatrix} \quad , \tag{8.6}$$

and rotations are fully described by the orientation angle $\phi(t)$ in $[0, 2\pi]$, initialized to $\phi(0) = -\pi/2$ to satisfy eq. (8.5). Notice that during fronto-parallel interaction the head DOF are reduced from six to four — namely, a translation 3-vector and a rotation in the face plane. The head DOF can be conveniently referred to the ρ-frame as $\boldsymbol{t}(0) - \boldsymbol{t}(t)$ and $\phi(t)$, and related to 2D quantities as follows:

$$\boldsymbol{t}(0) - \boldsymbol{t}(t) = 1/\kappa(0) \left(\begin{bmatrix} \boldsymbol{h}(0) \\ \lambda \end{bmatrix} - \frac{\kappa(0)}{\kappa(t)} \begin{bmatrix} \boldsymbol{h}(t) \\ \lambda \end{bmatrix} \right) \quad ; \tag{8.7}$$

$$\begin{bmatrix} \sin \phi(t) & \cos \phi(t) \\ -\cos \phi(t) & \sin \phi(t) \end{bmatrix} = -\frac{\kappa(0)}{\kappa(t)} \mathrm{L}(t) \quad . \tag{8.8}$$

Given focal length λ and an estimate of $\mathrm{L}(t)$, $\boldsymbol{h}(t)$ and $\boldsymbol{h}(0)$, from

---

† The fronto-parallel is a very natural way to stand in front of a computer, as it is optimal in terms of ergonomics.

eq. (8.8) it is possible in principle to recover rotation $\phi(t)$ and relative scaling $\kappa(0)/\kappa(t)$: the latter can be used into eq. (8.7) to recover translation parameters up to an unknown scale factor‡ $1/\kappa(0)$.

However, we prefer to use a more direct approach to evaluate relative scale and rotation from the current and reference trackers — see Figures 8.6 (*a* through *d*). The approach does not involve eq. (8.8) but instead exploits the ocular centers as located in the image. Observe in fact that relative scaling can be estimated as the interocular distance ratio $\delta(0)/\delta(t)$ (Fig. 8.6, *c*). Similarly, as shown in Fig. 8.6 (*d*), the relative inclination of the line connecting the ocular centers can be used to estimate rotation.

The estimated 3D parameters correspond one-one to the four basic head displacements which the user can mix together during frontoparallel interaction.

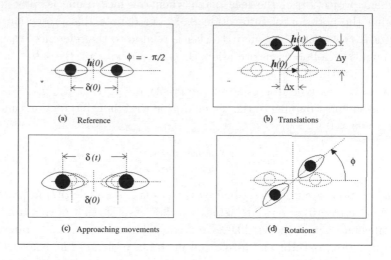

Fig. 8.6. The four head DOFs considered for the experiments.

Calibrating and using the 2D pointer. Remapping the 2D pointer has a more quantitative nature. The key idea for such a pointer is in fact to be able to know where the user is actually looking in the screen. Such a strategy is usually implemented using precise but otherwise intrusive infrared light equipment [157, 152] and allows the eye pupil to be used as a 2D mouse.

‡ This indeterminacy originates from modeling not the eyes themselves in the face plane but, instead, their image appearance.

Having denoted the affine eye projection map by $(K, \boldsymbol{k})$, having defined a new camera projection map as $(H', \boldsymbol{h}')$, with $\boldsymbol{h}'$ the projection of the ocular center of the eye where the pupil is located†, and having expressed image and screen points $\boldsymbol{c}$ and $\boldsymbol{a}$ as 2-vectors using their native coordinate frames γ and α respectively, it follows that:

$$^{\alpha}\boldsymbol{a} = M^{\gamma}\boldsymbol{c} + \boldsymbol{m} \quad , \tag{8.9}$$

where $M = \left[H'K\right]^{-1}$ and $\boldsymbol{m} = -M\boldsymbol{h}' - K^{-1}\boldsymbol{k}$.

Fig. 8.7. 2D calibration. *Left*: Calibration grid. *Right*: Remapped points.

The camera-to-screen map $(M, \boldsymbol{m})$ involves time-dependent quantities, some of which — e.g., the distance from eye to screen and eye focal length — are not known or difficult to measure. Nevertheless, this transformation can be estimated at startup via a plane-to-plane calibration procedure:

(i) *Observation.* A set of $M \geq 6$ image observations of pupil positions is collected and recorded, obtained by tracking the pupil while letting the user execute a sequence of gaze fixations on M given screen locations. Fig. 8.7 (*left*) shows the case $M = 9$, where the locations to fix are organized in a 3×3 calibration grid covering the entire screen. To reduce errors during this phase, each new observation is obtained as an average of subsequent image measurements.

(ii) *Estimation.* The affine model is then estimated using data and observations, as the LS solution of an overdetermined system obtained from eq. (8.9). LS computations are carried out in two steps, by first computing data and observation centroids $^{\alpha}\boldsymbol{a}_{\mathrm{B}}$ and

---

† Such a projection is also the centroid of the external eye sub-tracker including the pupil's image. Vectors h of eq. (8.7) and h' differ by the centroid of the remaining sub-tracker.

$^{\gamma}c_{\mathrm{B}}$ and estimating the matrix M from $(^{\alpha}a-^{\alpha}a_{\mathrm{B}}) = \mathrm{M}\,(^{\gamma}c-^{\gamma}c_{\mathrm{B}})$, and then obtaining the translation as $m = {}^{\alpha}a_{\mathrm{B}} - \mathrm{M}\,{}^{\gamma}c_{\mathrm{B}}$.

At run-time, pupil positions in the image are remapped onto the screen using the calibrated map. Fig. 8.7 (*right*) shows the qualitative results of a test on calibration accuracy. In the test, the user is asked to fix the calibration grid points successively, while the corresponding image pupil positions, suitably averaged, are remapped onto the screen using eq. (8.9). The few remapped points in the figure which are halfway between grid crossings are due to user eye movements between successive fixations.

Quantitative results on the same calibration test are shown in Table 8.1. This reports the average and maximum mismatch between the set of calibration points ("ground truth") and the remapped points both in the two coordinate directions and in magnitude. Magnitude errors provide us with a resolution limit for our 2D pointer, which must be taken into account in the design of the graphic interface. To reduce map reconstruction errors during calibration, head motions can be compensated by normalizing the image plane observations with respect to the reference ones. Similarly, the calibrated map can be updated at run-time based on current visual data [86].

Calibration Accuracy	Error on x	Error on y	Uncertainty radius
Average (mm)	6.23	10.69	12.38
Maximum (mm)	17.51	19.93	26.53

Table 8.1. *Calibration accuracy.*

Pointer timing. Choosing the right threshold value is of key importance for a good balance between speed of operation and naturality of interaction. If the threshold value is too low, then every action is interpreted as a click command, an undesirable situation usually referred to as *Midas touch* [157]. A good dwell time for the 2D pointer, which takes into account the high mobility of the pupil, is 1 second, which on the one hand guarantees a fast response, and on the other limits the occurrence of false alarms. Since head motions are slower, a time threshold about three times longer can be used for the 3D pointer.

A second timing mechanism is implemented in the interface, avoiding the occurrence of "interference" between the pointers. Consider for example the case of a 3D click, which occurs when the head persists in a fixed position for one second or more. If, in the same time period, the pupil is also fixed, then a 2D click event is generated, which is most probably involuntary. To solve the interference problem, the 2D and 3D pointers are decoupled, by letting the pupil be actually remapped only if the head is in a suitable neighborhood of its reference position — i.e., if the current tracker is not too different from the reference tracker.

8.4 Interface

An interface has been implemented to support interaction using our visual pointers within a virtual museum containing a digital collection of canvases by famous 20th century artists such as Klimt, Picasso, Modigliani, etc. The virtual environment is complemented by a 2D on-screen hypertext providing the museum with on-line catalogue facilities.

The graphic interface uses the OpenGL graphic libraries and runs on a Silicon Graphics Indy workstation (MIPS R4000/R4010 with 100 MHz clock). The vision subsystem software also runs on the Indy, and gets raw image data through a VINO frame grabber board from an off-the-shelf B/W camera.

To achieve natural interaction, the loop delay must be short enough to provide the user with feedback about his latest action. The overall interaction loop time for our system is the sum of the time spent doing visual computations and graphic environment manipulation. Initializing visual algorithms involves automatic eye extraction and template initialization and takes around 450 ms to complete. At run-time visual tracking runs almost at video rate (50 ms) instead, using $N = 64$ sampling points for both external eye and iris search. Without special hardware for graphics acceleration, most of the loop time is taken by graphic remapping (several 100ms at an intermediate image quality).

3D viewpoint control and navigation. Examples of a typical interaction session using the 3D pointer are illustrated in Figures 8.8 and 8.9 (time flows top to bottom and left to right). The screen content and a mirrored image of the user's eye region are shown, in order to emphasize the relationship between user action and environment changes.

Fig. 8.8 shows a zoom-in sequence. Zooming is obtained by approaching the screen with the head; this causes the painting in the middle of

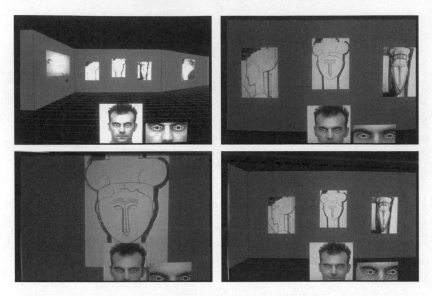

Fig. 8.8. 3D pointer: zoom sequence.

the wall to be displayed at full resolution. A new viewpoint can always be selected by head fixation. However, in this case the user decides to go back to the initial view by moving away from the screen (last image of the sequence).

Another kind of viewpoint adjustment can be obtained by head rotation around the visual axis (Fig. 8.9). This proves to be useful when interesting on-screen features do not have the right orientation. Thanks to the remapping semantics, a clockwise head rotation produces a natural counterclockwise rotation of the environment.

Viewpoint changes are produced by navigational actions corresponding to head translations parallel to the screen. This excludes, in principle, the possibility of executing head pan movements, as the constraint on fronto-parallel interaction would not be met. For example, panning the head leftwise would be interpreted in our interface as a rigid leftward head translation (correctly remapped as a rightward environment shift), *and* a decrease of interocular distance, incorrectly remapped as a zoom-out. Thus, the correct image resolution must be recovered by an additional zoom-in action.

Furthermore, notice that proper semantics must be introduced to generate rotations in the environment using our 4-DOF pointer. In our in-

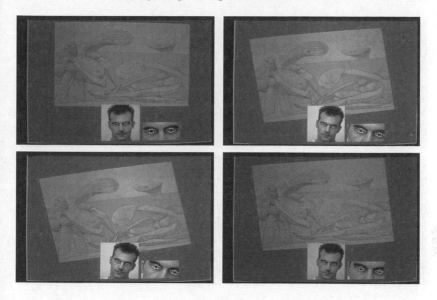

Fig. 8.9. 3D pointer: rotation sequence.

terface, if a side museum wall is reached by a translational movement, an environment rotation is automatically generated, so as to show the paintings on that wall.

2D inspection and selection. Once a specific viewpoint has been selected by head rotation, the user can go back to the reference position, inspect the on-screen scene, and possibly learn more about a given painting in it, or about its author, by selecting a canvas by pupil pointing (Fig. 8.10).

An important aspect of the interface concerns the screen regions which can accept eye-gaze commands, which we refer to as *active windows*. At menu level 0, as commands are issued directly by fixing a canvas, each canvas is an active window. At menu level 1 (Fig. 8.10, *bottom right*), the screen is partitioned in two regions. The left-hand region has six active windows, four of which allow access to information about the author, the historical period, selected and related paintings; the remaining two windows are used for paging control ("back," "next"). The right-hand side of the screen contains output information, and as such it can be fixed by the user without timing constraints (passive window). As the first menu level is accessed, the passive window is filled by default with the painting which was selected in the museum. Fig. 8.11 shows the process

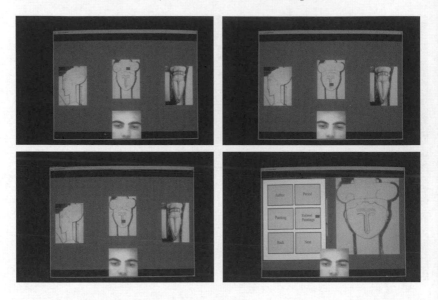

Fig. 8.10 2D selection. The 1st menu level is accessed from level 0 by steadily pointing the eye to a specific painting.

of getting information about the author of the painting: the "author" button is repeatedly fixed, and this causes the author information to be pasted into the passive window to be read.

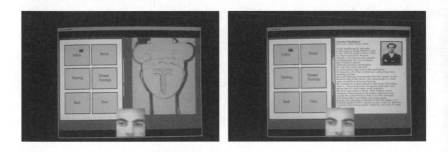

Fig. 8.11. 2D selection: second menu level.

The spacing and size of active windows strictly depend on the magnitude of the pupil remapping error (see again Table 8.1). The average pointing error can be used to properly design the 2D interface and size-up active windows in order to reduce the risk of false alarms during slightly incorrect pointing.

8.5 Innovation

In this chapter, we have presented an approach to advanced human-machine interfacing based on computer vision and computer graphics. The key idea is to use computer vision to develop non intrusive pointer devices based on user head and eye motions, and to couple them with a simple drag and click semantics for interaction in graphic 2D and 3D environments. Basically, the pointers capture significant parameters of user action, which are then remapped onto the environment. The main operations which the user can perform are environment exploration and data selection. Head tracking is used to interact with a 3D environment, while eye pupil tracking allows to control interaction with 2D-based interfaces. To implement the 3D pointer, we continuously track the image of the external part of the user's eyes, and use its deformations to infer head motion parameters. Concerning the 2D pointer, we propose an approach derived from infrared technology applications, and novel to computer vision, i.e., to track eye pupils so as to measure gaze pointing actions in terms of observed screen points rather than simply as directions in the 3D space.

Some directions for future work with our visual pointer technique can finally be outlined. One way to cope with uncertainty in measurements and human intentions alike is to use *adaptive interfaces*. Such interfaces should cooperate with the user in making a decision, either by allowing him to refine a command, or by suggesting a series of alternatives during interaction. The interaction framework can be extended to deal with *remote environments*. Indeed, while interaction with the on-screen environment always takes place locally, the displayed scene needs not to be necessarily a graphic environment, but could for example be the output of a remote, possibly motorized, camera. Thus our approach can be effectively extended to applications such as teleconferencing, telepresence and teleoperation. Other interesting applications are in the field of *augmented reality*. Think of replacing the screen plane with a real-world plane, say a desk, an office wall or some other work panel. The approach can be easily adapted to this new scenario. Another extension of the approach is to allow for *richer semantics at the user level*. That is, besides the basic interaction capabilities offered by our approach, the user could be provided with other means of interfacing with the machine. A way to extend semantics naturally in a computer vision context can be that of interpretation of gestures and expressions.

9

Monocular Tracking of the Human Arm in 3D

E. Di Bernardo, L. Goncalves and P. Perona

Abstract

The motion of the human body can in itself be a useful human-machine interface, and computer vision can provide a method for tracking the body in an unobtrusive fashion. In this chapter, we describe a system capable of tracking the human arm in 3D using only a single camera and no special markers on the body. The real-time implementation has a manipulation resolution of 1 cm and has been tested as a novel 3D input device.

9.1 Introduction and Motivation

Visual estimation and tracking of the motion and gestures of the human body is an interesting and exciting computational problem for two reasons: (a) from the engineering standpoint, a non-invasive machine that could track body motion would be invaluable in facilitating most human-machine interactions and, (b) it is an important scientific problem in its own right. Observing the human body in motion is key to a large number of activities and applications:

Security In museums, factories and other locations that are either dangerous or sensitive it is crucial to detect the presence of humans and monitor/classify their behavior based upon their gait and gestures.

Animation – The entertainment industry makes increasing use of actor-to-cartoon animation where the motion of cartoon figures and rendered models is obtained by tracking the motion of a real person.

Virtual reality – The motion of the user of a virtual reality system is necessary to adjust display parameters and animations.

Human-machine interfaces – The motion of the human body may be used as a convenient interface between man and machine, for example, the hand could be used as a 3D mouse.

Biomechanics – Reconstructing the 3D motion of human limbs is used for clinical evaluation of orthopedic patients and for training of both professional and amateur athletes.

Signaling – In airports, at sea, and in other high-noise environments the arms and torso are used for signaling.

Camera control – Active camera control based on the motion of humans can be used for sport events, conferences and shows, thus replacing human operators. It may also be used to make human operators more effective in security monitoring.

Traffic monitoring – Pedestrians are often a component of street traffic. They need to be detected and their behavior understood (e.g., intention to cross at a traffic light, gesture signaling for emergency help) in order to help avoid collisions and dangerous situations, and in order to detect accidents immediately.

Customer monitoring – Data on the behavioral pattern of exploration and purchasing of store customers is extremely valuable to advertising companies, producers, and sales management.

Current techniques for tracking the human body involve a large variety of methods. *Security, traffic monitoring, signaling, and customer monitoring* are typically implemented using human observers that survey the scene either directly or via a multiple camera closed circuit TV system. For *animation and biomechanics* multiple camera systems and manual tracking of features across image sequences is used. For *virtual reality* an assortment of gloves, suits, joysticks and inductive coils is used. For *human-machine* interfaces we have joysticks, mice and keyboards.

All of these methods require either employing dedicated human operators or using ad hoc sensors. This results in a number of limitations:

(i) *Practicality* – the user needs to wear markers or other ad hoc equipment which may be impractical, uncomfortable, constrain the user to a limited work space, be difficult to transport;

(ii) *Cost* – computational and sensory hardware and human operator time;

(iii) *Timeliness* the data may not be available in real-time, but only after a lag required to process a batch of images, allow communication between human operators etc.

If tracking the human body could be made automatic and non-invasive, and therefore cheaper, more practical and faster, not only the applications listed above could be better performed, but also a number of new applications would be feasible.

9.1.1 Automatic Human Motion Estimation

Previous work on human motion estimation can be coarsely grouped into three types :

- gesture classification, [129, 128]
- systems which track or classify periodic motions with 1 degree of freedom, [259, 228, 245]
- estimation of 3D unconstrained motion; of the hand from a monocular view [251]; of the body, with the use of multiple cameras [131, 163] and special markers [51].

We are interested in estimating 3D unconstrained motion. The most accurate system at the moment is ELITE [51], which is able to estimate position with an accuracy of 0.1% of the workspace diameter. However, to achieve such accuracy, it is necessary to use a system composed of special-purpose markers, infrared lighting, and 4-8 cameras that need to be accurately calibrated. As in [251], we explore the opposite side of the spectrum of approaches to the problem: how accurately can one track in 3D the human body with the simplest, cheapest, and most convenient setup – a single grayscale camera and no special markers.

In this chapter we study the more constrained problem of estimating the motion of the human arm. This is a good starting point because arm estimation is very useful in numerous applications (e.g., human-machine interaction, human factors analysis); it's also easily extendible to the whole body since leg structure is very similar to that of the arm and so only torso and head tracking remain to be done.

In the next section we present some theoretical considerations on the accuracy achievable in depth reconstruction from a monocular view. Afterwards, we describe our arm model, the estimation method, and the results of experiments with the system.

9.2 The Accuracy Achievable from a Monocular View

We will not attempt to give a full analysis, but rather to provide some intuition. From a monocular view, the depth of an isolated point is impossible to recover; it is information on relative structure which allows

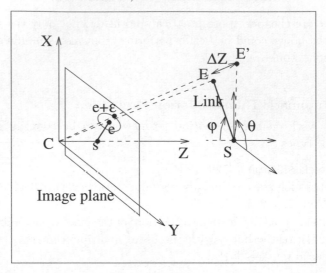

Fig. 9.1 Estimating depth sensitivity: What is the change in depth (ΔZ) for a given image coordinate error (ϵ) given the angle ϕ from the optical axis?

depth to be determined. The simplest structure to study is that of a line segment. In our analysis, we keep one endpoint of the segment fixed in space and calculate the dependence of the depth estimation of the other endpoint with respect to deviations in its image plane coordinates. This calculation is performed for the second endpoint positioned thoughout the hemisphere of possible positions towards the camera. In order to facilitate comparison with our experiment, we calculate image coordinates using the camera parameters of the camera in the experiment. Furthermore, we place the fixed endpoint of the line segment along the optical axis at the same depth as the location of shoulder during the experiment, and the length of the line segment is the length of the upper-arm of the subject performing the experiment.

Fig. 9.1 shows the coordinate system used in calculating the sensitivity. The angle ϕ is the angle between the segment and the optical axis. Fig. 9.2(top) shows the error of the endpoint's depth estimate when its image coordinates are disturbed by 1 pixel (in the worst direction). The qualitative nature of the results agree with one's initial intuition; when the line segment is pointing towards the camera, the depth error is quite small, and when the segment endpoints are equidistant from the camera the depth error increases quickly to infinity. From this plot we calculate as a function of image coordinate error the maximum angle of deviation

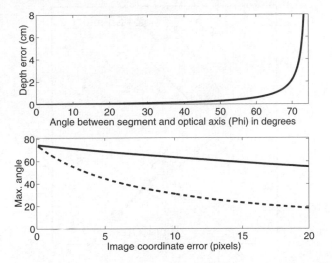

Fig. 9.2 Sensitivity Analysis: (Top): Typical error in depth estimate of the free endpoint of a line segment when there is 1 pixel error in its image plane coordinates. (Bottom) An example of the maximum permissible angle between the segment and the optical axis as a function of image plane coordinate error, so that relative error is less than 7.5% (solid), 1.0% (dashed)

from pointing straight at the camera permissible so that the relative depth error is less than 7.5% and less than 1% (Fig. 9.2(bottom)). It can be seen that as the accuracy required increases, the range of acceptable positions decreases significantly.

Of course, since our estimation method (described below) does not use measurements of endpoint position in the image plane, a direct application of these results is not possible; however, it gives us some idea of how sensitive the depth estimation is with respect to the information in the image. One can improve upon pure length measurements by using both the dynamics of the system being estimated (i.e., the existence of a smooth trajectory, velocity), and more of the structure of the object (i.e., even if one arm segment is in an ill-conditioned position, the other may not be, and so the position of the arm can still be estimated accurately).

9.3 The Estimation System

We model the arm in 3D and use the current estimate of arm position to predict the arm projection in the image. The difference between the

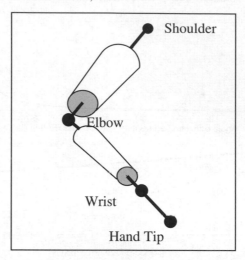

Fig. 9.3 The arm model: Limbs are modeled as truncated right-circular cones. The elbow and shoulder joints are modeled as spherical joints, and the hand tip is assumed to be along the forearm axis

predicted image and the actual arm image is used as an error measurement to update the estimated arm position with a recursive estimator. Thus, rather than extracting features explicitly from the image, we make direct comparisons between the actual image and the expected image. This method is inspired by Dickmann's work on lane following [107].

9.3.1 The Arm Model

In order to generate the predicted image, we need to render a 3D model of the arm from the camera's point of view. We choose a simple 3D model (Fig. 9.3) in which the upper and lower arm are modeled as truncated right-circular cones, and the shoulder and elbow joints are modeled as spherical joints.

In order to keep the model as simple as possible and to have as few degrees of freedom as possible (only four positional DOF with two spherical joints), we chose not to model (or render) the shape of the hand, but simply assume it to extend along the axis of the forearm. This strong simplification provided us with a reasonable starting point for experimentation.

Our model thus requires seven fixed parameters to describe its shape: the longitudinal lengths of the hand, forearm and upper arm (three), and the diameters of the two limb segments at each end (four). Each of these parameters was measured with approximately 5% accuracy (we have not yet systematically studied the effect of model inaccuracies). Furthermore, we assume that the 3D position of the shoulder is known. There is a natural hierarchy to the segmentation of the human body, and shoulder position is determined by tracking the torso. Since we attempt to track only the arm, we assume the shoulder position is known.

9.3.2 The Recursive Estimator

The state of the system consists of the four spherical joint angles and their velocities. In order to recursively estimate it, we use an implicit version of the Extended Kalman Filter [164, 63, 158]. The dynamics of the system is described by a random walk in the spherical joint velocities:

$$\begin{cases} \vec{\theta}(t + \Delta T) &= \vec{\theta}(t) + \vec{\theta_v}\Delta T \\ \vec{\theta_v}(t + 1) &= \vec{\theta_v}(t) + \vec{w} \end{cases} \tag{9.1}$$

where $\vec{\theta}$ is the vector of spherical coordinates, $\vec{\theta_v}$ is the vector of the angular velocities and $\vec{w}$ is a vector of Gaussian noise.

The measurement equation, instead of being in the standard form

$$\vec{y} = \vec{h}(\vec{\theta}, \vec{\theta_v}) \tag{9.2}$$

is an implicit and non-linear relation between the state and the image values

$$\vec{h}(\vec{y}, \vec{\theta}, \vec{\theta_v}) = \vec{0} \tag{9.3}$$

This kind of problem can be transformed to the classical formulation of the Extended KF. The key is to obtain a linearization of the measurement equation. This involves calculating the Jacobian of the measurements with respect to the state (and the image intensities), which in turn involves knowing a precise camera calibration.

9.3.3 The Error Measurements

The measurement process is explained in detail in [137]. We pre-process the image with a background subtraction scheme; based on accumulated statistics of background-only images, a decision is made as to whether each pixel is part of the background or something else. This produces

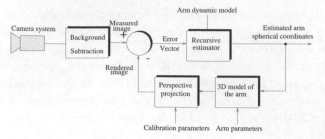

Fig. 9.4 The estimation system: Real and rendered arm views are compared to provide an error signal to a recursive estimator

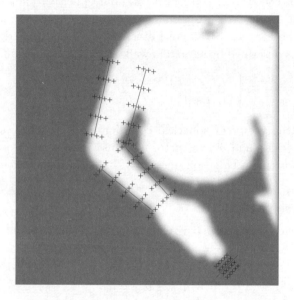

Fig. 9.5 The measurements for the recursive estimator: The (+) indicate locations on the segmented and blurred image where intensity values are compared with those from the predicted arm position (outlined by lines)

an image which assumes value 1 where the arm and the body are and value 0 elsewhere. The last step of pre-processing is to blur the image with a 2D guassian kernel with $\sigma = 10/6$ pixels. This blurring generates a smooth 10 pixel-wide step along the contour of the arm. The difference between this pre-processed image and the image predicted by the recursive filter is calculated at 20 points on both sides of each (predicted) limbs' contours and the (predicted) hand tip position (Fig. 9.5). If the predicted and the real image align exactly (and in the absence of

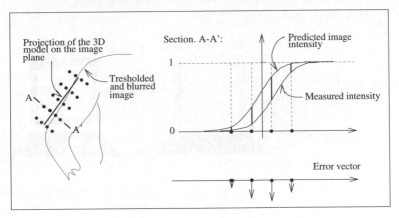

Fig. 9.6 Detail of the measurement process: Transverse to the predicted arm contour, the acquired and pre-processed image is sampled at 4 points. The difference between the expected and measured intensity values generates an error vector

measurement noise and modeling error), all these differences are zero, otherwise, the deviations from this ideal value constitutes the innovation process used by the Kalman filter for the update of the state estimate (Fig. 9.6).

9.4 Real-Time Implementation

In an initial batch experiment [137], we found that our system could track the human arm with an error of at most 5 cm along the line-of-sight (an 8% relative error). A human-machine interface must of necessity operate in real-time, and so we implemented our system in real-time (Fig. 9.7). A C80 image processing board (a 5 CPU TI-TMS320C80-based DSP board) receives the camera input, and performs the pre-processing (background subtraction algorithm) to obtain the foreground/background segmented image The board communicates with a host Pentium computer, receiving a list of locations where to make measurements, and returning the respective image intensity values. The Pentium PC uses the measurements from the C80 to perform recursive estimation, and communicates the currently estimated arm pose to an SGI Workstation. The SGI Workstation runs a test application. The C80 and Pentium run at a 30 Hz frame-rate, and transmit every 5th estimate to the SGI application.

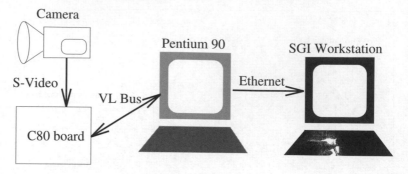

Fig. 9.7 System configuration: the hardware architecture comprises a commercial camera, a video board, a Pentium 90 and an SGI workstation

9.5 System Evaluation

There are several performance criteria that can be considered in assessing the usability of a real-time system. In this section we introduce some such criteria and evaluate our system according to them.

9.5.1 Robustness

Of foremost importance is the system's robustness. An ideal system would be able to track the arm at all times, whereas our system so far still loses track of the arm every now and then if the user is not experienced. The main reason for the loss of tracking is that typical arm movements are too quick. If between one frame and the next the subject's arm moves so much that there isn't much overlap between the predicted arm position in the new frame and the actual arm position, the measurements from the new frame will not carry any information, and thus the estimation process will fail.

Since our system incorporates a model of the dynamics of arm motion, losing track of the arm does not translate into a maximum allowable arm velocity. Rather, with the current dynamic model of a random walk in joint velocities, a more correct measure would be the maximum allowable joint accelerations. However, the amount of mismatch in joint space necessary to cause enough mismatch in the image plane for the hand/arm to be lost depends on the relative configuration of the arm as well as the orientation of the arm with respect to the camera. Because of this, it is difficult to quantify the maximum allowable joint accelerations (or more in line with the mechanisms of tracking loss, the 3D acceleration of the hand tip). Based on our experimentation, movements need to be made approximately 2 times slower than normal. With some practice, a user is able to adapt his movement so that the system does not loose track of his arm.

One may improve the system's tracking ability in several ways. Multi-resolution measurements on a pyramid of down-sampled images could increase the range over which a mismatch in arm positions can still give useful measurements. Also, an improved dynamic model of arm motion may increase the prediction accuracy of the recursive filter.

Another factor limiting the robustness of our system is due to the pre-processing block currently in use. Not only the arm but also the rest of the body is detected as foreground, and thus, if some part of the arm crosses over into the image region occupied by, say, the torso, the measurements coming from that part of the arm will be incorrect. Fortunately, the Jacobian of the estimated state of the system with respect to those image intensities will be zero, so that those measurements do not affect the update of the estimated state. Therefore, the system is insensitive to occlusions overall. However, if enough of the arm is occluded, tracking may be lost. To correct this problem, a more sophisticated pre-processing block must be used. Loss of tracking also occurs because of the problem of shadows. Although the pre-processing block was designed to compensate for the presence of shadows, sometimes it fails. When this occurs, some of the background is considered as foreground, and if the arm is nearby, some of the measurements may be affected.

9.5.2 Quality of Data

Robustness issues aside, there are several performance measures that can be used to assess the quality of the output produced by the system. Their relative weight depends on the intended use of the system.

9.5.3 Absolute Positioning Accuracy

We compared the computed 3D position of the hand-tip with the actual 3D position, with the arm held still in a certain pose. Using a pre-recorded sequence for which a ground-truth trajectory was known, we found that our system had a maximum absolute positioning accuracy of 8% along the line-of-sight. Note that for many applications, this kind of measure is irrelevant. For instance, for the purposes of a human-

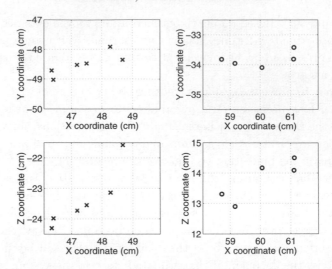

Fig. 9.8 Repeatability of hand-tip position estimation: scatter plots of estimated hand-tip position when the user repeatedly moves to the same locations in the workspace. Left: a location on the tabletop. Right: a location along a tightly strung string between the tabletop and the ceiling. The coordinates are relative to the shoulder position; X is forwards (towards camera), Z is upwards, and Y to the left. The camera was 130 cm from the shoulder, looking downwards with an inclination of 30 degrees to the horizon, and viewing angles of 65 degrees horizontally, 50 degrees vertically

machine interface, it is often sufficient that different poses be identified as unique. The virtual space can be distorted and it is not essential that there be an exact correspondence with points in real space, since the user can correct the position using visual feedback.

9.5.4 Repeatability

A more useful performance measure for a human-machine interface is one which measures the repeatability with which a given position can be reached. We measured the variance of the virtual hand-tip position when the user places his hand-tip at a specified location in 3D. Using this measure, we found our system to produce results which are repeatable with a standard deviation of approximately 1 cm (less than 1% of the distance to the camera). The data for this calculation was obtained by having a user repeatedly move his hand-tip between four marked locations distributed in the arm's workspace. Fig. 9.8 shows scatter plots of the repeatability measurements for two of the locations.

9.5.5 Resolution

The final performance measure that we consider is one which measures the resolution of positional control. In our specific case, we chose to measure the resolution with which the virtual hand-tip position can be controlled. The data was generated by having a user repeatedly try to line up his virtual hand-tip coordinates with those of a randomly chosen virtual point. This virtual point was shown on the SGI display by hi-lighting its XYZ coordinates on the scales (recall Fig. 9.9). We found the system to have a resolution standard deviation of approximately 1cm.

9.5.6 Static Versus Dynamic Performance Measures

The three measures described above are all "static" performance measures, that is, measures applied when the arm is stationary, rather than moving. "Dynamic" measures would take into account, for example, the joint angles, velocities and accelerations as a function of time (over complete trajectories). Since we did not have available a method for determining the ground truth of those quantities as a function of time, we were unable to compute any dynamic performance measures. Note that it is necessary to use a dynamic performance measure to asses the tracking qualities of the recursive estimator (such as convergence, stability). We can, however, remark qualitatively on the estimator's tracking: because of the random walk velocity arm dynamics model, there was an obvious "lagging behind" of the estimator whenever a sudden change in direction occurred.

9.5.7 Practicality

In the introduction we claimed that a system like this would be more practical to use than the usual tools. We set up an experiment: we render in the virtual 3D space (represented on the SGI screen using perspective projection) a small cube in a random location inside the arm's reachable space. The task consists of reaching this location with the hand, grabbing the cube and moving it to a new random location (Figure 9.9). It takes an experienced user between 5 to 20 seconds to complete the task. The difficulty in executing the task derives from two factors. First, sudden accelerations can cause the tracking to be lost, and second, the estimator sometimes locks on to an incorrect solution (a monocular projection of 2 links can have up to 4 possible solutions). In

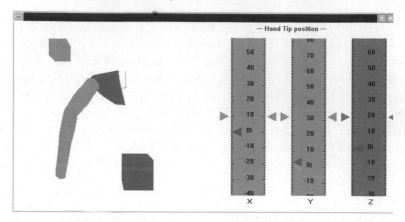

Fig. 9.9 An experimental task: the user has to grab hold of a virtual box and relocate it to a target position. The SGI display shows a perspective view of arm, box, and target location. To further aid the user, target and initial box locations are indicated on the XYZ scales as well

either case, the user must then "restart" the tracking from a predefined initial arm position. Furthermore, although rendered in a perspective view, it is still difficult to accurately perceive the position of the target. The displaying of XYZ scales aids this, but the user then moves his arm sequentially, along one axis at a time. Using a 3D trackball instead of our system, the same task is typically done in less than 3 seconds.

9.6 Conclusions and Future Work

We have shown how it is possible to use computer vision techniques to track a human arm in 3D in an unencumbered fashion using a monocular view. These techniques provide an intuitive human-machine interface which can be useful for such application areas as human factor engineering, where virtual object manipulation in 3D is necessary.

In the future we expect to increase the robustness of the system with two improvements. First, we can remove the assumption that the shoulder position is fixed in 3D, and instead track it in the image plane (perhaps with the use of a more anatomically correct model of the shoulder kinematics). This will allow the projected model to fit better to each frame, and hopefully avoid a lot of the incorrect solutions (convergence to the wrong 3D arm pose). Second, with a better model of arm dynamics, it may be possible to increase robustness without increasing the frame rate. There is much knowledge from studies of human motion which we may be able to incorporate into our system. For instance, we could incorporate knowledge of joint limits [193]. There is also the knowledge that some postures are more common than others, and that, say, when you are reaching in free space, there is a "standard" position for the elbow [187]. Another example is the fact that for ballistic arm movements there is a standard hand speed profile which is common to all such movements, modulo a time and amplitude scaling [11].

10

Looking at People in Action – An Overview

Y. Yacoob, L. Davis, M. Black, D. Gavrila,
T. Horprasert and C. Morimoto

Abstract

Using computers to watch human activity has proven to be a research area having not only a large number of potentially important applications (in surveillance, communications, health, etc.) but also one the had led to a variety of new, fundamental problems in image processing and computer vision. In this chapter we review research that has been conducted at the University of Maryland during the past five years on various topics involving analysis of human activity.

10.1 Introduction

Our interest in this general area started with consideration of the problem of how a computer might recognize a facial expression from the changing appearance of the face displaying the expression. Technically, this led us to address the problem of how the non-rigid deformations of facial features (eyes, mouth) could be accurately measured even while the face was moving rigidly.

In section 10.2 we discuss our solution to this problem. Our approach to this problem, in which the rigid head motion is estimated and used to stabilize the face so that the non-rigid feature motions could be recovered, naturally led us to consider the problem of head gesture recognition. Section 10.3 discusses two approaches to recognition of head gestures, both of which employ the rigid head motion descriptions estimated in the course of recognizing expressions.

In section 10.4 we discuss recent work addressing the problem of estimating the 3D orientation of a face from video. In that section we focus on the geometric model that is employed to create an instantaneous estimate of face orientation from a single image. This algorithm has been integrated into a tracking system that recovers the features needed for face orientation estimation. Finally, section 10.5 presents a model-based approach for recovering the three-dimensional pose of a human in action from multi-camera video sequences of the human in action.

10.2 Recognizing Facial Expressions

The problems of modeling and recognizing facial actions has been the subject of much recent study [29, 38, 120, 197, 211, 261, 285, 290, 323]. Two early systems for recognition of facial expressions were developed at the University of Maryland. They were based on the analysis of the optical flow fields computed from image sequences of human subjects and recognized expressions by constructing mid- and high-level representations of facial actions [261, 323] (e.g., mouth opening, eyebrow raising etc.). The optical flow vectors were computed at the high intensity gradient points of the primary features (i.e., mouth, eyes, eyebrows, and nose) and were used as input to both systems. The primary facial features were tracked automatically throughout the image sequence based on a spatio-temporal approach. The approach described in [323] was based on a rule-based system guided by psychological findings. A neural network architecture that learns to recognize facial expressions from an optical flow field was reported in [261]. These systems made the limiting assumption that the head was not undergoing any rigid motion during the display of facial expressions.

The recognition of facial expressions in image sequences with significant head motion is a challenging problem due to the co-occurrence of non-rigid and rigid motions. Black and Yacoob [38] recently proposed a model of rigid and non-rigid facial motion using a collection of local parametric models. The image motion of the face, mouth, eyebrows, and eyes are modeled using image flow models with only a few parameters. The motions of these regions are estimated over an image sequence using a robust regression scheme [37] which makes the recovered motion parameters stable under adverse conditions such as motion blur, saturation, loss of focus, etc. These recovered parameters correspond simply and intuitively to various facial expressions.

To model the rigid motion of a face in the image the simple assumption that the majority of the face can be modeled by a plane was made. The image motions of the facial features (eyes, mouth and eyebrows) were modeled relative to the head motion using different parametric models.

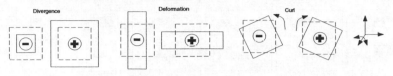

Fig. 10.1 The figure illustrates the motion captured by the various parameters used to represent the motion of the regions. The solid lines indicate the deformed image region and the "–" and "+" indicate the sign of the quantity.

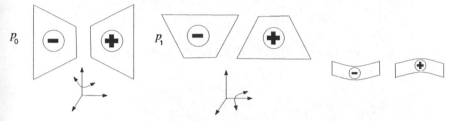

Fig. 10.2. Parameters for planar motion and curvature.

For the eyes a simple affine model was used. For the brows and mouth an affine model was augmented with an additional curvature parameter to account for the arching of the brows and curvature of the mouth when smiling.

The approach can be summarized as follows. Given an initial location of the face, eyes and brows, and mouth, the rigid motion of the face region (excluding the deformable features) between two frames using a planar motion model is estimated. The motion of the face is used to register the images via warping and then the relative motion of the feature regions is estimated in the coordinate frame of the face. The estimated motion parameters provide a simple abstraction of the underlying facial motions and be used to classify the type of rigid head motion.

The parameterized motion models are fully described in [38]. These models measure the horizontal and vertical translation, *divergence* (isotropic expansion), *curl* (rotation about the viewing direction), *deformation* (squashing or stretching), *yaw, pitch* and *curvature* (see Figs. 10.1 and 10.2).

The deformation and motion parameters were used to derive mid- and high-level descriptions of facial actions similar to our original system.

Fig. 10.3 illustrates a sequence with a complex rigid face motion due to rapid head rotations. In addition to the rapid motion, the sequence contains sections of motion blur, loss of focus, and saturation. Despite the low quality of the sequence the tracking of the head and features is

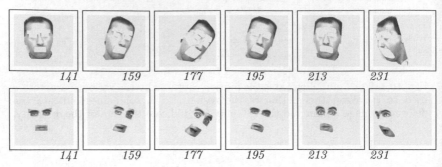

Fig. 10.3. Rotation experiment. Rigid head tracking, every 18th frame.

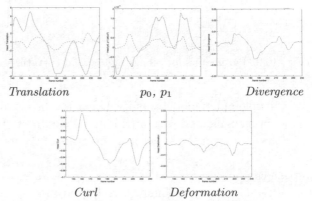

Fig. 10.4 The rotate face motion parameters. Translation: solid = horizontal, dashed = vertical, yaw, solid = p_0, pitch, dashed = p_1.

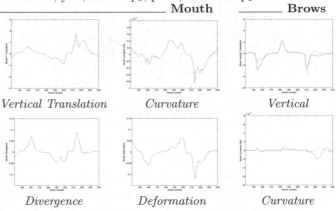

Fig. 10.5 The rotate sequence. For the brows, the solid and dashed lines indicate left and right brows respectively.

robust. In Fig. 10.4 the plot of curl shows that the face rotates clock-wise in the image plane, then rotates counterclockwise, pauses briefly, and continues the counterclockwise motion. The plot of the yaw (p_0 solid line) indicates that the head is rotating about the neck axis roughly in conjunction with the curl. Fig. 10.5 indicates that two surprise expressions take place during the sequence as characterized by the eyebrow motion and mouth deformation.

Two sets of experiments were conducted. In the first, tens of expressions of forty subjects (having varied race, culture, and appearance) displaying their own choice of expressions were recorded. The expressions 'fear' and 'sadness' were hard to elicit compared to 'happiness,' 'surprise,' 'disgust' and 'anger.' The subjects were also asked to move their heads; but avoid a profile view. In the second set of experiments digitized video-clips of talk shows, news and movies were used. TV broadcasting, reception, video-recording and digitization made the data quite noisy.

A database of 70 image sequences of forty participants was collected. Each sequence is about 9 seconds long and contains 1-3 expressions (taken at 30Hz). On these 70 image sequences displaying a total of 128 expressions, the system achieved a successful recognition rate of 89% for 'smile,' 94% for 'surprise,' 100% for 'anger,' 100% for 'fear,' 87% for 'sadness,' and 89% for 'disgust' where success rate is defined as correct/(correct + false-alarm). Failure rate, defined as miss/(miss + correct) was 5%, 9%, 10%, 17%, 0%, and 7%, respectively.

Table 10.1 shows the details of our results. The category of 'False' refers to false positives of an expression, and is further divided into positives that happened to be another expression (see category 'Substitution') and the rest are expressions that were recognized when the face was neutral (mostly due to motion and tracking inaccuracies). 'Miss' refers to an expression that the system failed to identify. Some confusion of expressions occurred between the following pairs: 'fear' and 'surprise,' and 'anger' and 'disgust.' These distinctions rely on subtle shape and motion information that were not always accurately detected.

Fig. 10.6 shows four frames (taken as every fourth frame from the sequence) of the beginning of an 'anger' expression of a six year old boy. The text that appears on the left side of each image represents the mid-level descriptions of the facial deformations, and the text that appears on the right side represents the mid-level descriptions of the head motion.

Expression	Corr.	False	Miss	Subst.	Succ.	Fail
Happiness	58	7	3	2	89%	5%
Surprise	32	2	3	2	94%	9%
Anger	18	-	2	-	100%	10%
Disgust	14	2	1	1	100%	17%
Fear	5	-	1	-	87%	0%
Sadness	8	1	-	1	89%	7%

Table 10.1. *Facial expression recognition results on forty subjects*

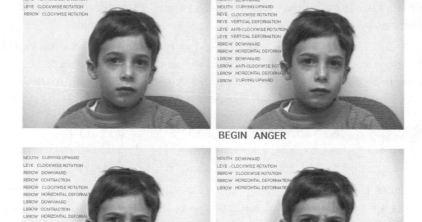

Fig. 10.6 Four frames (four frames apart) of the beginning of an 'anger' expression displayed by a six year old boy.

The text below each image displays the high-level description of the facial deformations and the head motions.

10.3 Head Gesture Recognition

The planar face motion model can also be used to recognize head gestures. We developed a rule-based system and a Hidden Markov Model system for this purpose.

10.3.1 A Rule-based System

The motion rotation parameters estimated for the face plane are used to derive mid-level predicates that characterize its motion. The parameter values are first thresholded to filter out most of the small and noisy estimates of deformation and motion. The mid-level representation describes the observed facial changes at each frame.

We focused on recognizing six head gestures: *nodding (agreeing), negating (disagreeing), approximating (as in 'more-or-less' or 'maybe'), greeting, shifting attention* and *expressing joy*. These gestures were selected from several psychology and behavior science sources [64, 264]. In a laboratory environment our subjects had little difficulty showing these gestures upon request (with some unnatural gestures in attempts to express joy).

Fig. 10.7 illustrates the values of the primary rotation parameters of the head (*image-curl, image-yaw* and *image-pitch*) for two image sequences (284 frames in each). Each sequence contains three head gestures. The left column graphs show the results for a sequence that includes 'nodding,' 'negating' and 'approximating,' respectively. The right column graphs show the results for a sequence that includes 'greeting,' 'shifting attention' and 'expressing joy,' respectively. Notice that the vertical axes differ in range for each sequence to enhance the clarity of the display.

A 'nod' opens the first sequence (left column), indicated by cyclic change in *image-pitch* (dashed line). Afterwords, a 'negating' gesture occurs and is captured by cyclic change in *image-yaw*. The third gesture is 'approximating' and is best described as a motion in the image plane and captured by the *image-curl* parameter. Notice that during each gesture some non-zero component of rotation may be estimated in directions other than expected due to approximating the head as an independent rigid body (which is inaccurate due to the constraints imposed by the neck on the head motion), and due to errors in the planar face model.

A 'greeting' gesture opens the second sequence (right column), detected by a single cycle of a 'nodding' sequence (usually a relatively slow cycle), as seen in *image-pitch* (dashed line). Afterwords, a 'shift attention' gesture occurs since there are simultaneous rotations in both *image-yaw* and *image-pitch*; these motions are subsequently reversed (since we assume that 'shifting attention' is sustained for a few seconds). The third gesture is that of 'expressing joy' and it is recognized by significant rotations in both the image plane (*image-curl*) and around the neck (*image-yaw*) (and possibly in *image-pitch*). Table 10.2 provides a description of the motions associated with each gesture.

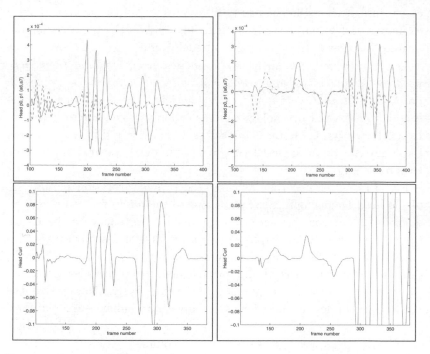

Fig. 10.7 Motion estimation results of two image sequences (each column is for a sequence) for nod, negative, and approximate (left column), greet, shift attention and express joy (right column). The dashed parts denote p_1, dotted p_0.

A large set of experiments was performed to verify and evaluate the performance of the recognition procedure. On the image sequences of 20 subjects displaying a total of 110 gestures, the system achieved a perfect recognition rate on 'nodding', 'negating', 'approximating' and 'greeting', 67% for 'shifting attention', and 88% for 'expressing joy' (see Fig. 10.8).

Gesture	Observed Head Motion
Nod	Cyclic rotations in *image-pitch* (a minimum of two cycles is required)
Negate	Cyclic rotations in *image-yaw* (a minimum of two cycles is required)
Approximate	Cyclic rotations *image-curl* (a minimum of two cycles is required; no other rotations should occur)
Greet	A single rotation cycle in *image-pitch*
Shift Attention	A single rotation cycle in *image-yaw* and in *image-pitch* (relatively long pause before reversal of action)
Express joy	Cyclic rotations in *image-curl* (minimum of two cycles is required; other rotations *image-pitch* and *image-yaw* must occur)

Table 10.2. *The cues for head gesture*

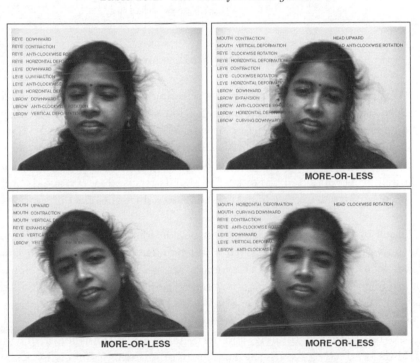

Fig. 10.8. A 'more-or-less' sequence, the images are 20 frames apart

10.3.2 Hidden Markov Models

The block diagram of the HMM head gesture recognition system is given in Figure 10.9. The vector quantization module transforms the motion parameters into observation sequences that are used by the HMMs. The HMMs, after training, score the input observation sequence, and the model with the highest score (i.e., maximum likelihood) determines the output symbol.

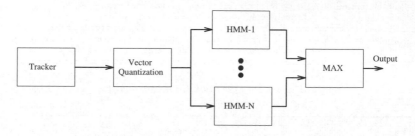

Fig. 10.9. Block diagram of the head gesture recognition system.

We use a dynamic mechanism for selecting an appropriate threshold before the quantization process. First, a low threshold is used to localize gestures in the input sequence. It is assumed that periods of silence (i.e., all image rotations close to zero) separate the presentation of a gesture. After the localization of a gesture in the sequence, the energy of each parameter is computed. High energy signals receive low thresholds and low energy signals receive high thresholds to reduce the effect of spurious noise.

Each of these image rotations can be considered to be positive ($+$), negative ($-$), or zero (0). With 3 independent parameters which can assume 3 different values, 27 symbols are necessary to code a single state (e.g., the symbol "0" can be used to code the parameter state ($+$, $+$, $+$), the symbol "1" to code ($+$,$+$,$-$), and so on, until all combinations are coded).

To facilitate the training and recognition operation modes of the HMMs, we further reduce the number of observation symbols by mapping the image rotation parameters into the seven symbols: UP, DOWN, LEFT, RIGHT, CLOCKWISE, ANTICLOCKWISE, and REST. A symbol is selected as output based on the dominant motion which is determined by the signal with highest energy. UP or DOWN are selected when image-pitch is dominant, LEFT or RIGHT when image-yaw is dominant, and CLOCKWISE or ANTICLOCKWISE when image-curl is dominant. When none of the signals is dominant, the symbol REST is selected.

The image rotations are thresholded and mapped to the seven possible observation symbols, depending on the instantaneously highest energy band. Although the system could work by directly considering the overall highest energy band, we choose this approach of selecting the instantaneous highest band to be able to model more complex gestures.

For our experiments we developed one HMM for each of nod (YES), negate (NO), approximate (MAYBE) and greet (HELLO). The models were trained using 28 sequences taken from 5 people. The test data consisted of 33 sequences taken from 6 other people. Due to the simplicity of the models, the parameters of each model were initially "guessed" and then tuned by the Baum-Welch iterative process.

Table 10.3 shows the results for the trained HMMs using the test data. Observe that the HELLO gesture is confused most of the time with the YES gesture. This is caused by the definition of the HELLO gesture, that is considered to be a single nod. Looking at the input sequence data for the HELLO gesture, most subjects present more than a single nod, at least 1.5 cycles which characterizes the YES gesture. The YES gesture is also confused with the HELLO gesture because some subjects when told to perform the YES gesture, executed only one image-pitch cycle. Changing the definitions in order to allow the HELLO gesture to have up to 2 cycles and considering the YES gestures to be those sequences with more the 2 image-pitch cycles would solve this problem for this particular data set.

	YES	NO	MAYBE	HELLO
YES	13		2	3
NO		5		
MAYBE	1	1	4	
HELLO	2			2
TOTAL	16	6	6	5

Table 10.3. *Confusion matrix of test data for trained HMMs*

10.4 Head Orientation Estimation

In this section we present an algorithm for estimating the orientation of a human face from a single monocular image. The algorithm takes advantage of the geometric symmetries of typical faces to compute the yaw and roll components of orientation, and anthropometric modeling [122, 325] to estimate the pitch component. The approach requires no prior knowledge of the exact face structure of the individual being observed. The diversity of face and head appearances due to hair (head and facial) and eyeglasses in addition to articulated jaw motion and facial surface deformations leave very few features geometrically stable and predictable across individuals and head orientations. The nose is the only feature subject to no significant deformations. In addition, the eyes are often visible (although occasionally covered by eye-glasses). For estimating head orientation, we assume that both eyes and the nose are visible, thus avoiding near-profile poses. Our approach consists of the following stages:

(i) Region tracking of the face and the face features based on parameterized motion models (see [38]).

(ii) Sub-pixel estimation of eye-corners and nose-tip.

(iii) Computing 3D orientation from these five points.

Our model for head estimation assumes that the four eye-corners are co-linear in 3D; this assumption can be relaxed to account for a slight horizontal tilt in the eyes of Asian subjects (see [122, 325] for statistics on the deviation of the eye corners from co-linearity). The details of the algorithm can be found in [149]

Some frames of an image sequence are shown in Figures 10.10 and 10.11. In Fig. 10.10, the plots of pitch (α), yaw (β), and roll (γ) are shown.

Fig. 10.11 illustrates an experiment to compare pitch recovery using anthropometric models and an individual's actual face structure. For this purpose, two image sequences of a Caucasian male and an Asian female were captured. The plots show the differences between using individual structure (true 3D measurement of the subject's features) and the anthropometry in the computational models. The means of the face structures of adult American Caucasian male and female are employed in this experiment. In both cases, the pitch is recovered with an error predicted by our model.

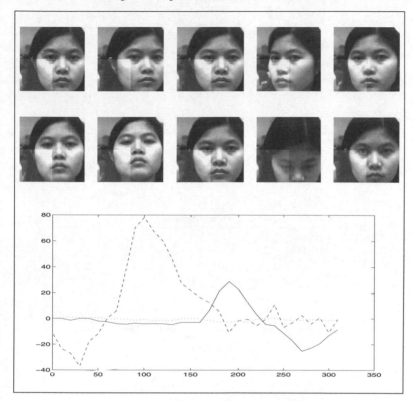

Fig. 10.10 Some images in a sequence, and the result of pose estimation. The plots show the sequences of rotation angles through the image sequence.

10.5 Model-based Tracking and Analysis

In this section a vision system for 3D model-based tracking of unconstrained human movement is described. Using image sequences acquired simultaneously from multiple views, we recover the 3D body pose at each time instant. The pose-recovery problem is formulated as a search problem and entails finding the pose parameters of a graphical human model whose synthesized appearance is most similar to the actual appearance of the real human in the multi-view images. The models used for this purpose are acquired from the images. We use a decomposition approach and a best-first technique to search through the high-dimensional pose parameter space. A robust variant of chamfer matching is used as a fast similarity measure between synthesized and real edge images.

By using a multi-view approach we achieve tighter 3D pose recovery and tracking of the human body than from using one view only; body

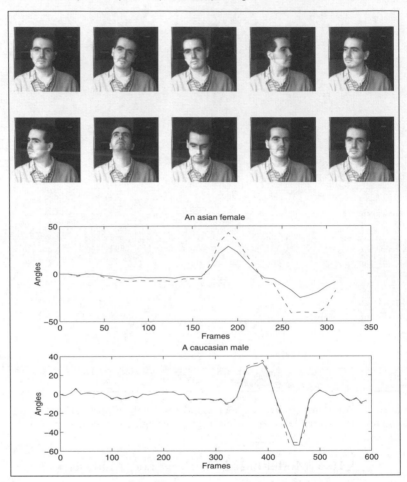

Fig. 10.11 The error when applying our approach to different face structures. (*solid line*) is the plot of α computed by employing statistics from anthropometry, while (*dash line*) is the plot of α computed by utilizing the real measurements of model's face structure.

poses and movements that are ambiguous from one view can be disambiguated from another view. We synthesize appearances of the human model for all the available views, and evaluate the appropriateness of a 3D pose based on the similarity measures for the individual views.

For our purposes of tracking 3D whole-body motion, we currently use a 22 DOF model (3 DOF for the positioning of the root of the articulated structure, 3 DOF for the torso and 4 DOF for each arm and each leg), without modeling the palm of the hand or the foot, and using a rigid head-torso approximation. We employ the class of *tapered super-quadrics* [220]; these include such diverse shapes as cylinders, spheres, ellipsoids and hyper-rectangles to represent body parts.

We derive the shape parameters from the projections of occluding contours in two orthogonal views, parallel to the zx- and zy-planes. This involves the human subject facing the camera frontally and sideways. We assume 2D segmentation in the two orthogonal views; a way to obtain such a segmentation is proposed in [162]. Back-projecting the 2D projected contours of a quadric gives the 3D occluding contours, after which a coarse-to-fine search procedure is used over a reasonable range of parameter space to determine the best-fitting quadric. Fitting uses chamfer matching as a similarity measure between the fitted and back-projected occluding 3D contours.

The general framework for our tracking component is adopted from the early work of O'Rourke and Badler [263]. Four main components are involved: *prediction, synthesis, image analysis* and *state estimation.* The prediction component takes into account previous states up to time t to make a prediction for time $t + 1$. It is deemed more stable to do the prediction at a high level (in state space) than at a low level (in image space), allowing an easier way to incorporate semantic knowledge into the tracking process. The synthesis component translates the prediction from the state level to the measurement (image) level, which allows the image analysis component to selectively focus on a subset of regions and look for a subset of features. Finally, the state-estimation component computes the new state using the segmented image.

We compiled a large data base containing multi-view images of human subjects involved in a variety of activities. These activities are of various degrees of complexity, ranging from single-person hand waving to the challenging two-person close interaction of the Argentine Tango. The data was taken from four (near-) orthogonal views (FRONT, RIGHT, BACK and LEFT) with the cameras placed wide apart in the corners of a room for maximum coverage. The background is fairly complex; many regions contain bar-like structures and some regions are highly textured The subjects wear tight-fitting clothes. Their sleeves are of contrasting colors, simplifying edge detection somewhat in cases where one body part occludes another.

Fig. 10.12 illustrates tracking for persons Dariu (D)and Ellen (E). The movement performed can be described as raising the arms sideways to a 90 degree extension, followed by rotating both elbows forward. The current recovered 3D pose is illustrated by the projection of the model in

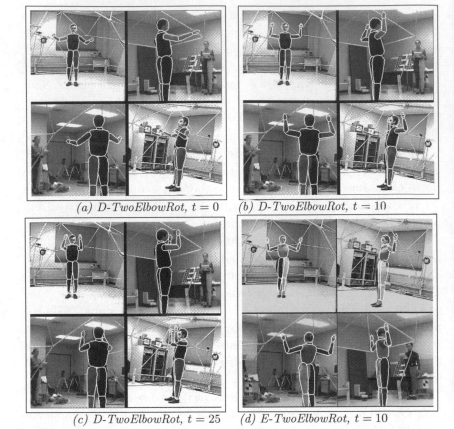

(a) *D-TwoElbowRot, t = 0*   (b) *D-TwoElbowRot, t = 10*

(c) *D-TwoElbowRot, t = 25*   (d) *E-TwoElbowRot, t = 10*

Fig. 10.12 (a)-(c) Tracking sequence D-TwoElbowRot ($t = 0, 10, 25$), (d) Tracking sequence E-TwoElbowRot ($t = 10$); cameras FRONT, RIGHT, BACK and LEFT

the four views, shown in white. The displayed model projections include for visual purposes the edges at the intersections of body parts; these were not included in the chamfer matching process. It can be seen that tracking is quite successful, with a good fit for the recovered 3D pose of the model for the four views.

10.6 Ongoing Research

We conclude with a brief description of ongoing research projects. The motions observed in video sequences of humans cover a wide range of scales. For example, when observing the motion of the leg during walking, the image motion near the hip might be only a fraction of a pixel per frame, while the motion at the foot is typically many pixels per frame. In order to measure this wide range of motions we developed a temporal scale space approach to motion estimation. While our research has relied heavily on motion, it is clear that motion alone cannot account for the changes we observe in human action. For example, when viewing the mouth, there is lip motion but also appearance change as the mouth opens, for example. We are developing an approach for representing an image sequence as a mixture of motion and appearance change, and applied this model to the analysis of video clips of mouth motions.

Part three

Gesture Recognition and Interpretation

11

A Framework for Gesture Generation and Interpretation

J. Cassell

Abstract

In this chapter I describe ongoing research that seeks to provide a common framework for the generation and interpretation of spontaneous gesture in the context of speech. I present a testbed for this framework in the form of a program that generates speech, gesture, and facial expression from underlying rules specifying (a) what speech and gesture are generated on the basis of a given communicative intent, (b) how communicative intent is distributed across communicative modalities, and (c) where one can expect to find gestures with respect to the other communicative acts. Finally, I describe a system that has the capacity to interpret communicative facial, gestural, intonational, and verbal behaviors.

11.1 Introduction

I am addressing in this chapter one very particular use of the term "gesture" – that is, hand gestures that co-occur with spoken language. Why such a narrow focus, given that so much of the work on gesture in the human-computer interface community has focused on gestures as their own language – gestures that might replace the keyboard or mouse or speech as a direct command language? Because I don't believe that everyday human users have any more experience with, or natural affinity for, a "gestural language" than they have with DOS commands. We have plenty of experience with actions and the manipulation of objects. But the type of gestures defined as (Väänänen & Böhm, 1993) "body movements which are used to convey some information from one person to another" are in fact primarily found in association with spoken language (90% of gestures are found in the context of speech, according to McNeill, 1992). Thus, if our goal is to get away from learned, predefined interaction techniques and create *natural* interfaces for normal human users, we should concentrate on the type of gestures that come naturally to normal humans.

Spontaneous (that is, unplanned, unself-conscious) gesture accompanies speech in most communicative situations and in most cultures (despite the common belief to the contrary). People even gesture while they are speaking on the telephone (Rimé, 1982). We know that listeners attend to such gestures, and that they use gesture in these situations to form a mental representation of the communicative intent of the speaker.

What kinds of meanings are conveyed by gesture? How do listeners extract these meanings? Will it ever be possible to build computers that can extract the meanings from human gesture in such a way that the computers can understand natural human communication (including speech, gesture, intonation, facial expression, etc.)? When computers can interpret gestures, will they also be able to display them such that an autonomous communicating agent will act as the interlocutor in the computer? We imagine computers that communicate like we do, producing and understanding gesture, speech, intonation, and facial expression, thereby taking seriously the currently popular metaphor of the computer as conversational partner.

11.2 Background

11.2.1 The Communicative Function of Hand Gestures

A growing body of evidence shows that people unwittingly produce gestures along with speech in many different communicative situations. These gestures have been shown to elaborate upon and enhance the content of accompanying speech (McNeill, 1992; Kendon, 1972), often giving clues to the underlying thematic organization of the discourse or the speaker's perspective on events. Gestures have also been shown to identify underlying reasoning processes that the speaker did not, or could not, articulate (Church and Goldin-Meadow, 1986).

Do gestures play any role in human-human communication? We know that gestures are still produced in situations where there is no listener, or the listener cannot see the speaker's hands (Rimé, 1982), although more gestures may be produced when an addressee is present (Cohen, 1977; Cohen & Harrison, 1973). Thus it appears that gestures must serve some function for the speaker, independent of any communicative intent. In addition, we know that information appears to be just about as effectively communicated in the absence of gesture – on the telephone, or from behind a screen (Short, Williams & Christie, 1976; Williams, 1977) – and thus gesture is not *essential* to the interpretation of speech. But it has been shown that when speech is ambiguous (Thompson & Massaro, 1986) or in a speech situation with some noise (Rogers, 1978), listeners do rely on gestural cues (the higher the noise-to-signal ratio, the more facilitation by gesture). And, when adults are asked to assess a child's knowledge, they are able to use information that is conveyed in the child's gesture (that is not the same as that conveyed by the child's speech) to make that assessment (Goldin-Meadow, Wein & Chang, 1992; Alibali, Flevares & Goldin-Meadow, 1994). Finally, when people are exposed to gestures and speech that convey slightly different information, whether additive or contradictory, they seem to treat the information conveyed by gesture on an equal footing with that conveyed by speech, ultimately seeming to build one single representation out of information conveyed in the two modalities (Cassell, McNeill & McCullough, in press).

We suspect that hand gestures must be integral to communication when we examine their temporal relationship to other communicative devices. Hand gestures co-occur with their semantically parallel linguistic units, although in cases of hesitations, pauses, or syntactically complex speech, it is the gesture which appears first (McNeill, 1992). At the most local level, individual gestures and words are synchronized in time so that the *stroke* (the most energetic part of the gesture) occurs either with or just before the intonationally most prominent syllable of the accompanying speech segment (Kendon, 1980; McNeill, 1992). At the most global level, we find that the hands of the speaker come to rest at the end of a speaking turn, before the next speaker begins his/her turn. At the intermediate level, we find the phenomenon of co-articulation of gestural units, whereby gestures are performed rapidly, or their production is stretched out over time so as to synchronize with preceding and following gestures and the speech these gestures accompany. An example of gestural co-articulation is the relationship between the two gestures in the phrases "if you [write the check]† then I'll [withdraw] the money for you." After performing the gesture that depicts writing a check, the hands do not completely relax. Instead, the right hand remains in space

---

† Square brackets indicate the extent of the hand gesture with respect to speech.

and depicts withdrawing something (like a letter from a mailbox). Thus the occurrence of the word "withdraw," with its accompanying gesture, affects the occurrence of the gesture that accompanies "write the check."

The essential nature of gestures in the communicative situation is demonstrated by the extreme rarity of *gestural errors*. That is, although spoken language is commonly quite disfluent, full of false starts, hesitations, and speech errors, gestures virtually never portray anything but the speaker's communicative intention. Speakers may *say* "left" and mean "right," but they will probably *point* towards the right. Listeners may correct speakers' errors on the basis of the speaker's gestures (McNeill, 1992).

So, we can conclude that hand gestures serve a communicative function in face-to-face communication. Hand gestures are ubiquitous in face-to-face communication and appear to be integral to the production and comprehension of language in face-to-face contexts. In fact, listeners take into account the information conveyed by gesture, even when this information is not redundant to the information conveyed in speech. We next ask whether all gestures function in the same way in communicative contexts, and which types of gestures are most common.

11.2.2 Kinds of Gestures Found in Human-Human Communication

Let us first look at the types of gestures that have been covered primarily in the extant literature on computer vision and human-computer interface, and then contrast that with the type of gestures that have been covered in the extant psychological and linguistic literature on gestures as an integral part of communication.

When we reflect on what kinds of gestures we have seen in our environment, we often come up with a type of gesture known as *emblematic*. These gestures are culturally specified in the sense that one single gesture may differ in interpretation from culture to culture (Efron, 1941; Ekman & Friesen, 1969). For example, the 'V-for-victory' gesture can be made in 'American' either with the palm or the back of the hand towards the listener. In Britain, however, a 'V' gesture made with the back of the hand towards the listener is inappropriate in polite society. Examples of emblems in American culture are the thumb-and-index-finger ring gesture that signals 'okay' or the 'thumbs up' gesture. Many more of these emblems appear to exist in French and Italian culture than in America (Kendon, 1993), but in few cultures do these gestures appear to constitute more than 10% of the gestures produced by speakers. That is, in terms of *types*, few enough different emblematic gestures exist to make the idea of co-opting emblems as a gestural language untenable. And in terms of *tokens*, we simply don't seem to make that many emblematic gestures on a daily basis. Why, then, do emblematic type gestures (such as putting up one hand to mean 'stop,' or making a 'thumbs up' gesture to mean that everything is okay) appear so often in the human-computer interface literature? I think it is because emblematic gestures are *consciously produced* and therefore easier to remember.

Another conscious gesture that has been the subject of some study in the interface community is the so-called propositional gesture (Hinrichs & Polanyi, 1986). An example is the use of the hands to measure the size of a symbolic space while the speaker says, "it was this big." Another example is pointing at a chair and then pointing at another spot and saying, "move that over there." These gestures are not unwitting and in that sense not spontaneous, and their interaction with speech is more like the interaction of one grammatical constituent with another than the interaction of one communicative channel with another; in fact, the demonstrative "this" may be seen as a place holder for the syntactic role of the accompanying gesture. These gestures can be particularly important in certain types of task-oriented talk, as discussed in the well known paper, "Put-That-There: Voice and Gesture at the Graphics Interface" (Bolt, 1987). Gestures such as these are found notably in communicative situations where the physical world in which the conversation is taking place is also the topic of conversation. These gestures do not, however, make up the majority of gestures found in spontaneous conversation, and I believe that, in part, they received the attention that they have because they are *conscious witting* gestures available to our self-scrutiny.

We have, however, still ignored the vast majority of gestures: those that although unconscious and unwitting are the gestural vehicles for our communicative intent – with other humans, and potentially with our computer partners as well. These gestures, for the most part, are not available to conscious access, either to the person who produced them or to the person who watched them being produced. This, I believe, is the reason that so many of these gestures have been ignored by the human-computer interface community: these gestures do not come immediately to mind when we reflect on the gestures we see around us.

In case the fact of losing access to the form of a whole class of gestures seems odd, consider the analogous situation with speech. For the most part, in most situations, we lose access to the *surface structure* of utterances immediately after hearing or producing them. That is, if listeners are asked whether they heard the word "couch" or the word "sofa" to refer to the same piece of furniture, unless one of these words sounds odd to them, they probably will not be able to remember which they heard. Likewise, slight variations in pronunciation of the speech we are listening to are difficult to remember, even right after hearing them (Levelt, 1989). That is because, so it is hypothesized, we listen to speech in order to extract meaning, and we throw away the words once the meaning has been extracted. In the same way, we appear to lose access to the form of gestures (Krauss, Morrel-Samuels & Colasante, 1991), even though we attend to the information that they convey (Cassell, McNeill & McCullough, in press).

The more common, spontaneous, unplanned gestures are of four types:

- *Iconic* gestures depict by the form of the gesture some feature of the action or event being described – such as the gesture of holding a tube with a handle that accompanies, "Press the [handle of the caulking gun slowly as you move the nozzle across the window ledge that needs caulk]."

Iconic gestures may specify the manner in which an action is carried out, even if this information is not given in accompanying speech. For example, only in gesture does the narrator specify the essential information of how the handle of the caulk gun is to be manipulated.

Iconic gestures may also specify the viewpoint from which an action is narrated. That is, gesture can demonstrate who narrators imagine themselves to be and where they imagine themselves to stand at various points in the narration, when this is rarely conveyed in speech, and listeners can infer this viewpoint from the gestures they see. For example, one speaker at the Computer Vision Workshop was describing to his neighbor a technique that his lab was employing. He said, "and we use a wide field cam to [do the body]," while holding both hands open and bent at the wrists with his fingers pointed towards his body, and the hands sweeping up and down. His gesture shows us the wide field cam "doing the body" and takes the perspective of somebody whose body is "being done." Alternatively, he might have put both hands up to his eyes, pantomiming holding a camera, and playing the part of the viewer rather than the viewed.

- *Metaphoric* gestures are also representational, but the concept they represent has no physical form; instead, the form of the gesture comes from a common metaphor. An example is, "the meeting went on and on" accompanied by a hand indicating rolling motion. There need not be a productive metaphor in the speech accompanying metaphoric gestures; sometimes the metaphors that are represented in gesture have become entirely conventionalized in the language. There does need to be a recognizable vehicle that mediates between the form of the gesture and the meaning of the speech it accompanies.

Some common metaphoric gestures are the *process metaphoric* just illustrated, and the *conduit metaphoric*, which objectifies the information being conveyed, representing it as a concrete object that can be held between the hands and given to the listener. Conduit metaphorics commonly accompany new segments in communicative acts. An example is the box gesture that accompanies, "In this [next part] of the talk I'm going to discuss new work on this topic." Metaphoric gestures of this sort contextualize communication; for example, placing it in the larger context of social interaction. In this example, the speaker has prepared to give the next segment of discourse to the conference attendees. Another typical metaphoric gesture in academic contexts is the metaphoric pointing gesture that commonly associates features with people. For example, one speaker at the Computer Vision Workshop pointed to Sandy Pentland and said, "the work was based on work in [appearance-based constraints]." Here, Sandy is representing – or standing in for – work on appearance-based constraints.

- *Deictics* spatialize, or locate in the physical space in front of the narrator, aspects of the discourse. These can be discourse entities that have a physical existence, such as the tube of caulk that the narrator pointed to on the workbench, or non-physical discourse entities. An example of the latter might be pointing left, and then right, while saying, "well, Roberto was looking at Pietro across the table ..."

Deictic gestures populate the space between the speaker and listener with discourse entities as they are introduced and continue to be referred to. Deictics do not have to be pointing index fingers. One can also use the whole hand to represent entities or ideas or events in space. An example from the conference comes from one speaker who named another researcher's technique of modeling faces and then said, "We [don't] do that; we [bung] them all together." During the word "don't," this speaker used both hands to demarcate or wave away the space to his right, and during "bung," he brought both hands together to demarcate a space directly in front of him. In this example, the speaker is positioning the techniques that he chose not to use to one side, and the techniques that he did use directly in front of him.

- *Beat gestures* are small baton like movements that do not change in form with the content of the accompanying speech. They serve a pragmatic function, occurring with comments on one's own linguistic contribution, speech repairs, and reported speech. An example is, "she talked first, I mean second" accompanied by a hand flicking down and then up.

Beat gestures may signal that information conveyed in accompanying speech does not advance the "plot" of the discourse, but rather is an evaluative or orienting comment. For example, the narrator of a home repair show described the content of the next part of the TV episode by saying, "I'm going to tell you how to use a caulking gun to [prevent leakage] through [storm windows] and [wooden window ledges]. . ." and accompanied this speech with several beat gestures to indicate that the role of this part of the discourse was to indicate the relevance of what came next, as opposed to imparting new information in and of itself.

It is natural to wonder about the cultural specificity of these types of gestures. We often have the impression that Italians gesture more, and differently, than British speakers. As far as the question of quantity is concerned, it is true that some cultures may embrace the use of gesture more than others – many segments of British society believe that gesturing is inappropriate, and therefore children are discouraged from using their hands when they speak. But the effect of these beliefs and constraints about gesture is not as strong as one might think. In my experience videotaping people having conversations and telling stories, many speakers claim that they never use their hands. These speakers are then surprised to watch themselves on video, where they can be seen using their hands as much as the next person.

As far as the nature of gesture is concerned, as mentioned above, emblems do vary widely. The four gesture types described, however, have appeared in narrations in a variety of languages: English, French, Spanish, Tagalog, Swahili, Georgian, Chinese, etc. Interestingly, and perhaps not surprisingly, the *form* of metaphoric gestures appears to differ from language community to language community. Conduit metaphoric gestures are not found in narrations in all languages: neither Chinese nor Swahili narrators use them. These narratives do contain abundant metaphoric gestures of other kinds, but do not depict abstract ideas as

Fig. 11.1. Complex Gesture Generation

bounded containers. The metaphoric use of space, however, appears in all narratives collected, regardless of the language spoken. Thus, apart from emblematic gestures, the use of gesture appears to be more universal than particular.

11.3 The Problem

In Fig. 11.1, Seymour Papert is talking about the advantages of embedding computing in everyday objects and toys. He says, "A kid can make a device that will have *real behavior* ... that the two of them [will interact] in a - to - to do a dance together." When he says "make a device," he looks upward; when he says "real behavior," he stresses the words. He also stresses "will interact" while looking towards the audience, raising his hands to chest level, and pointing with each hand towards the other as if each hand is a device that is about to interact with the other. The concept of interaction, of course, does not have a physical instantiation. The gesture produced by Papert is a metaphoric depiction of the notion of interaction. Note that this communicative performance comprises speech with intonation, facial movements (gaze), and hand gestures, all three behaviors in synchrony.

How could we possibly interpret such a gestural performance? How could we have understood that two index fingers pointing towards the center were two Lego robots preparing to dance with one another (the example that he gave of interaction)?

Unlike language, gesture does not rely on a one-to-one mapping of form to meaning. Two fingers pointing towards the center may convey dancing robots at one point, while at another point in the very same discourse that same gesture may indicate rolling up a carpet in a room. Of course, the fact that gesture is not a code is what makes it a powerful index of human mental representation. Spoken languages are constrained by the nature of grammar, which is arbitrary and non-iconic (for the most part). Language is mediated by the ratified social code. Gesture, on the other hand, can play out in space what we imagine in our minds.

And yet the psycholinguistic literature tells us that humans attend to gestures of just this sort, and interpret them in real-time. When speech and gesture do not convey the same information, listeners do their best to reconcile the two modalities. How is this done?

In what follows, I suggest that (a) gesture interpretation may be bootstrapped by its synchronization with intonation and the information structure of an utterance; (b) gesture takes up the parts of a semantic representation not taken up by the speech, and that listeners may use gesture to fill in empty feature slots in a semantic frame; and (c) our experience with objects in the world provides action frames that may be used to inform the semantic frames needed for gesture interpretation.

11.3.1 Previous Solutions

Implementations of Gesture in Multi-modal Systems

As I said above, vision systems have tended to concentrate on gestures as a language, rather than gesture as a part of a multimodal communicative event. So-called multimodal systems have to some extent suffered from the same problem, concentrating on gestures as replacements for words in the stream of meaning. Nonetheless, some of these systems have been quite successful in combining speech and gesture at the computer interface. One of the first such systems was *Put-That-There*, developed by Richard Bolt, Christopher Schmandt, and their colleagues (Bolt, 1987; Bolt, 1980). *Put-That-There* used speech recognition and a six-degree-of-freedom space sensing device to gather input from a user's speech and the location of a cursor on a wall-sized display, allowing for simple deictic reference to visible entities. Recently, several systems have built on this attempt. Koons et al. (1993) uses a two-dimensional map allowing spoken commands, deictic hand gestures, and deictic eye movement analysis (indicating where the user is looking on the display). In this system, nested frames are employed to gather and combine information from the different modalities. As in *Put-that-There*, speech drives the analysis of the gesture: if information is *missing* from speech (e.g., "delete that one"), then the system will search for the missing information in the gestures and/or gaze. Time stamps unite the actions in the different modalities into a coherent picture. Wahlster (1991) uses a similar method, also depending on the linguistic input to guide the interpretation of the other modalities. Bolt & Herranz (1992) describe a system that allows a user to manipulate graphics with semi-iconic gestures. Bers (1996) presents a system that allows the user to combine speech and pantomimic gesture to direct a bee on how to move its wings – the gestures are mapped onto the bee's body, making it move as prescribed by the user's pantomimic example. The gesture segmentation scheme for his system utilizes the kinetic energy of body part motion. Using a cutoff point and time stamping, motions can be selected that relate to the intended movement mentioned in speech. Sparrell (1993) uses a scheme based on stop-motion analysis: whenever there is a significant stop or slowdown in the motion of the user's hand, then the preceding motion segment is grouped and analyzed for features such as finger posture and hand position. In all of these systems interpretation is not carried out until the user has finished the utterance.

Missing from these systems is a concept of non-verbal function with respect to discourse function. That is, in the systems reviewed thus far, there is no discourse structure over the sentence (no notion of "speaking turn" or "new information"). Therefore, the role of gesture and facial expression cannot be analyzed at more than a sentence-constituent-replacement level. What is needed is a discourse structure that can take into account turn-taking and the increasing accumulation of information over the course of a discourse. In the following sections I describe a discourse framework for the generation of multimodal behaviors, and then how such a framework is being used to integrate and interpret multimodal behaviors incrementally (that is, before the user has finished the utterance).

11.4 The Current Solution

11.4.1 A Discourse Framework for Gesture

What I am suggesting is that gesture fits into the entire context of communicative activities in particular rule-governed ways, and that understanding the interaction of those communicative modalities will help us build systems that can interpret and generate gesture. In particular, understanding the parallel and intersecting roles of information structure, intonation (the prosody or "melody" of language), and gesture will give us a discourse framework for predicting where gestures will be found in the stream of speech.

Information Structure

The information structure of an utterance defines its relation to other utterances in a discourse and to propositions in the relevant knowledge pool. Although a sentence like "George withdrew fifty dollars" has a clear semantic interpretation, which we might symbolically represent as *withdrew'(george', fifty-dollars')*, such a simplistic representation does not indicate how the proposition relates to other propositions in the discourse. For example, the sentence might be an equally appropriate response to the questions "Who withdrew fifty dollars?" "What did George withdraw?" "What did George do?" or even "What happened?" Determining which items in the response are most important or salient clearly depends on which question is asked. These types of salience distinctions are encoded in the information structure representation of an utterance.

Following Halliday and others (Halliday 1967; Hajicova, 1987), we use the terms *theme* and *rheme* to denote two distinct information structural attributes of an utterance. The theme/rheme distinction is often referred to in the literature by the terms *topic/comment* or *given/new*. The theme roughly corresponds to what the utterance is about, as derived from the discourse model. The rheme corresponds to what is new or interesting about the theme of the utterance. Depending on the discourse context, a given utterance may be divided on semantic and pragmatic grounds into thematic and rhematic constituents in a variety of ways. That is, depending on what question was asked, the contribution of the current answer will be different. The following examples illustrate the coupling of intonational "tunes" with themes and rhemes.†

    Q: Who withdrew fifty dollars?

† Boldface type indicates pitch accents (stressed words).

A: (**George**)$_{RHEME}$ (withdrew fifty dollars)$_{THEME}$

Q: What did George withdraw?

A: (George withdrew)$_{THEME}$ (**fifty dollars**)$_{RHEME}$

If you speak these examples aloud to yourself, you will notice that even though the answers to the two questions are identical in terms of the words they contain, they are uttered quite differently: in the first the word "George" is stressed, and in the second it is the phrase "fifty dollars" which is stressed. This is because in the two sentences different elements are marked as rhematic or difficult for the listener to predict. For the project at hand, an understanding of the relationship between information structure and intonation is crucial because information structure may predict in which utterances gestures occur, and intonation predicts the timing of gestures with respect to the utterance in which they occur.

It has been suggested that "intonation belongs more with gesture than with grammar" (Bolinger, 1983). Not only do intonation and hand and face gestures function in similar ways, they also stand in similar relationships to the semantic and information structures underlying spoken language. That is, we believe that the distribution of gestural units in the stream of speech is similar to the distribution of intonational units in three ways.

- First, gestural domains are isomorphic with intonational domains. The speaker's hands rise into space with the beginning of the intonational rise at the beginning of an utterance, and the hands fall at the end of the utterance along with the final intonational marking.

- Secondly, the most effortful part of the gesture (the *stroke*) co-occurs with the pitch accent, or most effortful part of enunciation.

- Third, we hypothesize that one is most likely to find gestures co-occuring with the rhematic part of speech, just as we find particular intonational tunes co-occuring with the rhematic part of speech. We hypothesize this because the rheme is that part of speech that contributes most to the ongoing discourse, and that is least known to the listener beforehand. It makes sense that gestures, which convey additional content to speech, would be found where the most explanation is needed in the discourse. This does not mean that one never finds gestures with the theme, however.

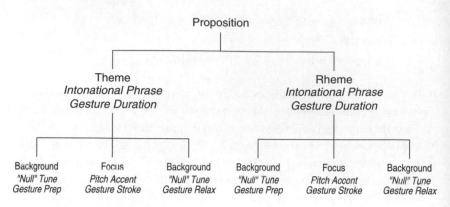

Fig. 11.2. Discourse Framework

The Role of the Discourse Framework in Generation

Let's turn to how this framework might allow us to automatically generate gestures along with speech and intonation. In the system "Animated
Conversation" (Cassell *et al*, 1994), we automatically generated speech
content, intonation, and hand gestures (and facial expression, which I
won't address further here) on the basis of the information given above.
In particular, gestures were generated along with words or phrases that
the discourse model had marked as rhematic. The domain we addressed
was banking; that is, the conversation generated was between a bank
teller and a customer desiring to withdraw money. As far as *which kind*
of gesture was generated in a given context, we relied on the taxonomy
of gesture discussed above, and implemented it in the following way:

- Concepts that referred to entities with a physical existence in the
  world were accorded iconics (concepts such as "checkbook," "write,"
  etc.).
- Concepts with common metaphoric vehicles received metaphorics (concepts such as "withdraw [money]," "bank account," "needing help").
- Concepts referring to places in space received deictics ("here," "there").
- Beat gestures were generated for items where the semantic content
  cannot be represented but the items were still unknown, or *new*, to
  the hearer (the concept of "at least").

The timing of gestures was also implemented according to the psycholinguistic findings described above. Information about the duration
of intonational phrases acquired in speech generation was then used to

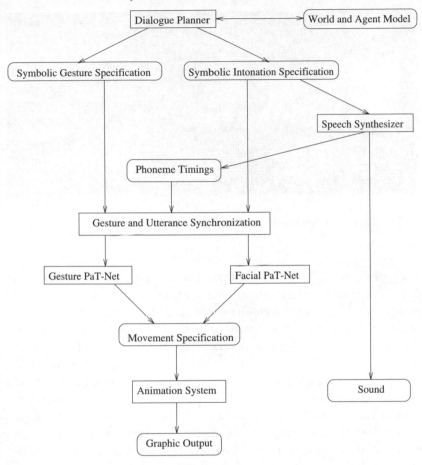

Fig. 11.3. Animated Conversation System Architecture

time gestures. If there was a non-beat gesture in an utterance, its preparation was set to begin at or before the beginning of the intonational phrase, and to finish at or before the first beat gesture in the intonational phrase or the nuclear stress of the phrase, whichever came first. The stroke phase was set to coincide with the nuclear stress of the phrase. Finally, the relaxation was set to begin no sooner than the end of the stroke or the end of the last beat in the intonational phrase, with the end of relaxation to occur around the end of the intonational phrase. Beats, in contrast, were simply timed to coincide with the stressed syllable of the word that realizes the associated concept.

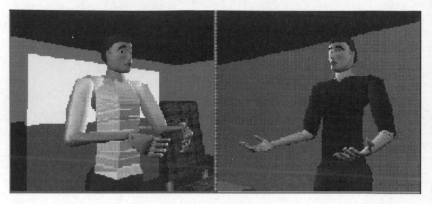

Fig. 11.4. (a) "Do you have a blank check?"; (b) "Can you help me?"

All of the modalities were generated on an equal footing. That is, we based our system on the claims that gesture and speech are generated by humans at the same computational stage (McNeill, 1992), and that gesture is not a *translation* of speech, but its equal partner in communication. Thus, the dialogue generation engine at the top of the system, shown in Fig. 11.3, was enriched with explicit representations of the structure of the discourse and the relationship of the structure to the agents' domain plans. These added representations, which describe the entities that are of discourse concern and the purposes for which agents undertake communicative actions, figure crucially in the determination of the appropriate gesture and intonation to accompany agents' utterances.

This heuristic for generating verbal and nonverbal behaviors was successful to a certain extent. Gestures looked natural and occurred in natural looking places. They appeared timed correctly with respect to intonation. Fig. 11.4 and Fig. 11.5 reproduce excerpts from the conversation generated by the "Animated Conversation" system.

Fig. 11.4(a) shows the automatic generation of an iconic gesture representing a check or checkbook, along with the phrase, "Do you have a blank check?"; (b) shows the generation of a metaphoric gesture representing supplication, along with the phrase, "Can you help me?"

Fig. 11.5(a) shows the automatic generation of an iconic gesture indicating writing on something, along with the phrase, "You can write the check"; (b) shows the the generation of a beat gesture, along with the phrase, "Yes, I have eighty dollars in my account."

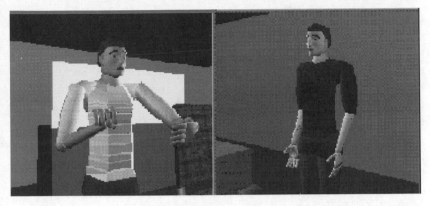

Fig. 11.5. (a) "You can write the check"; (b) "I have eighty dollars"

However, although the distribution of gestures in the discourse and the choice of type of gestures were generated automatically, we relied on a provisional and unsatisfactory method for generating the form of particular gestures. A gesture "dictionary" was accessed, which provided particular gesture forms for the domain of the dialogue.

11.4.2 A Semantic Framework for Gesture

The next step, then, is to further deconstruct gestures so as to understand how particular forms of gesture are generated in particular instances. Once again, I start by attempting to generate gesture, but keep in mind the goal of a framework that will also allow interpretation of naturally occurring gesture. This goal will be partially addressed by the system described in the last section of the chapter.

We start from the premise that we don't have access to a speaker's communicative intentions, and we don't always have access to the scene or events being described by a speaker, but we do have access to language – to the common linguistic code that we share with our interlocutors. An essential part of the knowledge of language is the knowledge of lexical semantics.

Lexical Semantics

The lexicon is our mental vocabulary, the words that we know, in all of their forms (I write, you write, she writes), along with their meanings. When we speak, we choose words from the lexicon, make them fit the other words around them, and then utter them. Semantics is the study of, or a theory of, how the meanings of words are related to one another and to our thinking processes, and how particular words are chosen. The concept that underlies the verb "go" includes the concepts that underlie the verbs "walk," "run," "drive," etc. because those are different manners of going somewhere. Here we are particularly interested in the issue of *lexical choice*, or how one word is chosen over another. Why do we say, "I *hightailed* it out of the room," rather than, "I *left* the room"? Why do we choose to say, "Sandy walked to the conference," one day, and another day, "Sandy went to the conference on foot"? In the first sentence the manner of locomotion is conveyed in the verb, and in the second sentence the manner of locomotion is conveyed in the prepositional phrase.

A Lexical Semantics that Includes Gesture

What does any of this have to do with gesture? Well, we have rejected the idea of a dictionary of gestures that speakers draw from to produce gestures and that listeners draw from for gesture interpretation, because of evidence about the absence of a one-to-one mapping between form and meaning in everyday gesture. We know, however, that gestures do sustain a tight link with the semantics of speech. I described above the evidence on the non-overlapping and yet complementary nature of the information conveyed in speech and gesture. Here I hypothesize that, for material that has been chosen to be conveyed, the concepts are represented mentally in terms of a complex of semantic features, and some of those features are conveyed in speech, and some are conveyed in gesture.

We are currently implementing this model by building a dialogue generation system that annotates for theme and rheme (Prevost, 1996) and takes semantic features into account when distributing information across speech and gesture. This resolves some of the problems seen in "Animated Conversation."

Thus, in some cases one would hear, "Hannes walked to the store," while in other cases one would hear, "Hannes went to the store" and see a gesture indicating the manner of locomotion, as illustrated in Fig. 11.6.

The examples given thus far account for the choice of gestures that accompany verbs of motion, primarily. These gestures mostly represent the viewpoint of an observer on the action. That is, the speaker's hand as a whole represents a characters feet or body (such as in Fig. 11.6). Many gestures, however, are more pantomimic and involve the representation of an action, where the speaker's hands represent someone else's

Fig. 11.6 Distribution of Semantic Features in Speech and Gesture: "Hannes went to the store."

hands. For example, a speaker might say, "and then I saw him pound in the nail" and with her hands represent somebody holding a hammer and hammering. In this case, although the sentence refers to the speaker herself ("I") as well as some third person, the gesture represents action on the part of the third person. Gestures such as these involve representation and knowledge of action. In order for such gestures to be accounted for in a theory of lexical choice, the semantics must be of a form that allows knowledge of the world.

11.4.3 The Link between Gesture and Action

If the form of gestures is partially determined by semantic features, how are those semantic features represented mentally such that they can be instantiated in gesture? I believe that some of the semantic features that are represented in iconic gestures are acquired through action schemata. In order to illustrate this process, let's look at the development of gestural semantic features from a series of actions.

The Acquisition of Gestural Features in Real-Time

Imagine the following scenario. Lucinda is watching "This Old House," a television show about do-it-yourself home renovation.† During the introductory credits we see the hero of the show repairing windows in a beautiful old home. During the show, the narrator, talking about weatherproofing a Victorian home, is describing the caulking gun. The

---

† This example – as with the earlier examples from Lucinda's life – is fictive, but constructed on the basis of an intimate and long-term association with how-to gestures, instructions concerning old home renovation, and caulk guns.

narrator picks up a caulking gun from the table in front of him and introduces its use:

"This is a caulking gun, which one fills with tubes of caulk, and which is used to fill and waterproof exposed wood."

As the narrator speaks, he lifts the handle to show where the caulk tube is inserted, and lowers the handle to show how to extrude the caulk. He also points to a tube of caulk on the workbench. He then replaces the tool on the workbench and continues his discussion of exposed wood by explaining how to waterproof window ledges. In this second part of the discussion, the narrator describes how to use the caulking gun. The narrator starts, however, by framing the relevance of his talk:

"In this [next part]$_A$ I'm going to tell you how to use a caulking gun to [prevent leakage]$_B$ through [storm windows]$_C$ and [wooden window ledges]$_D$ (...) Press the [handle of the caulking gun slowly as you move the nozzle across the window ledge that needs caulk]$_E$."

The narrator makes the following gestures during this segment of talk:

A. The narrator opens his hands, with the palms facing one another and the fingers facing away from his body, and then moves his wrists so that his fingers are facing down – as if he is delineating a box.

B, C, D. The narrator's right hand is lax, but he flips it over and back so that the palm is facing first upward and then downward.

E. The narrator forms his left hand into a fist to represent the body of the caulking gun, holding it diagonally in front of his body, and uses his right hand to represent the hand of the user, pumping an imaginary handle up and down.

Lucinda goes to Home Depot to pick up materials to repair her leaking windows. She says to the salesperson "where do I find that . . . [gesture 'E'] to fill the cracks in my window ledges?"

Lucinda has learned the concept of 'caulking gun' from a linguistic-action-gestural performance.† Two things should be noted about the performance that Lucinda observes:

- The description of the concept of caulking proceeds by first *demonstrating* caulking on an actual house (during the introductory credits), next *defining* caulking through a generic description of a caulking gun, and finally *describing* how to caulk. The passage is, therefore, from a particular present event of caulking the narrator's house, to a generic

† The following terminological distinction is useful here: I will refer to speech as linguistic, manipulations of objects as action, and hand movements that do not interact with objects in the real world as gestures.

event of caulking, to another particular future event of caulking the listener's house.

- While the narrator first defines the caulking gun in speech, he adds non-redundant features to that definition with his actions. Only in his actions does he show the relationship between the caulking gun and the tube of caulk (e.g., that the tube is fit into the cradle of the caulking gun), and the manner of using the caulking gun (e.g., that pushing down the handle extrudes the caulk). Likewise, in the second part of the narrator's description, when he describes how to caulk, the speech and gesture are non-redundant: only in gesture is the manner of movement demonstrated. By this second part of the performance, the hands have become a *symbol* of the object spoken of – an iconic representation of the tool and the home owner's interaction with it.[†] Note that not just representational gestures are used here; three other qualitatively different gestures are also a part of this communicative act. These four gesture types enable the construction of a sensorimotor schema for adults – a semantic frame or schema that encompasses the knowledge types that allow the listener to understand the talk about home repair, and will allow the listener to caulk her own house later on.

In the time of one communicative event, the context of talk has gone from being the world itself – as populated by do-it-yourself-show hosts, caulking guns, and tubes of caulk – to being a representation of the world. This representation by the speaker is what allows the listener to construct a representation of the activity herself, including new lexical items, images of tools and activities, and motor knowledge (knowledge of how-to). Thus, the background against which talk is being interpreted by the listener has gone from being the Victorian home in the country, to the studio of "This Old House," to an imaginary event of home renovation. Although the *focal event* (Goodwin & Duranti, 1992) has remained the same – the use of a caulking gun – the *background* has changed several times.

The relevance of such an action schema approach to gestural meaning for our concerns here is twofold. First, as far as gesture generation is concerned, we might envisage the generation of task-oriented dialogues that share semantic features between the simulation of physical actions

---

† The interpretation of passage from action to symbol (as well as the idea of looking for examples of this movement in home improvement TV shows) is from Streeck, 1995.

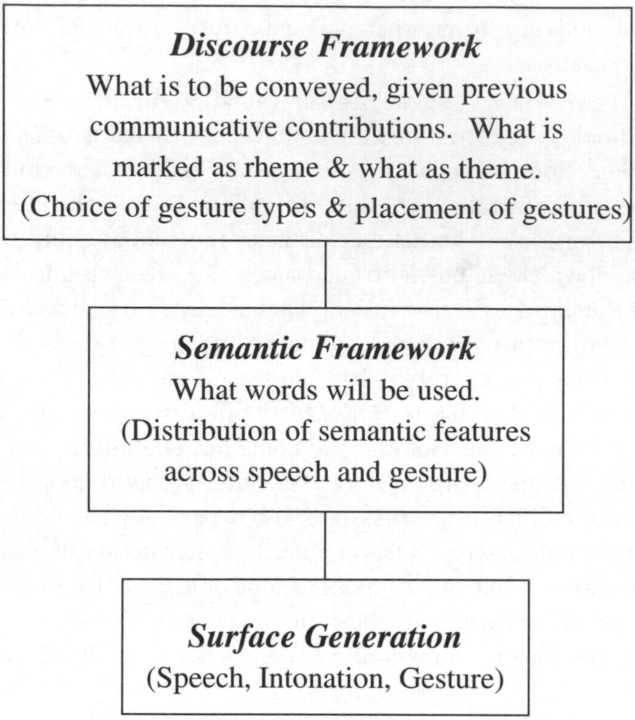

Discourse Framework
What is to be conveyed, given previous communicative contributions. What is marked as rheme & what as theme.
(Choice of gesture types & placement of gestures)

Semantic Framework
What words will be used.
(Distribution of semantic features across speech and gesture)

Surface Generation
(Speech, Intonation, Gesture)

Fig. 11.7. Model of Multimodal Generation

and the instruction talk (and gestures) that accompanies the actions. The animated agents that we create may be able to follow instructions (Webber, 1994; Webber *et al*, 1995) and also use their knowledge of the world and objects around them to give instructions. Secondly, as far as interpretation is concerned, we can envisage a discourse understanding system that learns semantic information from task-oriented talk and physical actions, and then goes on to apply that knowledge to the understanding of gestures in talk about the same domain.

So far, then, we have a discourse framework and a semantic framework, as in Fig. 11.7.

11.5 Applying the Solution to Interpretation

The framework above provides a general theory of the relationship between verbal and nonverbal behavior, but our implementations up until this point have been in the form of dialogue generation systems. In what follows, I turn to the issue of *interpreting* multimodal behavior of the spontaneous unplanned sort that we have described.

I use the word "interpretation" rather than "recognition" or "perception" because we will beg the issue of vision by using input gathered through data gloves, a body tracker, a gaze tracker, and a microphone for speech.

Supposing a perceptual system, we still need an interpretation layer that can integrate information from gaze, hand gesture, intonation, and speech. Ymir is a testbed system especially designed for prototyping multimodal agents that understand human communicative behavior and generate integrated spontaneous verbal and nonverbal behavior of their own (Thórisson, 1995, 1996). Ymir is constructed as a layered system. It provides a foundation for accommodating any number of interpretive processes, running in parallel, working in concert to interpret and respond to the user's behavior. Ymir thus offers opportunities to experiment with various computational schemes for handling specific subtasks of multimodal interaction, such as natural language parsing, natural language generation, and selection of multimodal acts.

Ymir's strength is the ability to accommodate two types of behavior. On the one hand, some communicative behavior controls the *envelope of communication*. For example, gaze is an indicator to the participants of a conversation for deciding who should speak when; when the current speaker looks at the listener and pauses, this serves as a signal that the speaker is giving up the turn (Duncan, 1972). On the other hand, some communicative behavior controls the *content of communication*. For example, the content of speech and the content of iconic gestures determine the direction that the conversation is taking. Ymir has layers dedicated to *reactive* behaviors, such as gaze and other turn-taking signals, and *reflective* behaviors, such as speech and contentful gestures. Reactive behaviors require fast "automatic" reactions to maintain the conversation (when the other interlocutor stops speaking and looks at me, I should begin to speak). This reactive layer in Ymir is differentiated from the reflective layer, which attends to speech input, the content of gestures, and other types of information that will need to be understood and responded to.

Gandalf (Thórisson, op cit.) is the first agent constructed in this architecture. It has been provided with the minimal behaviors necessary for face-to-face dialogue. It can understand limited utterances (currently using a grammar-based speech recognizer), intonation, body stance (oriented towards Gandalf or towards the task at hand), and the function

Fig. 11.8 Gandalf understands and responds to speech, gaze & hand gestures

of some hand gestures. It understands the social conventions of gaze and head/face direction and integrates them to provide the correct feedback behaviors at the correct time. The prototype primarily serves to demonstrate Ymir's treatment of the timing of multimodal acts, and to illustrate Ymir's ability to accept and integrate data from independent modules that work on partial input data, and to integrate data at multiple levels. We are currently adding the ability to understand and generate additional behaviors.

The Ymir system, as noted above, relies on gestural input gathered by way of cybergloves and a body tracker. We chose the hardware route because of the difficulty of using vision systems to recognize the handshape and, consequently, the meaning of gestures (due to occlusion, etc.). But not all discourse tasks require a recognition of gesture handshape. A *classification* of gestures into iconics, deictics, and beats would also be helpful as a way of bootstrapping the understanding of the concurrent speech. In addition, if one could distinguish iconics from beats, then one could concentrate the vision resources of a system on recognizing the form of iconics, and simply acknowledge the presence of beats. To this end, I am currently exploring a more *perception-based* approach to the classification of gesture, in terms of temporal phase. I believe that gestures classified by temporal phase will turn out to correlate significantly with gestures classified by function, thus facilitating the use of computer vision to extract meaning from gesture. A preliminary attempt to implement this theory in a vision system has met with encouraging although limited results (Wilson, Bobick & Cassell, 1996).

11.6 Conclusions

In this chapter, I described the characteristics of natural spontaneous human gestures and contrasted the types of gestures that have served as the focus for many human-computer interface systems with the types of gestures that are found in human-human communication. Although there are good reasons for focusing on the former type of gesture – they are the types of gestures more accessible to reflection, and easier to treat as linguistic units – I argued that it is time to address in our human-computer interfaces the whole range of gesture types. To this end, I presented a framework that allows for the understanding of gesture in the context of speech. I then described several implementations of this framework. The more advanced system deals with the generation of multimodal communicative behaviors, but a new system provides a context for the interpretation of gestures in the context of speech. Although the systems presented are by no means complete, they encourage us to push forward in the use of natural spontaneous gesture and speech in our communication with computers.

12

Model-Based Interpretation of Faces and Hand Gestures

C.J. Taylor, A. Lanitis, T.F. Cootes, G. Edwards and T. Ahmad

Abstract

Face and hand gestures are an important means of communication between humans. Similarly, automatic face and gesture recognition systems could be used for contact-less human-machine interaction. Developing such systems is difficult, however, because faces and hands are both complex and highly variable structures. We describe how flexible models can be used to represent the varying appearance of faces and hands and how these models can be used for tracking and interpretation. Experimental results are presented for face pose recovery, face identification, expression recognition, gender recognition and gesture interpretation.

12.1 Introduction

This chapter addresses the problem of locating and interpreting faces and hand gestures in images. By interpreting face images we mean recovering the 3D pose, identifying the individual and recognizing the expression and gender; for the hand images we mean recognizing the configuration of the fingers. In both cases different instances of the same class are not identical; for example, face images belonging to the same individual will vary because of changes in expression, lighting conditions, 3D pose and so on. Similarly hand images displaying the same gesture will vary in form.

We have approached these problems by modeling the ways in which the appearance of faces and hands can vary, using parametrised deformable models which take into account all the main sources of variability. A robust image search method [90, 89] is used to fit the models

217

to new face/hand images recovering compact parametric descriptions. Given this compact coding, standard statistical pattern recognition techniques can be used to perform the task of interpretation.

For our face interpretation experiments we have used a database containing 690 face images from 30 individuals. We have described the contents of the database elsewhere [189]. The database is publicly available on the Word Wide Web at:

http://peipa.essex.ac.uk/ftp/ipa/pix/faces/manchester

In the remainder of the chapter we review some of the most relevant literature on face coding and interpretation, describe our approach in more detail, and present results for coding and reconstruction, pose recovery, person identification, gender recognition, and expression recognition. We also describe how our approach can be applied to the problem of gesture recognition and present preliminary results for this problem.

12.2 Background

In this section we briefly review previous work on face image interpretation and coding. Comprehensive reviews for these topics can be found elsewhere [31, 71, 266, 297].

12.2.1 Locating Facial Features

Methods based on deformable templates have proved useful for locating facial features. Kass et al [169] describe the use of active contour models – snakes – for tracking lips in image sequences. They initialize a snake on the lips in a face image and show that it is able to track lip movements accurately. Because snakes do not incorporate prior knowledge about expected shapes, this approach is, however, easily confused both by other structures present in the image and occlusion. Yuille et al [328] describe the use of deformable templates, based on simple geometrical shapes, for locating eyes and mouths. These templates are similar to snakes, in that they can deform and move. Yuille's models incorporate shape constraints but it is difficult to ensure that the form of a given model is sufficiently general or that an appropriate degree of variability has been allowed.

Human faces are characterized by constrained geometrical relationships between the positions of facial features. Some systems exploit these constraints to locate groups of features [62, 95]. For example, once one feature has been located, the positions of other features can be predicted and their search areas reduced significantly.

12.2.2 Coding and Reconstruction

Kirby and Sirovich [178] propose the decomposition of face images into a weighted sum of basis images (or eigenfaces) using a Karhumen–Loeve expansion. They code a face image using 50 expansion coefficients and subsequently reconstruct an approximation using these parameters.

Model-based coding and reconstruction has also received a considerable attention in the literature. Models based on the physical and anatomical structure of faces [285] and 3D models [197] have been used to account for the variability in appearance due to changes in pose and expression.

12.2.3 Identification

Face image identification techniques can be divided into two main categories: those employing geometrical features and those using grey-level information.

Techniques based on geometrical features use a number of dimensional measurements [62], or the locations of a number of key points [94, 132, 322] in single images or in image sequences, for face image interpretation.

Techniques based on grey-level information show more promise. Turk and Pentland [291] describe face identification using an eigenface expansion. The eigenface weights are used for classification. Many researchers have built on this approach [92, 94], which is perhaps the most successful to date. Other approaches based on grey-level information, include template matching [62] and filtering with multi-scale Gabor filters [188].

12.3 Overview of our Approach

Our approach can be divided into two main phases: modeling, in which flexible models of facial appearance are generated, and interpretation, in which the models are used for coding and interpreting face images.

12.3.1 Modeling

We model the shapes of facial features and their spatial relationships using a single 2D flexible shape model (a Point Distribution Model) [90].

The model is generated by a statistical analysis of the positions of land-mark points over a set of training face shapes. The model describes the mean shape and a set of linearly independent *modes* of shape variation. Any face shape can be represented using a weighted sum of the mean and modes of variation, controlled by a small number of model parameters.

We have augmented our shape model with flexible grey-level models (of similar form to the shape model) using two complementary approaches. In the first we generate a flexible grey-level model of "shape-free" appearance by deforming each face in the training set to have the same shape as the mean face. In the second approach we use a large number of local profile models, one at each landmark point of the shape model. The first approach is more complete but the second is more robust to partial occlusion.

Shape and grey-level models are used together to describe the overall appearance of each face; collectively we refer to the model parameters as appearance parameters. It is important to note that the coding we achieve is reversible – a given face image can be reconstructed from its appearance parameters.

12.3.2 Interpretation

When a new image is presented to our system, facial features are located automatically using Active Shape Model (ASM) search [90, 89] based on the flexible shape model obtained during training. This results in automatically located model points which are transformed into shape model parameters. Grey-level information at each model point is collected and transformed to local grey-level model parameters. Then the face is deformed to the mean face shape and the grey-level appearance is transformed into the parameters of the shape-free grey-level model. The resulting set of appearance parameters can be used for image reconstruction, person identification (including gender recognition), expression recognition and pose recovery.

12.4 Modeling Faces

We have described elsewhere [189, 191] the generation of flexible models of facial appearance. In this section we provide a brief introduction.

12.4.1 Flexible Models

A flexible model [90] can be generated from a set of training examples, each represented by N variables. The average example ($\hat{\mathbf{X}}$) is calculated and the deviation of each example from the mean is computed. A principal component analysis of the covariance matrix of deviations reveals the main modes of variation. Any training example $\mathbf{X}_i$ can be approximated using:

$$\mathbf{X}_i = \hat{\mathbf{X}} + \mathbf{Pb}$$

where $\mathbf{P}$ is a matrix of unit eigenvectors of the covariance of deviations and $\mathbf{b}$ is a vector of eigenvector weights (these are referred to as model parameters). By modifying $\mathbf{b}$, new instances of the model can be generated. Since the columns of $\mathbf{P}$ are orthogonal, $\mathbf{P}^T\mathbf{P} = \mathbf{I}$, and we can be solve with respect to $\mathbf{b}$:

$$\mathbf{b} = \mathbf{P}^T(\mathbf{X}_i - \hat{\mathbf{X}})$$

Thus, training examples can be transformed to model parameters. Usually, the number of eigenvectors needed to describe the variability within a training set is much smaller than the original number of parameters, so that training examples can be approximated with a small number of model parameters $b_1 \ldots b_t : t < N$. The same method can be used to train both shape and grey-level models. For shape models the variables are point coordinates and for grey-level models the variables are based on grey-level intensities.

12.4.2 Modeling Shape

We have built a flexible shape model (or Point Distribution Model) [90] representing a line drawing of the face using 152 points (see Fig. 12.1) on each of 160 training examples. The model can approximate the shape of any face in the training set using just 16 modes of variation/parameters; the effect of varying some of the model parameters is shown in Fig. 12.2.

12.4.3 Modeling Shape-Free Appearance

We wish to model grey-level appearance independently of shape. To do this we have applied a warping algorithm [50] to deform all training images to the mean shape, in such a way that changes in grey-level intensities are kept to a minimum. Training images were deformed to the

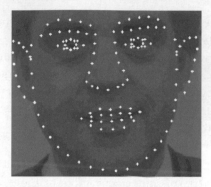

Fig. 12.1. Shape model points

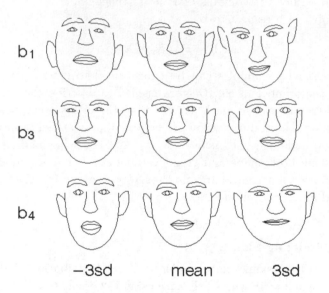

b_1

b_3

b_4

−3sd   mean   3sd

Fig. 12.2. The main modes of shape variation

mean shape and grey-level intensities within the face area were extracted. Each training example was represented by a vector containing the normalized grey-level at each pixel in the patch. A flexible grey-level model was generated for our database; only 79 modes of variation/parameters were needed to explain 95% of the variation. Each parameter is responsible for a specific mode of variation, as shown in Figure 12.3.

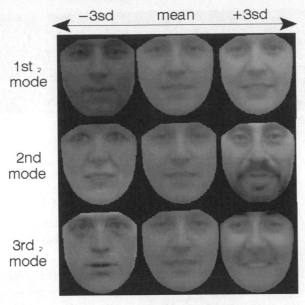

Fig. 12.3. The main modes of grey-level variation

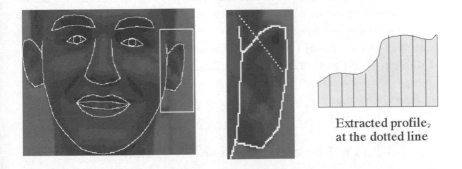

Extracted profile
at the dotted line

Fig. 12.4. Extraction of a grey profile at a model point

12.4.4 Modeling Local Appearance

To model local grey-level variations we overlaid shape model points on the corresponding training images and extracted grey-level profiles perpendicular to the boundary, as shown in Figure 12.4. A flexible grey-level model was built for the profile at each model point; most of these models needed four modes of variation/parameters to explain 95% of the variation.

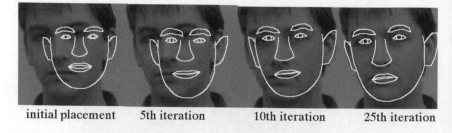

initial placement   5th iteration   10th iteration   25th iteration

Fig. 12.5. Fitting the shape model

12.5 Locating Facial Features

The shape model and local grey-level models described above can be used to locate all the modeled features simultaneously [90, 89]. The mean shape model is placed in the image and is allowed to interact dynamically until it fits to the image evidence. Each iteration involves two main steps: calculating a new suggested position for each model point, based on matching the local grey-level models, followed by moving and deforming the model in order to place each point as close as possible to its new preferred position. During this process the shape model is only allowed to deform in ways which are consistent with the training set. The robustness, speed and accuracy of this basic algorithm can be improved using a multi-resolution approach [89]. The fitting procedure is illustrated in Fgure 12.5 and described in detail in [90, 89]. We have shown [89] that model points in new face images can be located with an average accuracy of about 3 pixels, using this method.

12.6 Recovering Appearance Parameters

New face images can be coded in terms of model parameters. This procedure is summarized in Figure 12.6. The shape model is fitted automatically to the new face and the shape model parameters corresponding to the extracted shape are computed. At each located shape model point, grey-level information from a profile perpendicular to the boundary is extracted and the model parameters of the local grey-level model are calculated. The warping algorithm is applied to produce a shape-free face and the shape-free grey-level model parameters are calculated. Together the three sets of model parameters constitute a full set of appearance parameters; in the following sections we describe how we use these parameters to reconstruct and interpret face images.

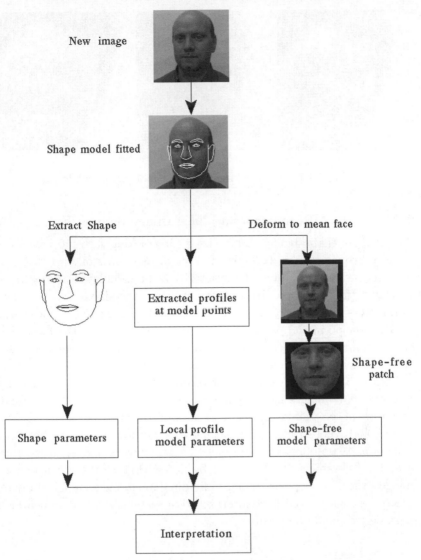

Fig. 12.6. Calculating the appearance parameters

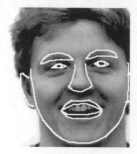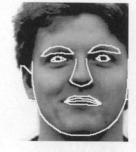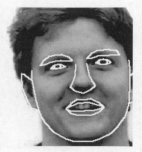

Fig. 12.7. Face tracking using a flexible shape model

12.7 Reconstructing Face Image Sequences

The flexible shape model can be used for tracking face movements in a video sequence. An example of tracking is shown in Fig. 12.7. At each frame the appearance parameters can be calculated and used for reconstructing the face. To reconstruct a face the shape-free grey-level parameters are used to generate the shape-free grey-level appearance, and the shape model parameters to define the shape of the face. The warping algorithm [50] is applied to deform from the average face shape to the shape corresponding to the shape parameters given.

Figure 12.8 shows examples of reconstructions from face image sequences. The images in these sequences are *new* images of individuals who were in the training set. The total number of parameters needed for coding and reconstructing faces using this method, is 99 (16 shape parameters, 4 two-dimensional orientation parameters and 79 shape-free-grey-level parameters). It should be noted that in the reconstructed images, the pose, expression and individual appearance are faithfully reproduced thus a face image interpretation system based on appearance parameters should be feasible.

12.8 Recovering Pose

Once the shape model has been fitted to a new face, the recovered shape model parameters can be used to determine the pose. As shown in Figure 12.2, the first (b1) and third (b3) shape model parameters are responsible for controlling the apparent changes in shape due to nodding and turning. Pose recovery can be based on the values of these parameters, calculated for a new face outline. To calibrate the system, we captured a series of face images in which an individual was asked to rotate his head

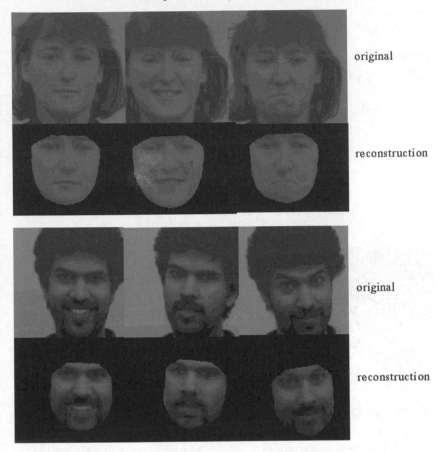

Fig. 12.8. Example of tracking and reconstruction of face image sequences

in both the vertical and horizontal direction, from -20 degrees to +20 degrees by looking at a number of grid points on a wall; each grid point corresponded to a known combination of horizontal and vertical rotation angles. We fitted the shape model to these images automatically and recorded the values of the first and third shape parameters. When a new face is presented the shape model is fitted, the resulting numerical values for b1 and b3 are recorded and the pose angles are calculated based on the calibration.

We tested the accuracy of pose recovery on 30 new test images obtained similarly to the calibration set. The results are summarized in

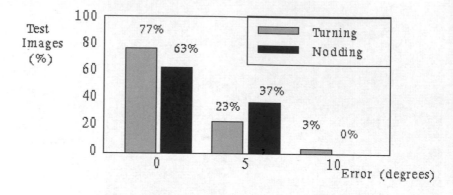

Fig. 12.9. Pose recovery results

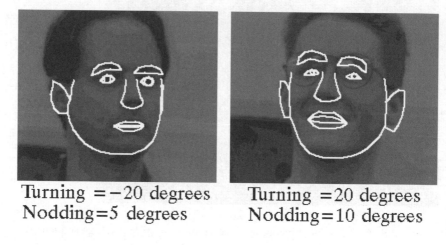

Turning = −20 degrees
Nodding = 5 degrees

Turning = 20 degrees
Nodding = 10 degrees

Fig. 12.10. Pose recovery example

Figure 12.9 and show robust recovery of pose angles. Fig. 12.10 shows examples of test images and the pose angles computed.

12.9 Identifying Individuals

We have developed a face identification system which uses appearance parameters. A classifier was trained by computing the appearance parameters for all training images (10 images for each of the 30 individuals) in our database and establishing the distribution of appearance parameters for each individual. Discriminant analysis techniques were applied

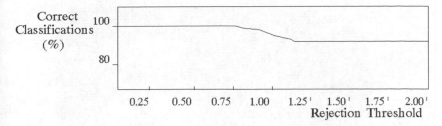

Correct Classifications (%)

Rejection Threshold

Fig. 12.11. The effect of changing the rejection threshold

in order to enhance the effect of the inter-class (between person) variation parameters using the Mahalanobis distance measure.

We performed person identification experiments on the test set of our face database which contains images with a wide range of expressions, poses and lighting conditions. When all three types of appearance parameters were used, 92% of the test images were classified correctly. (More detailed results of the classification experiments are given in [189]).

For access control applications it is important that person identification systems have the ability to reject faces which do not look similar to any of the database entries. We performed a preliminary experiment in which images were rejected if the minimum Mahalanobis distance was not within acceptable limits. The results of this experiment are shown in Fig. 12.11. When the threshold was set to 0.8 the correct classification rate was 100%. In this case, about 55% of the test images are rejected since they are not similar enough to any of the individuals in the training set, which is not surprising bearing in mind the appearance variations between training and test images in our database.

12.10 Gender Recognition

Gender recognition can also be implemented in our framework, since some appearance parameters reflect inter-gender differences. We trained the system using the appearance parameters of images from 16 male and 4 female subjects in our database, using a similar approach to the person identification experiments. A correct classification rate of 94% was obtained when we tested the system on 100 images of unseen individuals.

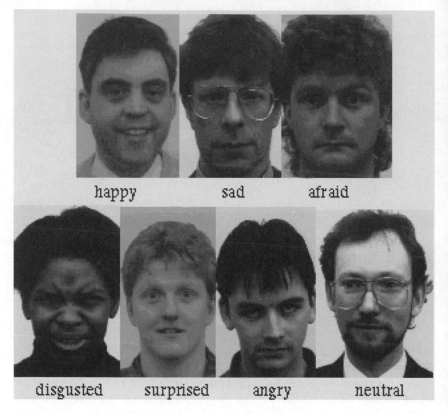

Fig. 12.12 Faces displaying the seven expressions we used in the expression recognition experiment

12.11 Expression Recognition

Expression recognition, particularly from static images, is a difficult problem. Even human observers often fail to agree in expression classification experiments. We have addressed the problem by establishing the distribution of appearance parameters over a selected training set for each expression category, so that the appearance parameters calculated for a new face image could be used for determining the expression.

We asked five observers to classify the expression of each of our training and test face images using the seven psychologically recognized categories [116] shown in Figure 12.12. For our experiments we used the images for which at least four of the observes agreed (139/300 training and 118/300 test images). A peak classification rate of 74% was obtained. We also asked two more observers to classify the expression of

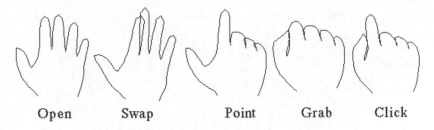

Open   Swap   Point   Grab   Click

Fig. 12.13. The gestures used in our experiments

the faces in each of the 118 test images on which we tested our classification system. They achieved 80% and 83% correct classification. The classification rate obtained from the automatic system compares well with these results.

12.12 Gesture Recognition

The framework we have described can also be used for gesture recognition [5, 145]. We trained a flexible shape model using hand shapes extracted from a sequence of moving hands, using 89 landmarks on each training shape; just nine shape parameters were needed to explain most of the variability in the training set. In the sequence the subject was asked to animate the five gestures shown in Fig. 12.13. These gestures were intended to be useful in mouse-less interaction with a windows-based operating system and represent actions such as point, point-and-click, grab, and swap.

The main modes of shape variation of the model are shown in Figure 12.14. Since shape information is sufficient for classifying gestures, we used just a shape model for classification, though local grey-level models were used for model fitting. Tracking was performed using model-based image search as described earlier for face images. The resulting shape parameters were used to determine the gesture in each frame using a Mahanabolis distance classifier. In practice, the constraints imposed by the multi-gesture shape model were relatively weak because, in order to span the full range of training examples, the linear sub-space of the model also included regions which corresponded to "illegal" examples of the hand shape. This lack of specificity (to legal hand configurations) led to lack of robustness in model-based tracking. We dealt with the problem by using five models for tracking, each trained using a large

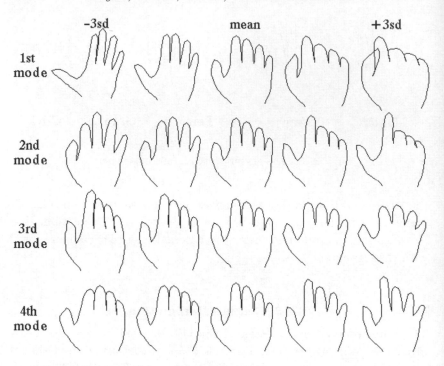

Fig. 12.14. The main modes of shape variation for the hand model

number of examples of one gesture and fewer examples of the other gestures. Each model was thus reasonably specific to the particular class of gesture but was able to model transitions to the other gestures. During tracking, each frame was classified using the multi-gesture model and the resulting gesture class was used to select the gesture-specific model to use for tracking the hand shape in the following frame. Fig. 12.15 shows results of hand tracking using this method.

The system was tested on a previously unseen hand image sequence containing 811 frames; 480 of these frames were rejected because they contained transitions between gestures. The rest of the frames were classified correctly.

12.13 Conclusions

We have presented an automatic face processing system which can be used for locating facial features, coding and reconstruction, recovering

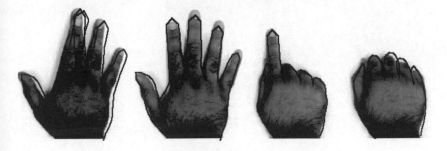

Fig. 12.15. Example of hand tracking

pose, recognizing expressions and identifying the individual in an image. We believe that our system is unusual in that it can cope successfully with almost all the aspects of face image processing, within a unified framework.

The face processing procedures described are fully automatic; errors in the classification experiments may be caused either by failure in locating landmarks accurately, or by failure of the classification algorithm. We do not distinguish between the two cases, since we believe that locating facial characteristics automatically is an important aspect of an integrated face processing system.

We have also described preliminary results for interpreting gestures, using a similar approach. Our results for most of the applications are promising, and demonstrate the potential of our approach in real life applications.

13

Recognition of Hand Signs from Complex Backgrounds

J.J. Weng and Y. Cui

Abstract

In this chapter, we present our approach to recognizing hand signs. It addresses three key aspects of the hand sign interpretation, the hand location, the hand shape, and the hand movement. The approach has two major components: (a) a prediction-and verification segmentation scheme to segment the moving hand from its background; (b) a recognizer that recognizes the hand sign from the temporal sequence of segmented hand together with its global motion information. The segmentation scheme can deal with a large number of different hand shapes against complex backgrounds. In the recognition part, we use multiclass, multi-dimensional discriminant analysis in every internal node of a recursive partition tree to automatically select the most discriminating linear features for gesture classification. The method has been tested to recognize 28 classes of hand signs. The experimental results show that the system can achieve a 93% recognition rate for test sequences that have not been used in the training phase.

13.1 Introduction

The ability to interpret the hand gestures is essential if computer systems can interact with human users in a natural way. In this chapter, we present a new vision-based framework which allows the computer to interact with users through hand signs.

Since its first known dictionary was printed in 1856 [61], American Sign Language (ASL) is widely used in the deaf community as well as by the handicapped people who are not deaf [49]. The general hand sign

235

interpretation needs a broad range of contextual information, general knowledge, cultural background, and linguistic capabilities.

Tremendous difficulties exist toward automatic hand-sign recognition in general settings. In order to concentrate on the focus of research with a manageable scope, we control the indoor environment so that the lighting is fixed and the human signer sits in front of the computer, facing the camera. In such an environment, the task of hand-sign recognition still involves a series of challenging tasks, including finding the location of the hand, segmenting hands from the complex backgrounds such as texture of various clothes, distinguishing various hand gestures, recognizing hand-signs which include location, shape, local motion, and global motion.

In our current research, we extract a set of hand gestures which have meaning in human communication. Twenty-eight different signs [52] used in our experiments are illustrated in Fig. 13.1. These hand signs have following characteristics: 1) they represent a wide variation of hand shapes; 2) they include a wide variation of motion patterns; 3) these hand signs are performed by one hand; 4) recognition of these signs does not depend on contextual information. The gestures which require the hand to perform in a certain environment or to point to a specific object are excluded.

In the linguistic description of ASL, Stokoe used a structural linguistic framework to analyze sign formation [279]. He defined three "aspects" that were combined simultaneously in the formation of a particular sign – what acts, where it acts, and the act. These three aspects translate into building blocks that linguists describe – the hand shape, the location, and the movement. There are two major components in our framework to deal with above three building blocks. We have a prediction-and-verification scheme to locate hands from complex backgrounds. The spatiotemporal recognition component combines motion understanding (movement) with spatial recognition (hand shape) in an unified framework.

13.2 Relation to Previous Work

Recently, there has been a significant amount research on vision-based hand gesture recognition (see [151] for a survey). The vision-based approaches acquire visual information of a gesture using a single video camera or a pair of cameras. Once the visual information is acquired, the sign is extracted by analyzing the temporal image sequence.

Fig. 13.1 The twenty eight different signs used in the experiment. (1) sign of "angry"; (2) "any"; (3) "boy"; (4) "yes"; (5) "cute"; (6) "fine"; (7) "funny"; (8) "girl"; (9) "happy"; (10) "hi"; (11) "high"; (12) "hot"; (13) "later"; (14) "low"; (15) "no"; (16) "nothing"; (17) "of course"; (18) "ok"; (19) "parent"; (20) "pepper"; (21) "smart"; (22) "sour"; (23) "strange"; (24) "sweet"; (25) "thank you"; (26) "thirsty"; (27) "welcome"; (28) "wrong" (Bornstein and Saulnier 1989).

The existing approaches typically include two parts: modeling hands and analysis of hand motion. Models of the human hand include the three dimensional model (e.g., Downton and Drouet [110] and Etoh *et al* [121]: generalized cylindrical model; Kuch and Huang [186]: NURBS-based hand model), the region-based model (e.g., Darrell and Pentland [102], Bobick and Wilson [44], and Cui *et. al.* [99]), the two-dimensional shape model (e.g., Starner and Pentland [278]: elliptic shape models; Cho and Dunn [74]: line segments shape model; Kervrann and Heitz [176] and Blake and Isard [40]: contour shape model), and the fingertip model (e.g., Cipolla *et al* [80] and Davis and Shah [104]).

Different models of hands lead to different models of hand motion. The system which uses the three dimensional hand model is capable of modeling the real hand kinematics (e.g., [186]). For the system which uses the two-dimensional hand model, the motion is described as two-dimensional rotation, translation and scaling in the image plane [176]. The trajectory of each fingertip is suitable to represent the motion in the case when the fingertip is used to model hands [104]. Typically, motion parameters are used to perform gesture classification.

The vision-based approach is one of the most unobtrusive ways to enable users to interact with computers in a natural fashion. However, it faces several difficult problems due to the limitations in machine vision today. Among them, the problem of segmenting moving hands from sometimes complex backgrounds is perhaps the most difficult one. Many current systems rely on markers or marked gloves (e.g. [80, 104, 278]). The others simply assume uniform backgrounds (e.g. [44, 99, 102]). Recently, Moghaddam and Pentland [221] proposed a maximum likelihood decision rule based on the estimated probability density of the hand and its 2D contour to detect hands from intensity images.

The human hand can change its shape tremendously in various hand signs. Furthermore, the signer can wear any clothes, which becomes a part of the background. Some of the backgrounds are shown in Figure 13.13. Therefore, segmentation and recognition must be tightly coupled — *without segmentation, reliable recognition is difficult; without recognition, reliable segmentation is difficult.* We address this fundamental problem using a prediction-and-verification scheme [96]. The prediction is based on partial views of the hand together with the learned relationship between each partial view and the global contour of the hand. The verification first extracts the actual observed hand from its background using the predicted global contour and then the extracted hand is verified based on the learned information about human hands.

Our segmentation scheme does not use any background pixels in the prediction and verification and therefore is applicable to very complex backgrounds.

Another major difference between our framework and most existing approaches is that in our framework, motion understanding is tightly coupled with spatial recognition. All the spatial and temporal information of the hand sign is treated in a unified way. We do not separate the hand modeling and the motion recognition into two different processes. The automatically computed, most discriminating features (MDF) will weight every spatial and temporal component in an optimal way. Thus, it can effectively deal with different cases, no matter which information is more important, hand shape or hand motion.

13.3 Overview of the Approach

A hand gesture is a *spatiotemporal event*. A spatiotemporal event involves an object of interest and the motion of the object. We treat hand sign recognition as a special case of spatiotemporal understanding. Our approach is called SHOSLIF (Self-Organizing Hierarchical Optimal Subspace Learning and Inference Framework) which as been applied to problems in several different application domains [312, 314]. We model the system at signal level and leave the complex knowledge-level learning task to the actual real-world training phase. As system designers, we minimize modeling knowledge level, but instead, emphasize modeling the system at signal level and designing efficient *ways* in which the system organizes itself. The tedious task of actual organizing the system is accomplished automatically by the system itself through interactive learning.

In this section, we give some general discussion on how to represent and recognize spatiotemporal events.

13.3.1 Time as a Dimension

A natural way to represent a spatiotemporal events is to consider input image sequence as data in space and time [91, 118] by associating the serial order of the pattern with the dimensionality of the pattern vector. The first temporal event is represented in the plane $t = 0$ and the second temporal event by plane $t = 1$, and so on. The entire spatiotemporal pattern vector is considered as a whole by the framework. Figure

13.2 shows an example in which the hand sign "no" is represented by a spatiotemporal sequence (three images).

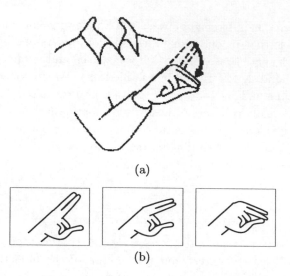

(a)

(b)

Fig. 13.2 The sign "no" and its image sequence representation: (a) the sign of "no", snap middle finger, index, and thumb together, (b) the sequence representation of the sign "no"

13.3.2 Recognition of Spatiotemporal Pattern

As shown in Figure 13.2, a spatiotemporal event includes two kinds of information: the object of interest and the movement of the object. The movement of the object can be further decomposed into two components: global and local motions. The global motion captures gross motion in terms of position. The local motion characterizes deformation, orientation, and gesture changes. In the case of sign language, the hand is the object of interest. The position change of the hand is a global movement and the change of the hand gesture and orientation is a local movement.

In this chapter, we propose a three stage framework for spatiotemporal event recognition, as illustrated in Figure 13.3. The first stage, sequence acquisition, acquires image sequences representing the event. This involves motion detection and motion-based visual attention. The start and end of motion mark the temporal attention window in which the event occurs. We map this temporal window to a standard temporal length (e.g., 5) to form what is called *motion clip*, while the speed

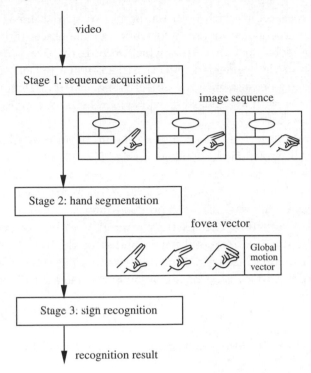

video

Stage 1: sequence acquisition

image sequence

Stage 2: hand segmentation

fovea vector

Global motion vector

Stage 3: sign recognition

recognition result

Fig. 13.3. The three-stage framework for spatiotemporal event recognition

information is available from the mapping performed in this stage. In a motion clip, only the temporal dimension is normalized.

The second stage is visual attention and object segmentation. This stage directs the system to focus on the object of interest in the image. If we assume that the object of interest is moving in a stationary environment, it is not difficult to roughly determine the position of a moving object in an image using motion information. However, it is not simple if the task is to extract the contour of the object from various backgrounds. Here, we present a prediction-and-verification segmentation scheme to locate hands from complex backgrounds. The scheme uses the past experience to guide the search of the valid segmentation and is more efficient and effective than other stochastic approaches such as simulated annealing.

After stage two, the object of interest in each image of a sequence is segmented and mapped to a fovea image of a standard fixed size. Segmented fovea images at different times form a standard *spatiotempo-*

ral fovea sequence, in which both temporal and spatial dimensions are normalized. The global motion information of the object of interest is placed in a global motion vector, which records the size and position information of the segmented object in the original image. This vec-tor is necessary because once the object is segmented and mapped to a fovea sequence with a standard spatiotemporal size, the global motion information is lost.

Let a fovea image f of m rows and n columns be an *(mn)*-dimensional vector. For example, the set of image pixels $\{f(i,j) \mid 0 \leq i < m, 0 \leq j < n\}$ can be written as a vector $\mathbf{V} = (v_1, v_2, \cdots, v_d)$ where $v_{mi+j} = f(i,j)$ and $d = mn$. Note that although pixels in an image are lined up to form a 1D vector $\mathbf{V}$ this way, 2D neighborhood information between pixels will be characterized by the scatter matrix of $\mathbf{V}$ to be discussed later. Let p be the standard temporal length and f_i be the hand fovea image corresponding to the frame i. Then we create a new vector $\mathbf{X}$, called the *fovea vector*, which is a concatenation of the hand foveas and global motion vector G,

$$\mathbf{X} = (f_1, f_2, ..., f_p, G). \tag{13.1}$$

The third stage is to recognize the spatiotemporal event from the fovea vector.

We focus on the second and third stages in this work. The outline of the chapter is as follows. We dedicate the next section to the hand seg-mentation. In Section 13.5, we present our recognition scheme. Exper-imental results are presented in Section 13.7. We end with conclusions and a brief discussion of the future work.

13.4 Hand Segmentation

A general object segmentation system accepts an input image $\mathbf{I}$ and an intention signal $\mathbf{P}$ which specifies the type of object that it is looking for and outputs the segmentation result $\mathbf{C} = S(\mathbf{I}, \mathbf{P})$. To check the validation of the segmentation result, we need a verifier f. In order to build such a segmentation system, we need to answer two questions: 1) how to find $\mathbf{C}$ and 2) how to construct f.

We present a prediction-and-verification scheme to answer the above questions. First, we introduce the concept of *valid segmentation* and provide criteria to evaluate whether a segmentation is valid or not. Sec-ondly, we develop a systematic approach to predict the valid segmenta-tion using attention images of multiple fixations as visual cues.

13.4.1 Valid Segmentation

Given an input image, we can construct an attention image of the hand as shown in Figure 13.4.

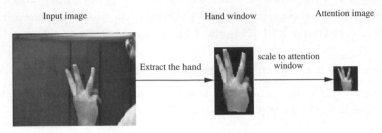

Fig. 13.4. The illustration of constructing attention images

The Most Expressive Features (MEF)

We describe an attention image F of m rows and n columns as an (mn)-dimensional vector. For example, the set of image pixels $\{f(i,j) \mid 0 \leq i < m, 0 \leq j < n\}$ can be written as a vector $\mathbf{V} = (v_1, v_2, \cdots, v_d)$ where $v_{mi+j} = f(i,j)$ and $d = mn$. Hand attention images in a training set can be considered as samples from a d-dimensional random vector $\mathbf{X}$. Typically d is very large. The Karhunen-Loeve projection [202] is a very efficient way to reduce a high-dimensional space to a low-dimensional subspace.

A d-dimensional random vector $\mathbf{X}$ can be expanded exactly by d orthonormal vectors, $\mathbf{v}_1, \mathbf{v}_2, \cdots, \mathbf{v}_d$, so that

$$\mathbf{X} = \sum_{i=1}^{d} y_i \mathbf{v}_i = V\mathbf{Y} \qquad (13.2)$$

where V is an orthogonal $d \times d$ square matrix consisting of orthonormal column vectors $\mathbf{v}_i$. Without loss of generality, we can assume that the mean of the random vector $\mathbf{X}$ is a zero vector, since we can always redefine $\mathbf{X} - E\mathbf{X}$ as the vector to consider. The approximate representation is $\hat{\mathbf{X}}(m) = \sum_{i=1}^{m} y_i \mathbf{v}_i$ $(m < d)$. It has been proved [202] that the best unit vectors $\mathbf{v}_1, \mathbf{v}_2, \cdots, \mathbf{v}_m$ that minimize

$$\epsilon^2(m) = E\|\delta\mathbf{X}(m)\|^2 = E\|\mathbf{X} - \hat{\mathbf{X}}(m)\|^2 \qquad (13.3)$$

are the m unit eigenvectors of the covariance matrix Σ_X of $\mathbf{X}$, associated with the m largest eigenvalues.

We can choose m so that the variation ratio $\sum_{i=m+1}^{n} \lambda_i / \sum_{i=1}^{n} \lambda_i$ is smaller than a given percentage (e.g., 5%). These m vectors are typically called the principle components. We call these m vectors $\{\mathbf{v}_i\}$ the *most expressive features* (MEF) in that they best describe the sample population in the sense of linear transform. For some earlier works on using MEF for recognition-related problems, the reader is referred to Turk and Pentland 1991 [291] and Murase and Nayar 1995 [226].

Approximation as Function Sampling and Interpolation

After projecting hand attention images to a low-dimensional MEF space, we are now ready to approximate the verifier f using function interpolation.

Definition 1 *Given a training vector* $\mathbf{X}_{k,i}$ *of gesture k in the MEF space, a Gaussian basis function* s_i *is* $s_i(\mathbf{X}) = e^{-\frac{\|\mathbf{X}-\mathbf{X}_{k,i}\|^2}{\sigma}}$, *where σ is a positive damping factor, and* $\| \cdot \|$ *denotes the Euclidean distance.*

A very small σ tends to reduce the contribution of neighboring training samples. Gaussian is one of the widely used basis functions [244].

Definition 2 *Given a set of n training samples* $L_k = \{\mathbf{X}_{k,1}, \mathbf{X}_{k,2}, \cdots, \mathbf{X}_{k,n}\}$ *of gesture k, the confidence level of the input $\mathbf{X}$ belongs to class k is defined as:* $g_k(\mathbf{X}) = \sum_{i=1}^{n} c_i s_i(\mathbf{X})$, *where the s_i is a Gaussian basis function and the coefficients c_i are to be determined by the training samples.*

The coefficients c_i's are determined as follows: given n training samples, we have n equations

$$g_k(\mathbf{X}_{k,i}) = \sum_{i=1}^{n} c_i s_i(\mathbf{X}_{k,i}), \qquad (13.4)$$

which are linear with respect to the coefficients c_i's. If we set $g_k(\mathbf{X}_{k,i})$ equal to 1, we can solve the above equations for c_i using Gauss-Jordan elimination method [246]. Figure 13.5 shows how the interpolation function would look like in the case when two training samples $(0,0)$ and $(1.4, 1.4)$ are used and $\sigma = 1$.

The confidence level defined in Definition 2 can be used to verify a segmentation result.

Definition 3 *Given a segmentation result $\mathbf{S}$ and a confidence level l, the verifier f outputs valid segmentation for gesture k if $g_k(\mathbf{S}) > l$.*

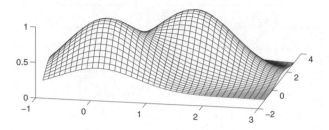

Fig. 13.5 Interpolation function with two training samples, (0,0) and (1.4,1.4)

Intuitively, a segmentation result **S** is valid if there is a training sample that is sufficiently close to it.

13.4.2 Predication for Valid Segmentation

This section investigates the problem how to find a valid segmentation. Our approach is to use the attention images from multiple fixations of training hand images. Given a hand attention image, an attention of a fixation is determined by its fixation position (s, t) and a scale r. Fig. 13.6 shows the attention images of the 19 fixations from one training sample. The scales s and positions (s, t) of these 19 fixations for an image with m rows and n columns are listed in Table 13.1.

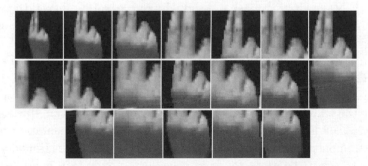

Fig. 13.6 The attention images from 19 fixations of a training sample. The first one is the same as the original hand attention image.

Table 13.1. *The list of fixation scale and position*

Scale	1.0	0.75	0.5	0.33
P1	$(\frac{m}{2}, \frac{n}{2})$	$(\frac{m}{2}, \frac{n}{2})$	$(\frac{m}{2}, \frac{n}{2})$	
P2			$(\frac{m}{3}, \frac{n}{3})$	$(\frac{m}{3}, \frac{n}{3})$
P3			$(\frac{m}{3}, \frac{n}{2})$	$(\frac{m}{3}, \frac{n}{2})$
P4			$(\frac{m}{3}, \frac{2n}{3})$	$(\frac{m}{3}, \frac{2n}{3})$
P5			$(\frac{m}{2}, \frac{n}{3})$	$(\frac{m}{2}, \frac{n}{3})$
P6			$(\frac{m}{2}, \frac{2n}{3})$	$(\frac{m}{2}, \frac{2n}{3})$
P7			$(\frac{2m}{3}, \frac{n}{3})$	$(\frac{2m}{3}, \frac{n}{3})$
P8			$(\frac{2m}{3}, \frac{n}{2})$	$(\frac{2m}{3}, \frac{n}{2})$
P9			$(\frac{2m}{3}, \frac{2n}{3})$	$(\frac{2m}{3}, \frac{2n}{3})$

Overview

Given a training set $L = \{I_1, I_2, \cdots, I_n\}$, where I_i is a training hand attention image, we obtain a set of attention images from multiple fixations for each I_i. We denote $F_{i,j}$ be an attention image from jth fixation of sample i in L. The attention images from the training set L_F is

$$L_F = \{F_{1,1}, \cdots, F_{1,m_1}, F_{2,1}, \cdots, F_{1,m_2}, \cdots, F_{n,1}, \cdots, F_{n,m_n}\},$$

where m_i is the number of the attention images generated from the training image I_i. Each attention image from a fixation is associated with the segmentation mask of original hand attention image, the scale r and the position of the fixation (s, t). These information is necessary to recover the segmentation for the entire object.

During the segmentation stage, we first use the motion information to select visual attention. Then, we try different fixations on the input image. An attention image from a fixation of an input image is used to query the training set L_F. The segmentation mask associated with the query result $F_{i,j}$ is the predication. The predicted segmentation mask is then applied to the input image. Finally, we verify the segmentation result to see if the extracted subimage corresponds to a hand gesture that has been learned. If the answer is yes, we find the solution. This solution can further go through a refinement process. Figure 13.7 gives the outline of the scheme.

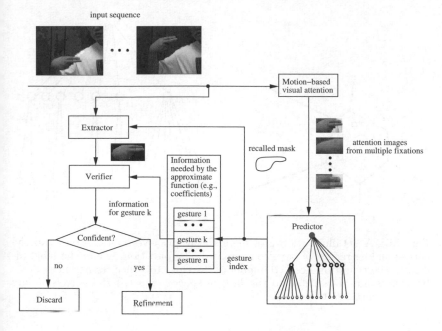

Fig. 13.7. Overview of the segmentation scheme

Organization of Attention Images from Fixations

Our objective is to achieve a retrieval with time complexity $O(\log n)$ for a learning set of size n. With this goal in mind, we build a hierarchical structure to organize the data.

Definition 4 *Given a set of points* $V = \{V_1, V_2, \cdots, V_n\}$ *in the space* S, *the* Voronoi diagram *partitions* S *into* $R = \{R_1, R_2, \cdots, R_n\}$ *regions, where* $R_i \cap R_j = 0$ *when* $i \neq j$, $\bigcup_{i=1}^{n} R_i = S$, *and for any* $x \in S$, $x \in R_i$ *if and only if* $\|x - V_i\| < \|x - V_j\|$ *for any* $j \neq i$. *We denote* V_i *be the center of the region* R_i.

Definition 5 *A* hierarchical quasi-Voronoi diagram P *of* S *is a set of partitions* $P = \{P_1, P_2, \cdots, P_m\}$, *where every* $P_i = \{P_{i,1}, \cdots, P_{i,n_i}\}$, $i = 1, 2, \cdots, m$ *is a partition of* S. $P_{i+1} = \{P_{i+1,1}, \cdots, P_{i+1,n_{i+1}}\}$ *is a finer Voronoi diagram partition of* P_i *in the sense that corresponding to every element* $P_{i,k} \in P_i$, P_{i+1} *contains a Voronoi partition* $\{P_{i+1,s}, \cdots, P_{i+1,t}\}$ *of* $P_{i,k}$.

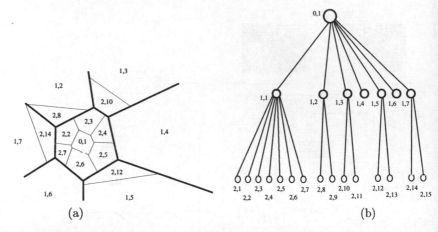

Fig. 13.8 A 2D illustration of a hierarchical quasi-Voronoi diagram and the corresponding recursive partition tree, (a) The partition, where the label indicates the center of a cell (the label of the child to which its parent's center belongs is not shown due to the lack of space), and (b) the corresponding recursive partition tree

The graphic description in Fig. 13.8 gives an simplified but intuitive explanation of the hierarchical quasi-Voronoi diagram. The structure is a tree. The root corresponds to the entire space of all the possible inputs. The children of the root partition the space into large cells, as shown by thick lines in Figure 13.8. The children of a parent subdivide the parent's cell future into smaller cells, and so on.

Prediction as Querying the Training Set

Given a training set L, a hierarchical quasi-Voronoi diagram $P = \{P_1, P_2, \cdots, P_n\}$ corresponding to L and a query sample $\mathbf{X}$, the prediction problem is to find a training sample $\mathbf{X}' \in L$, such that $\|\mathbf{X} - \mathbf{X}'\| \leq \|\mathbf{X} - \mathbf{X}''\|$ for any $\mathbf{X}'' \in L$ with $\mathbf{X}'' \neq \mathbf{X}'$.

The type of query mentioned above is a nearest neighbor problem, also known as *post-office* problem [182]. The nearest neighbor problem has been studied extensively in the past. There are efficient query algorithms $O(\log n)$ for two- or three- dimensional cases [70, 109]. However, there still lacks of efficient solutions for the case with dimension higher than three. k-d tree based nearest neighbor algorithms have been widely used in computer vision [28, 330]. k-d trees are extremely versatile and efficient to use in low dimensions. However, the performance degrades exponentially in high dimensions. R-tree and its variants [139, 272, 24,

59] have similar performance problem in nearest neighbor search for high dimensions. In this section, we present an efficient algorithm when the training set is d-supportive as defined below.

Definition 6 *Let S be a set which contains all possible samples. A training set $L = \{L_1, L_2, \cdots, L_n\}$ is a d-supportive training set if for any test sample $\mathbf{X} \in S$, there exist i such that $\|\mathbf{X} - L_i\| < d$, where $\| \cdot \|$ is the Euclidean distance.*

Next two theorems show the fact that if the training set is d-supportive, we have an efficient query algorithm.

Theorem 1 *Given a set of d-supportive training set $L = \{L_1, L_2, \cdots, L_n\}$, a hierarchical quasi-Voronoi diagram $P = \{P_1, P_2, \cdots, P_n\}$ corresponding to L and a query sample $\mathbf{X} \in S$, let the ith partition be $P_i = \{P_{i,1}, P_{i,2}, \cdots, P_{i,n_i}\}$ and $C = \{C_1, C_2, \cdots, C_{n_i}\}$ be the corresponding centers of regions in P_i. Assume C_1 be the center to $\mathbf{X}$ such that $\|C_1 - \mathbf{X}\| \leq \|C_i - \mathbf{X}\|$ for any $i \neq 1$. Let C_2 be any other center and P_1 be a boundary hyperplane between regions represented by C_1 and C_2 as illustrated in Fig. 13.9. Then the region of C_2 does not contain the nearest training sample to $\mathbf{X}$ if the distance between $\mathbf{X}$ and the hyperplane P_1 is greater than d.*

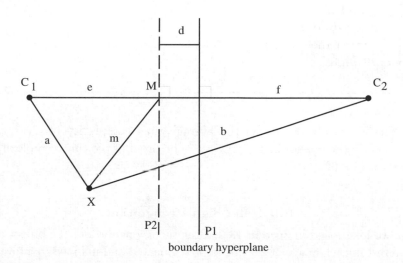

Fig. 13.9. A 2D illustration of nearest neighbor query theorems

In order to avoid to calculate the point to hyperplane distance in a high dimensional space, we can use following equivalent theorem.

Theorem 2 *Let* $\|C_1 - C_2\| = r$, $f = \frac{r}{2}$, $e = \frac{r}{2} - d$, $\|C_1 - \mathbf{X}\| = a$ *and* $\|C_2 - \mathbf{X}\| = b$ *as shown in Fig. 13.9. The region of C_2 does not contain the nearest training sample to* $\mathbf{X}$ *if* $a^2 - e^2 < b^2 - f^2$.

Given query sample $\mathbf{X}$, a hierarchical
quasi-Voronoi diagram P corresponding to
a d-supportive learning set with $C_{i,j}$ denotes to the center
of the partition region $P_{i,j}$.
begin
   $nodes\_list = root$;
   while $nodes\_list \neq$ **nil do**
      Pop the first node nd from $nodes\_list$;
      if nd is leaf **then**
         add center C_{nd} to the $center\_list$;
      else
         for regions under the node nd **do**
            Add region which is closest $\mathbf{X}$ to $nodes\_list$;
            Add regions which satisfy Theorem 3 to $nodes\_list$;
         end for
      end if
   end while
   Output the center in the $center\_list$ that minimizes $\|\mathbf{X} - C\|$.
end begin

The above algorithm has the average time complexity of $O(\log n)$ where n is the size of the training set. The proof of the time complexity is shown in [98].

13.5 Hand Sign Recognition

As we mentioned in Section 13.3, after the segmentation, the object of interest in each image of a sequence is segmented and mapped to a fovea image of a standard fixed size. These fovea images in a sequence and the global motion vector form a fovea vector.

An automatic hand gesture recognition system accepts an input fovea vector $\mathbf{X}$ and outputs the recognition result $\mathbf{C}$ which classifies the $\mathbf{X}$ into one of the gestures. Thus, a recognition system can be denoted by a function f that maps elements in the space of $\mathbf{X}$ to elements in the space of $\mathbf{C}$. Our objective of constructing a recognition system is equivalent to approximating function $f : S \mapsto C$ by another function $\hat{f} : S \mapsto C$. The error of a approximation can be indicated by certain measure of the error $\hat{f} - f$. One such measure is the mean square error:

$$E(\hat{f} - f) = \int_{X \in S} (\hat{f}(\mathbf{X}) - f(\mathbf{X}))^2 dF(\mathbf{X})$$

where $F(\mathbf{X})$ is the probability distribution function $\mathbf{X}$ in S. In other words, $\hat{f}$ can differ a lot from f in parts where $\mathbf{X}$ never occurs, without affecting the error measure. Another measure is the pointwise absolute error $\|\hat{f}(\mathbf{X}) - f(\mathbf{X})\|$ for any point $\mathbf{X}$ in S', where $S' \subset S$ is a subset of S that is of interest to a certain problem.

Of course, f is typically high-dimensional and highly complex. A powerful method of constructing $\hat{f}$ is using learning. Specifically, a series of cases is acquired as the learning data set:

$$L = \{(\mathbf{X}_i, f(\mathbf{X}_i)) | i = 1, 2, \cdots, n\}.$$

Then, construct $\hat{f}$ based on L. For notational convenience, the sample points in L is denoted by $X(L)$:

$$X(L) = \{\mathbf{X}_i | i = 1, 2, \cdots, n\}. \tag{13.5}$$

$X(L)$ should be drawn from the real situation so that the underlying distribution of $X(L)$ is as close to the real distribution as possible.

We propose a recursive partition tree in the most discriminating feature (MDF) space to approximate the function f.

13.5.1 The Most Discriminating Features (MDF)

In Section 13.4.1, we showed that using Karhunen-Loeve projection we can reduce a very high-dimensional image space to a lower dimensional MEF space. One way to approximate f is to use the nearest neighbor approximator [226, 291]. However, the MEF's are, in general, not the best ones for classification, because the features that describe some major variations in the class are typically irrelevant to how the subclasses are divided as illustrated in Figure 13.10.

In this work, multiclass, multivariate discriminant analysis [316] is

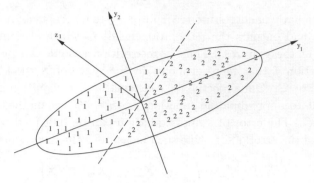

Fig. 13.10 A 2D illustration of the most discriminating features (MDF). The MDF is projection along z_1. The MEF along y_1 can not separate the two subclasses.

used to select the MDF's. It is a generalization of Fisher's linear discriminant [111]. Suppose samples of $\mathbf{Y}$ are m-dimensional random vectors from c classes. The ith class has a probability p_i, a mean vector $\mathbf{m}_i$ and a scatter matrix Σ_i. The *within-class scatter matrix* is defined by

$$S_w = \sum_{i=1}^{c} p_i E\{(\mathbf{Y} - \mathbf{m}_i)(\mathbf{Y} - \mathbf{m}_i)^t | \omega_i\} = \sum_{i=1}^{c} p_i \Sigma_i. \tag{13.6}$$

The *between-class scatter matrix* is

$$S_b = \sum_{i=1}^{c} p_i (\mathbf{m}_i - \mathbf{m})(\mathbf{m}_i - \mathbf{m})^t, \tag{13.7}$$

where the grand mean $\mathbf{m}$ is defined as $\mathbf{m} = E\mathbf{Y} = \sum_{i=1}^{c} p_i M_i$. The *mixture scatter matrix* is the covariance matrix of all the samples regardless of their class assignments:

$$S_m = E\{((\mathbf{Y} - \mathbf{m})(\mathbf{Y} - \mathbf{m})^t\} = S_w + S_b. \tag{13.8}$$

Suppose we use k-dimensional linear features $\mathbf{Z} = W^t \mathbf{Y}$ where W is an $m \times k$ rectangular matrix whose column vectors are linearly independent. The above mapping represents a linear projection from m-dimensional space to k-dimensional space. The samples $\mathbf{Y}_1, \mathbf{Y}_2, \cdots, \mathbf{Y}_n$ project to a corresponding set of samples $\mathbf{Z}_1, \mathbf{Z}_2, \cdots, \mathbf{Z}_n$ whose within-class scatter, and between-class scatter matrices are S_{Z_w} and S_{Z_b}, respectively. It is straightforward matter to show that

$$S_{Z_w} = W^t S_w W \tag{13.9}$$

$$S_{Z_b} = W^t S_b W. \tag{13.10}$$

These equations show how the within-class and between-class scatter matrices are transformed by the projection to the lower dimensional space. What we seek is a transformation matrix W that maximizes in some sense the ratio of the between-class scatter to the within-class scatter. A simple scalar measure of scatter is the determinant of the scatter matrix. The determinant is the product of the eigenvalues, and hence is the product of the variances in the principal directions, thereby measuring the square of the hyperellipsoidal scattering volume. Using this measure, we obtain the criterion function to maximize

$$J(W) = \frac{|W^t S_b W|}{|W^t S_w W|}. \tag{13.11}$$

It can be proved [316] that the optimal W that maximizes the above function are the generalized eigenvectors that correspond to the largest eigenvalues in

$$S_b \mathbf{w}_i = \lambda_i S_w \mathbf{w}_i. \tag{13.12}$$

In order to avoid compute the inverse of S_w, we can find the eigenvalues as the roots of the characteristic polynomial

$$|S_b - \lambda_i S_w| = 0 \tag{13.13}$$

and then solve

$$(S_b - \lambda_i S_w)\mathbf{w}_i = 0 \tag{13.14}$$

directly for the eigenvectors $\mathbf{w}_i$. Since the rank of S_b is at most $c - 1$, we know that only at most $c - 1$ features $\{\mathbf{w}_i\}$ are needed and we call these features the most discriminating features (MDFs).

13.5.2 Recursive Partition Tree

For large number of classes, the overall feature set may not be best for specific pairs of classes. An alternative classification scheme is the hierarchical classifier, where the most obvious discriminations are done first, postponing the more subtle distinctions to a later stage [224, 273]. Here, we present a recursive partition tree approximator in the MDF space. Unlike many other tree classifiers which have a fixed set of features, our feature set is adaptive. In the tree, each node is represented by a training sample and the related subregion and the samples under the subregion are used to generate the features. The graphic description in Figure 13.11 gives an simplified but intuitive explanation of the

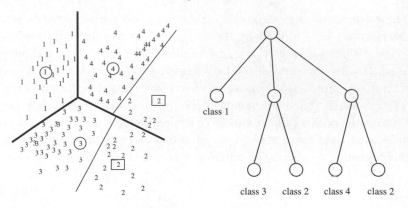

Fig. 13.11 A 2D illustration of a recursive partition tree. The samples surrounded by circles or rectangulars are the centers of the subregions. Left: the partition. Right: the corresponding recursive partition tree.

recursive partition tree. The leaves of the partition tree correspond to the regions which contain the training samples from a single class. The approximator uses the following decision rule to classify the query fovea vector $\mathbf{X}$ to the class of a leaf cell.

Definition 7 *Given a training set of fovea vectors $L = \{F_1, F_2, \cdots, F_n\}$ and corresponding recursive partition tree, for any query fovea vector $\mathbf{X}$, if the current level is not a leaf, the recursive partition tree approximator (RPTA) selects the cell with center C_i if for any other cell with center C_j, we have $R_d(\mathbf{X}, C_i) < R_d(\mathbf{X}, C_j)$. If the current level is a leaf node, RPTA designates the label of the leaf to the query $\mathbf{X}$.*

Since each local cell has its own projection, in order to logically compare between two different cells, we use a measurement called mixture distance (MD).

Definition 8 *Let C be the center of the region P, V be the projection matrix to the MEF space and W be the projection matrix to the MDF space. The mixture distance, $R_d(\mathbf{X}, C)$ from a query $\mathbf{X}$ fovea vector of the center C is defined as follows.*

$$\sqrt{\|\mathbf{X} - VV^t\mathbf{X}\|^2 + \|VWW^tV^tC - VWW^tV^t\mathbf{X}\|^2}$$

Intuitively, what is being measured can be seen in Fig. 13.12. In Figure 13.12, the original image space is a 3D space, the MEF space is a 2D subspace, and the MDF space is 1D subspace since two classes are well separated along the first MDF vector. The first term under the radical indicates the distance of the original vector from the population which indicates how well the MEF subspace represents the query vector **X**. This term is necessary since it is entirely possible that a query vector that is miles away from a particular subregion's MEF subspace would project very near to the region's center. The second term indicates the distance between the MDF components of the query vector and the MDF components of the center vector in the original image space.

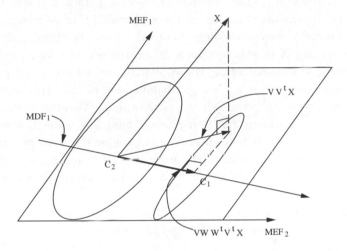

Fig. 13.12 Illustration of components in the mixture distance in a 3D original space

13.6 Convergence of the Approximators

An important issue to study here is how well the above approximators can approximate a function f. Its answer is closely related to the way samples are generated for the learning set L. In [313], Weng and Chen have shown that the nearest neighbor approximator approaches f *pointwise* in probability. In this section, we are going to show that the same result also holds for the recursive partition tree approximator.

Due to a high complexity and undetermined nature of the way in which a learning set L is drawn from the real world, it is effective to consider that $X(L)$, the set of samples in S, is generated randomly. We know that a fixed L is a special case of random L in that the probability distribution is concentrate at the single location. Thus, we consider **X** in $X(L)$ as a random sample from S. The learning set L is generated by acquiring samples from S with a d-dimensional probability distribution function $F(\mathbf{X})$.

Definition 9 *A point* $\mathbf{X}_0 \in S$ *is positively supported if for any* $\delta > 0$ *we have* $P\{\|\mathbf{X} - \mathbf{X}_0\| \leq \delta\} > 0$, *where* $P\{e\}$ *denotes the probability of the event* e.

If S consists of a finite number of discrete points, a point $\mathbf{X}$ in P is positively supported means that the probability of selecting $\mathbf{X}$ as a sample is not a zero-probability event. If S consists of infinitely many points, a point $\mathbf{X}$ in P is positively supported means that in any small neighborhood centered at $\mathbf{X}$, the probability of selecting any point in the neighborhood is not a zero-probability event. In practice, we are not interested in cases that almost never appears in a real-world application. An approximate function $\hat{f}$ can assume any value in subregions of S that will never be used in the application, without hurting the real performance of the system. Thus, we just need to investigate how well the approximation can do at points $\mathbf{X}$'s that are positively supported.

Definition 10 *A point* $\mathbf{X}_0 \in S$ *is an interior point of a region* $f(\mathbf{X}) = D$ *if there is a* $\delta > 0$ *such that for any* $\mathbf{X}$ *we have* $f(\mathbf{X}_0) = f(\mathbf{X}) = D$, *where* $\|\mathbf{X}_0 - \mathbf{X}\| < \delta$.

For a classification problem, we have a set of discrete number of categories to be assigned to the input. Then, $f(\mathbf{X})$ is continuous only at the interior points.

Theorem 3 *Suppose the query vector* $\mathbf{X}$ *is an interior and positively supported point in a bounded* S. *Let* n *be the size of a training set* L. *Given any small number* $\epsilon > 0$, *there is a number* N, *so that as long as we independently draw* $n > N$ *learning samples, the recursive partition tree approximator* $\hat{f}$ *has the following property*

$$P\{\hat{f}(\mathbf{X}) \neq f(\mathbf{X})\} < \epsilon,$$

where $\hat{f}'$ *the approximator based on the recursive partition tree.*

The proof of the above theorem is shown in [97]. Theorem 3 means that the RPTA approaches f *pointwisely* in probability: $P\{\hat{f}(\mathbf{X}) \neq f(\mathbf{X})\} \rightarrow 0$, as the size of training set L increases without bound.

13.7 Experimental Results

The framework has been applied to recognize the twenty eight different signs as illustrated in the Fig. 13.1. The image sequences are obtained while subjects perform hand signs in front of a video camera. The variation of hand size in images is limited. Two different lighting conditions are used. In the current implementation, each hand sign was represented by five images sampled from the video. Figure 13.13 shows several examples of these sequences.

13.7.1 Hand Segmentation

Two types of training were conducted in the experiments. The first type of training is to get the approximation for verifier f which would be used later to check the validation of the segmentation. For each gesture, a number (between 27 and 36) of training samples were used to obtained the approximation of the verifier f for that gesture. Figure 13.14 shows a representative subset of hand shapes learned by the system. Given a set of training samples $L = \{l_1, l_2, \cdots, l_n\}$ for gesture k, we empirically determined the damping factor σ in the interpolation function as follows:

$$\sigma = \frac{0.2 \sum_{i=1}^{n-1} \|\mathbf{X}_i - \mathbf{X}_{i+1}\|}{n-1}, \tag{13.15}$$

where $\mathbf{X}_i$ is a projection of a training sample in the MEF space.

The second type of training was to generate the attention images from multiple fixations of training samples. In the current implementation, the selection of the fixations is mechanical. In total 19 fixations were used for each training sample as illustrated in Figure 13.6.

In order to speed up the process of the segmentation, we utilize motion information to find a motion attention window. The attention algorithm can detect the rough position of a moving object, but the accuracy is not guaranteed. We solve this problem by doing some limited search based on the motion attention window. In the current implementation, given a motion attention window with m rows and n columns, we try the candidates with size from $(0.5m, 0.5n)$ to $(2m, 2n)$ using step size $(0.5m, 0.5n)$.

We tested the system with 802 images (161 sequences) which were not used in the training. A result was rejected if the system could not find a valid segmentation with a confidence level l. The segmentation was considered as a correct one if the correct gesture segmentation $\mathbf{C}$ was retrieved and placed in the right position of the test image. For the

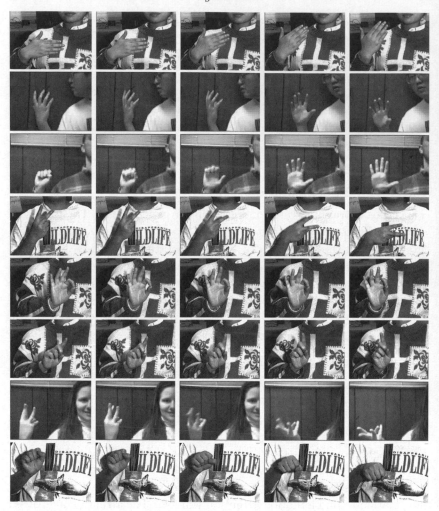

Fig. 13.13 Eight sample sequences. From top to bottom, they represent the signs "happy", "hot", "nothing", "parent", "pepper", "smart", "welcome", and "yes".

case of $l = 0.2$, we have achieved 95% correct segmentation rate with 3% false rejection rate. The results are summarized in Table 13.2. The time was obtained on a SGI INDIGO 2 (MIPS 4400 and clock 150 MHz) workstation. Figure 13.15 shows some segmentation results.

Fig. 13.14. A representative subset of hand shapes learned by the system

Table 13.2. *Summary of the segmentation results*

Training		Testing		
Number of fixation images	Number of test images	Correct segmentation	False rejection	Time per image
1742	805	95%	3%	58.3 sec.

13.7.2 Recognition of Hand Sign

The segmentation result was used as the input for sign recognition. The problem is now how to deal with the sequences which has some images that have been rejected by the segmentation routine. In this case, we still output those sequences because there are still good chances that they can be recognized if only one or two images in the sequences are rejected while the rest of them are fine. The number of images used in the training is 3300 (660 sequences). The number of testing images is 805 (161 sequences).

Results of the Nearest Neighbor Approximator in the MEF space

We show some experimental results to indicate the performance of the nearest neighbor approximator in the MEF space. We computed MEF's using 660 training sequences. Fig. 13.17 shows top 10 MEF's.

The number of MEF's was selected based on the variation ratio $r = \sum_{i=1}^{m} \lambda_i / \sum_{i=1}^{n} \lambda_i$, where m out of n MEF vectors were used, as defined in Section 13.4.1. Table 13.3 shows the number of MEF's corresponding to the variation ratio.

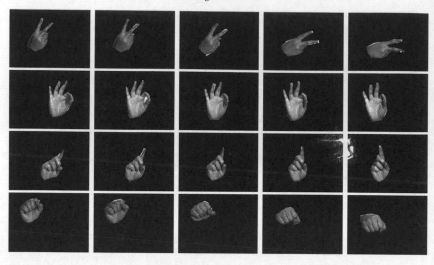

Fig. 13.15 The results of the segmentation are shown after masking off the background

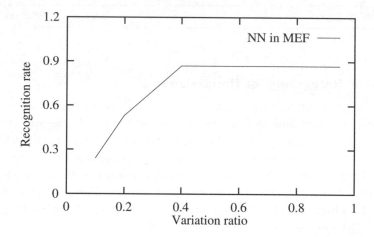

Fig. 13.16 Performance of the nearest neighbor approximator in the MEF space. The performance is given as a function of the number of MEF's used.

Fig. 13.16 shows the performance of the nearest neighbor approximator under the different variation ratio. The performance first improves when the ratio r increases. Then, at the point $r = 0.4$, the performance saturates at the recognition rate 87.0%. Table 13.4 shows average computation time for each sequence on the SGI INDIGO 2. The time was obtained based on the two different nearest neighbor query approaches,

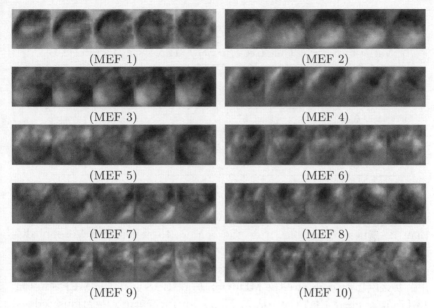

Fig. 13.17. Top ten MEF's

Table 13.3. *The number of MEF's vs. the variation ratio*

The variation ratio	The number of MEF's
10%	1
20%	2
40%	6
80%	48
95%	125

namely, the linear search and the hierarchical quasi-Voronoi diagram in Section 13.4.2. The use of the hierarchical quasi-Voronoi partition dramatically improves the query time.

Result of the Recursive Partition Tree Approximator in the MDF Space

In this experiment, same 660 training sequences were used to build a recursive partition tree. For each nonterminal region, we selected an adaptive radius r as defined in Section 13.5.2 to split the region into subregions. Given r for a nonterminal region, we have $k > 1$ training

Table 13.4. *Time of two nearest neighbor query approaches*

Variation ratio	Time (sec., linear)	Time (sec., hierarchical)
0.1	1.39	0.021
0.2	1.56	0.026
0.4	1.87	0.034
0.6	7.28	0.140
0.95	10.64	0.266

samples and the distance between each pair of these k samples is greater than r. These k samples were the centers to generate a Voronoi diagram. The distance here is the Euclidean distance in the MDF space corresponding to the region. Fig. 13.18 shows the top 10 MDF's at the root level. If we compare the MDF's in Fig. 13.18 with the MEF's in Fig. 13.17, it is clear that the top MDF's capture feature locations (edges) because it accounts for the major between-sign variations.

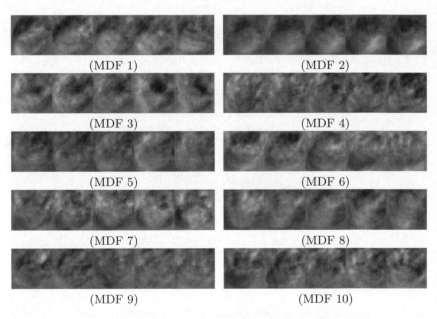

(MDF 1)　　　　　　　　　　　　(MDF 2)

(MDF 3)　　　　　　　　　　　　(MDF 4)

(MDF 5)　　　　　　　　　　　　(MDF 6)

(MDF 7)　　　　　　　　　　　　(MDF 8)

(MDF 9)　　　　　　　　　　　　(MDF 10)

Fig. 13.18. Top ten MDF's

Once we have created the recursive partition tree, we used it to rec-

Table 13.5. *Summary of the Experimental Data for RPTA*

Training		Testing	
Number of training samples	600 (3300 images)	Number of testing sequences	161 (805 images)
Height of the tree	7	Recognition rate	93.1 % (87% for MEF)
Number of nodes	90	Time per sequence (sec.)	0.63

ognize the sign. As we did in the experiments for the nearest neighbor approximator in the MEF space. The segmentation result was used as the input for sign recognition. The results are summarized in Table 13.5. The correct recognition rate of 161 testing sequences is 93.2% which is better than the recognition rate (87.0%) of the nearest neighbor approximator in the MEF space. The average recognition time per sequence is 0.63 second on the SGI INDIGO 2. The time is longer than the time (0.27 seconds) of nearest neighbor approximator when the quasi-Voronoi diagram is used in the query. This is because each nonterminal node in the recursive partition tree has its own version of projection matrices and each time the query vector traverses the node, it has to go through the local projection, whereas in the case of the nearest neighbor approximator, only one projection is necessary.

13.7.3 Experiments Related to MDF

We have shown that the approximator in the MDF space has better performance than the one in the MEF space. This is because the pixel-to-pixel distance, whether in the original image space or the MEF space, can not well characterize the difference between two signs due to the effects such as lighting, viewing angle, and hand variation between different subjects. On the other hand, the MDF's are the features that best characterize different categories. In this section, we show some experimental results to indicate quantitatively how the MEF and the MDF may perform very differently in classifying signs.

We computed MEF's and MDF's, respectively, using 50 sequences (10 for each signs). These signs are obtained from different subjects and the viewing positions are slightly different. Fig. 13.19(a) shows the samples

in the subspace spanned by the first two MEFs and Fig. 13.19 (b) shows
them in the subspace spanned by the first two MDFs.

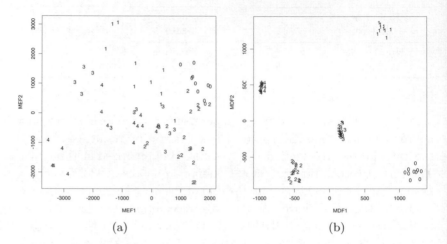

(a)   (b)

Fig. 13.19 The difference between MEF and MDF in representing samples,
(a) samples represented in the subspace spanned by the first two MEFs, (b)
samples represented in the subspace spanned by the first two MDFs, the numbers in the plot are the class labels of the samples.

As clearly shown, in the MEF subspace, samples from a single class
spread out widely and samples of different classes are not far apart. In
fact, some samples from different classes mingle together. However, in
the MDF subspace, samples of each class are clustered more tightly and
samples from different classes are farther apart. This shows that the
MDFs are better in terms of classification of signs.

13.8 Conclusions and Future Work

In this chapter, we have presented a new approach to recognizing hand
signs. The prediction-and-verification scheme for segmentation tightly
combines recognition with segmentation and it is able to deal with very
complex backgrounds. In our recognition method, motion understanding (the hand movement) is tightly coupled with spatial recognition
(hand shape) using a unified space. To achieve a high applicability
and adaptability to various conditions, we do not impose a priori features that the system must use, but rather the system automatically

selects features from images during learning. The system uses multi-class, multi-dimensional discriminant analysis to automatically select the most discriminating linear features for gesture classification. These features automatically weigh all the input components, through a linear combination, according to each component's relative importance in classification. The recursive partition tree approximator is proposed to perform classification with a large number of learned samples. With this tree, a large and complex many-class classification problem is recursively decomposed into smaller and fewer-class classification problems. This tree structure allows automatic feature selection in a coarse-to-fine fashion. Although the features we use belong to a linear type, the method realizes piecewise linear decision boundaries at leaf level, capable of approximating any smooth nonlinear decision boundary to a desired accuracy, as long as a sufficient number of training samples is available. In addition, the tree also allows pruning faraway samples from consideration in each query, realizing a logarithmic time complexity in the number of leaf nodes in the tree. The segmentation-recognition method addresses three key aspects of the moving hand sign interpretation, the hand shape, the location, and the movement.

In the current segmentation scheme, the fixations are generated mechanically. The number of fixations and the positions of fixation are the same regardless of the type of gesture. In order to achieve best possible performance, different gestures may require different fixation sequences. The later fixation depends on earlier ones. A future direction of research is to investigate dynamic generation of fixations based on learning.

14

Probabilistic Models of Verbal and Body Gestures

C. Bregler, S.M. Omohundro, M. Covell, M. Slaney,
S. Ahmad, D.A. Forsyth and J.A. Feldman

Abstract

This chapter describes several probabilistic techniques for representing, recognizing, and generating spatiotemporal configuration sequences. We first describe how such techniques can be used to visually track and recognize lip movements in order to augment a speech recognition system. We then demonstrate additional techniques that can be used to animate video footage of talking faces and synchronize it to different sentences of an audio track. Finally we outline alternative low-level representations that are needed to apply these techniques to articulated body gestures.

14.1 Introduction

Gestures can be described as characteristic configurations over time. While uttering a sentence, we express very fine grained verbal gestures as complex lip configurations over time, and while performing bodily actions, we generate articulated configuration sequences of jointed arm and leg segments. Such configurations lie in constrained subspaces and different gestures are embodied as different characteristic trajectories in these constrained subspaces.

We present a general technique called *Manifold Learning*, that is able to estimate such constrained subspaces from example data. This technique is applied to the domain of tracking, recognition, and interpolation. Characteristic trajectories through such spaces are estimated using Hidden Markov Models. We show the utility of these techniques on the domain of visual acoustic recognition of continuous spelled letters.

We also show how visual acoustic lip and facial feature models can be used for the inverse task: facial animation. For this domain we developed a modified tracking technique and a different lip interpolation technique, as well as a more general decomposition of visual speech units based on *Visemes*. We apply these techniques to stock-footage of a Marilyn Monroe scene and a news cast, where our technique is able to automatically modify a given utterance to a new sentence.

The models of verbal gestures that we use in the lip recognition and facial animation domain use low-level appearance-based and geometric representations. Lips and faces produce a relative constrained set of such features, which can be learned from data. In contrast, articulated objects, like hand and full body configurations, produce a much more complex set of image and geometric features. Constrained subspaces and sequences could be learned at higher levels of abstractions. Lower level representations should be based on much weaker and general constraints. We describe extensions to our gesture recognition approach that employ such low-level probabilistic constraints to image sequences of articulated gestures, and we outline how these new techniques can be incorporated into high-level manifold and HMM based representations.

Section 14.2 describes the constrained manifold representation using a mixture model of linear patches and a maximum likelihood estimation technique. Section 14.3 demonstrates an application to constrained tracking, and Section 14.4 describes a system that learns visual acoustic speech models for recognizing continuous speech. In Section 14.5 we briefly outline how to use the constrained space to interpolate lip images and in Section 14.6 we introduce a new set of techniques on how to use visual acoustic models for the *inverse task* of facial animation. Section 14.7 outlines the alternative low-level representations and how we plan to apply this to probabilistic gesture models of human body actions.

14.2 Constrained Lip Configuration Space

Human lips are geometrically complex shapes which smoothly vary with the multiple degrees of freedom of the facial musculature of a speaker. For recognition, we would like to extract information about these degrees of freedom from images. We represent a single configuration of the lips as a point in a feature space. The set of all configurations that a speaker may exhibit then defines a smooth surface in the feature space. In differential geometry, such smooth surfaces are called "manifolds".

For example, as a speaker opens her lips, the corresponding point in the lip feature space will move along a smooth curve. If the orientation of the lips is changed, then the configuration point moves along a different curve in the feature space. If both the degree of openness and the orientation vary, then a two-dimensional surface will be described in the feature space. The dimension of the "lip" surface is the same as the number of degrees of freedom of the lips. This includes both intrinsic degrees of freedom due to the musculature and external degrees of freedom which represent properties of the viewing conditions.

We would like to learn the lip manifold from examples and to perform the computations on it that are required for recognition. We abstract this problem as the "manifold learning problem": *given a set of points drawn from a smooth manifold in a space, induce the dimension and structure of the manifold.*

There are several operations we would like the surface representation to support. Perhaps the most important for recognition is the "nearest point" query: return the point on the surface which is closest to a specified query point (Fig. 14.1a). This task arises in any recognition context where the entities to be recognized are smoothly parameterized (e.g., objects which may be rotated, scaled, etc.) There is one surface for each class which represents the feature values as the various parameters are varied [226]. Under a distance-based noise model, the best classification choice for recognition will be to choose the class of the surface whose closest point is nearest the query point. The chosen surface determines the class of the recognized entity and the closest point gives the best estimate for values of the parameters within that class. The same query arises in several other contexts in our system. The surface representation should therefore support it efficiently.

Other important classes of queries are "interpolation queries" and "prediction queries". Two or more points on a curve are specified and the system must interpolate between them or extrapolate beyond them. Knowledge of the constraint surface can dramatically improve performance over "knowledge-free" approaches like linear or spline interpolation. (Fig. 14.1b)

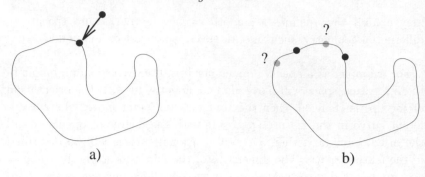

Fig. 14.1 Surface tasks a) closest point query, b) interpolation and prediction.

14.2.1 Mixtures of Local Patches

We present a manifold representation based on the closest point query [57]. If the data points were drawn from a *linear* manifold, then we could represent it by a point on the surface and a projection matrix. After the specified point is translated to the origin, the projection matrix would project any vector orthogonally into the linear subspace. Given a set of points drawn from such a linear surface, a principal components analysis could be used to discover its dimension and to find the least-squares best fit projection matrix. The largest principal vectors would span the space and there would be a precipitous drop in the principal values at the dimension of the surface (this is similar to approaches described [179, 291, 276]). A principal components analysis no longer suffices, however, when the manifold is nonlinear because even a one-dimensional nonlinear curve can span all the dimensions of a space.

If a nonlinear manifold is smooth, however, then each local piece looks more and more linear under magnification. Surface data points from a small local neighborhood will be well-approximated by a linear patch. Their principal values can be used to determine the most likely dimension of the patch. We take that number of the largest principal components to approximate the tangent space of the surface. The idea behind our representations is to "glue" such local linear patches together using a partition of unity.

The manifold is represented as a mapping from the embedding space to itself which takes each point to the nearest point on the manifold. K-means clustering is used to determine an initial set of "prototype centers" from the data points. A principal components analysis is performed on a specified number of the nearest neighbors of each prototype point. These

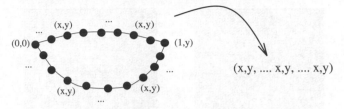

Fig. 14.2. Lip contour coding

"local PCA" results are used to estimate the dimension of the manifold and to find the best linear projection in the neighborhood of prototype i. The influence of these local models is determined by Gaussians centered on the prototype location with a variance determined by the local sample density. The projection onto the manifold is determined by forming a partition of unity from these Gaussians and using it to form a convex linear combination of the local linear projections:

$$P(x) = \frac{\sum_i G_i(x) P_i(x)}{\sum_i G_i(x)} \qquad (14.1)$$

This initial model is then refined to minimize the mean squared error between the training samples and the nearest surface point using EM optimization [105]. We have demonstrated the excellent performance of this approach on synthetic examples [58]. A related mixture model approach applied to input-output mappings appears in [161].

14.3 Constrained Tracking

To track the position of the lips we integrate the manifold representation with an "Active Contour" technique [169, 329, 190, 41]. In each image, a contour shape is matched to the boundary of the lips. The space of contours that represent lips is represented by a learned lip-contour-manifold. During tracking we try to find the contour (manifold-point) which maximizes the graylevel gradients along the contour in the image.

The boundary shape is parameterized by the x and y coordinates of 40 evenly spaced points along the contour. The left corner of the lip boundary is anchored at $(0,0)$ and all values are normalized to give a lip width of 1 (Fig 14.2). Each lip contour is therefore a point in an 80-dimensional "contour-space" (because of anchoring and scaling it is actually only a 77-dimensional space).

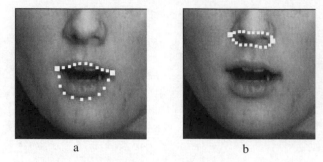

a   b

Fig. 14.3 Active contours for finding the lip contours: (a) a correctly placed snake; (b) a snake which has gotten stuck in a local minimum of the simple energy function.

Fig. 14.4 Two principle axes in a local patch in lip space: a, b, and c are configurations along the first principle axis, while d, e, and f are along the third axis.

The training set consists of 4500 images of 6 speakers uttering random words. The training images are initially labeled with a conventional *snake* algorithm. The standard *snake* approach chooses a curve by trying to maximize its smoothness while also adapting to certain image features along its length. These criteria are encoded in an energy function and the snake is optimized by gradient descent. Unfortunately, this approach sometimes causes the selection of incorrect regions (Fig. 14.3). We cull the incorrectly aligned *snakes* from the database by hand.

We then apply the manifold learning technique described above to the database of correctly aligned lip snakes. The algorithm learns a 5-dimensional manifold embedded in the 80-dimensional contour space. 5 dimensions were sufficient to describe the contours with single pixel accuracy in the image. Fig. 14.4 shows some of the lip models along two of the principal axes in the local neighborhood of one of the patches.

The tracking algorithm starts with a crude initial estimate of the lip position and size. In our training database all subjects positioned themselves at similar locations in front of the camera. The initial estimate

Fig. 14.5. A typical relaxation and tracking sequence of our lip tracker

is not crucial to our approach as we explain later. Currently work is in progress to integrate a full face finder, which will allow us to estimate the lip location and size without even knowing the rough position of the subject.

Given the initial location and size estimate, we backproject an initial lip contour from the lip-manifold back to the image (we choose the mean of one of the linear local patches). At each of the 40 points along the backprojected contour we estimate the magnitude of the graylevel gradient in the direction perpendicular to the contour. The sum of all 40 gradients would be maximal if the contour were perfectly aligned with the lip boundary. We iteratively maximize this term by performing a gradient ascent search over the 40 local coordinates. After each step, we anchor and normalize the new coordinates to the 80-dimensional shape space and project it back into the lip-manifold. This constrains the gradient ascent search to only to consider legal lip-shapes. The search moves the lip-manifold point in the direction which maximally increases the sum of directed graylevel gradients. The initial guess only has to be roughly right because the first few iterations use big enough image filters that the contour is attracted even far from the correct boundary.

The lip contour searches in successive images in the video sequence are started with the contour found from the previous image. Additionally we add a temporal term to the gradient ascent energy function which forces the temporal second derivatives of the contour coordinates to be small. Fig. 14.5 shows an example gradient ascent for a starting image and the contours found in successive images.

14.4 Learning and Recognizing Temporal Lip Configuration Sequences with Hidden Markov Models

In initial experiments we directly used the contour coding as the input to the recognition Hidden Markov Models, but found that the outer boundary of the lips is not distinctive enough to give reasonable recognition performance. The inner lip-contour and the appearance of teeth and tongue are important for recognition. These features are not very robust for lip tracking, however, because they disappear frequently when the lips close. For this reason the recognition features we use consist of the components of a graylevel matrix positioned and sized at the location found by the contour based lip-tracker. Empirically we found that a matrix of 24 × 16 pixels is enough to distinguish all possible lip configurations. Each pixel of the 24 × 16 matrix is assigned the average graylevel of a corresponding small window in the image. The size of the window is dependent of the size of the found contour. Because a 24 × 16 graylevel matrix is equal to a 384-dimensional vector, we also reduce the dimension of the recognition feature space by projecting the vectors to a linear subspace determined by a principal components analysis.

14.4.1 One Speaker, Pure Visual Recognition

The simplest of our experiments is based on a small speaker-dependent task, the "bartender" problem. The speaker may choose between 4 different cocktail names†, but the bartender cannot hear due to background noise. The cocktail must be chosen purely by lipreading. A subject uttered each of the 4 words, 23 times. An HMM was trained for each of the 4 words using a mixture of Gaussians to represent the emission probabilities. With a test set of 22 utterances, the system made only one error (4.5% error).

This task is artificially simple, because the vocabulary is very small, the system is speaker-dependent, and it does not deal with continuous or spontaneous speech. These are all state-of-the-art problems in the speech recognition community. For pure lip reading, however, the performance of this system is sufficiently high to warrant reporting here. The following sections describe more state-of-the-art tasks using a system based on combined acoustic and visual modalities.

14.4.2 Acoustic Processing and Sensor Fusion

For the acoustic preprocessing we use an off-the-shelf acoustic front-end system, called RASTA-PLP [146] which extracts feature vectors from the digitized acoustic data with a constant rate of 100 frames per second.

---

† We choose the words: "anchorsteam", "bacardi", "coffee", and "tequilla". Each word takes about 1 second to utter on average.

Psychological studies have shown that human subjects combine acoustic and visual information at a rather high feature level. This supports a perceptual model that posits conditional independence between the two speech modalities [216]. We believe, however, that such conditional independence cannot be applied to a speech recognition system that combines modalities on the phoneme/viseme level. Visual and acoustic speech vectors are conditionally independent given the vocal tract position, but not given the phoneme class. Our experiments have shown that combining modalities at the input level of the speech recognizer produces much higher performance than combining them on higher levels.

14.4.3 Multi-Speaker Visual-Acoustic Recognition

In this experiment, the aim is to use the the visual lipreading system to improve the performance of acoustic speech recognition. We focus on scenarios where the acoustic signal is distorted by background noise or crosstalk from another speaker. State-of-the-art speech recognition systems perform poorly in such environments. We would like to know how much the additional visual lip-information can reduce the error of a purely acoustic system.

We collected a database of six speakers spelling names or saying random sequences of letters. Letters can be thought of as small words, which makes this task a connected word recognition problem. Each utterance was a sequence of 3-8 letter names. The spelling task is notoriously difficult, because the words (letter names) are very short and highly ambiguous. For example the letters "n" and "m" sound very similar, especially in acoustically distorted signals. Visually they are more distinguishable (it is often the case that visual and acoustic ambiguities are complementary, presumably because of evolutionary pressures on language). In contrast, "b" and "p" are visually similar but acoustically different (voiced plosive vs. unvoiced plosive). Recognition and segmentation (when does one letter end and another begin) have additional difficulties in the presence of acoustical crosstalk from another speaker. Correlation with the visual image of one speaker's lips helps disambiguate the speakers.

Our training set consists of 2955 connected letters (uttered by the six speakers). We used an additional cross-validation set of 364 letters to avoid overfitting. In this set of experiments the HMM emission probabilities were estimated by a multi-layer-perceptron (MLP) [53]. The same MLP/HMM architecture has achieved state-of-the-art recognition

Task	Acoustic	AV	Delta-AV	relative err.red.
clean	11.0 %	10.1 %	11.3 %	-
20db SNR	33.5 %	28.9 %	26.0 %	22.4 %
10db SNR	56.1 %	51.7 %	48.0 %	14.4 %
15db SNR crosstalk	67.3 %	51.7 %	46.0 %	31.6 %

Table 14.1 *Results in word error (wrong words plus insertion and deletion errors caused by wrong segmentation)*

performance on standard acoustic databases like the ARPA resource management task.

We have trained three different versions of the system: one based purely on acoustic signals using nine-dimensional RASTA-PLP features, and two that combine visual and acoustic features. The first bimodal system (AV) is based on the acoustic features and ten additional coordinates obtained from the visual lip-feature space as described in section 14.4. The second bimodal system (Delta-AV) uses the same features as the AV-system plus an additional ten visual "Delta-features" which estimate temporal differences in the visual features. The intuition behind these features is that the primary information in lip reading lies in the temporal change.

We generated several test sets covering the 346 letters: one set with clean speech, two with 10db and 20db SNR additive noise (recorded inside a moving car), and one set with 15db SNR crosstalk from another speaker uttering letters as well.

Table 14.1 summarizes our simulation results. For clean speech we did not observe a significant improvement in recognition performance. For noise-degraded speech the improvement was significant at the 0.05 level. This was also true of the crosstalk experiment which showed the largest improvement.

14.4.4 Related Computer Lipreading Approaches

One of the earliest successful attempts to improve speech recognition by combining acoustic recognition and lipreading was done by Petajan in 1984 [242]. More recent experiments include [212, 327, 55, 319, 136, 275, 223, 227, 204, 1, 172]. All approaches attempt to show that computer lip reading is able to improve speech recognition, especially in noisy environments. The systems were applied to phoneme classification, isolated words, or to small continuous word recognition problems. Reported recognition improvements are difficult to interpret and compare because they are highly dependent on the complexity of the selected task (speaker-dependent/independent, vocabulary, phoneme/word/sentence recogntion), how advanced the underlying acoustic system is, and how simplified the visual task was made (e.g., use of reflective lipmarkers, special lipstick, or special lighting conditions). We believe that our system based on learned manifold techniques and Hidden Markov Models is one of the most complete systems applied to a complex speech recognition task to date but it is clear that many further improvements are possible.

14.5 Constrained Interpolation of Lip Sequences

So far we described how visual acoustic speech models can be used for recognition. In the next two sections we describe techniques that create new lip images which can be used for low-bandwidth video channels or facial animation applications.

First, we describe how the constrained manifold representation is applied to nonlinear image interpolation. This has applications to our domain of visual acoustic speech recognition where the different modalities are samples with different frequencies (30 images per second, 100 acoustic features per second). Another potential application of "model based" interpolation are video phone and video conference tasks, where the image frequency is usually lower then 30 frames per second.

Linear interpolated images are computed by traversing on a straight line between two key-feature vectors (images in our case). The interpolated image is the weighted average of two key images. Fig. 14.6 shows an example image which is the average of an open mouth and a closed mouth. The knowledge about the space of "legal" mouth shapes should constrain interpolated images to only lie in this space, similar to our tracking task. We like to traverse along the shortest curve that is embedded in the nonlinear manifold. We experimented with different techniques on how to traverse between two points on a nonlinear manifold representation and achieved the best performance with a technique that we call "manifold snakes".

The technique begins with the linearly interpolated points and iteratively moves the points toward the manifold. The *Manifold-Snake* is a

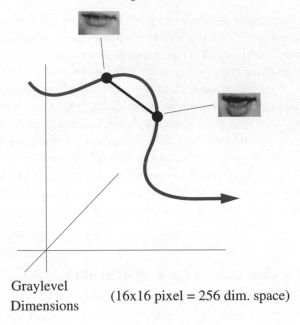

Graylevel Dimensions   (16x16 pixel = 256 dim. space)

Fig. 14.6. Linear versus nonlinear interpolation.

sequence of n points preferentially distributed along a smooth curve with equal distances between them. An energy function is defined on such sequences of points so that the energy minimum tries to satisfy these constraints (smoothness, equidistance, and nearness to the manifold):

$$E = \sum_i \alpha ||v_{i-1} - 2v_i + v_{i+1}||^2 + \beta ||v_i - proj(v_i)||^2 \qquad (14.2)$$

which has value 0 if all v_i are evenly distributed on a straight line and also lie on the manifold. In general E can never be 0 if the manifold is nonlinear, but a minimum for E represents an optimizing solution. We begin with a straight line between the two input points and perform gradient descent in E to find this optimizing solution.

Fig. 14.7 shows a case of linear interpolated and nonlinear interpolated 45×72 pixel lip images using this algorithm. The images were recorded with a high-speed, 100 frames per second camera†. Because of the much higher dimensionality of the images, we projected the images into a lower dimensional linear subspace. Embedded in this subspace we

† The images were recorded in the UCSD Perceptual Science Lab by Michael Cohen

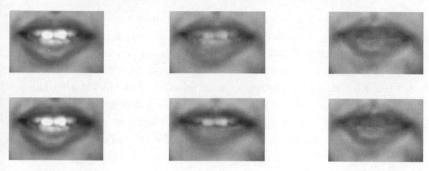

Fig. 14.7 45 × 72 images projected into a 16-dimensional subspace. Top row: linear interpolation. Bottom row: nonlinear "manifold-snake" interpolation.

induced a nonlinear manifold using a training set of 2560 images. The linearly interpolated lip image shows upper and lower teeth, but with smaller contrast, because it is the average image of the open mouth and closed mouth. The nonlinearly interpolated lip images show only the upper teeth and the lips half way closed, which is closer to the real lip configuration.

To learn the space of lip configurations in image space requires a relative large amount of example images. If we could code lip images using geometric features like we did for the tracking application, we could achieve a similar performance with less example shapes. Interpolating shapes is a "less nonlinear" task then interpolating graylevel images directly.

This leads to a different interpolation technique that is based on estimating geometric control points and using them for image morphing. We describe in the next section a facial animation system that uses such an alternative image interpolating technique.

14.6 Using Visual Acoustic Speech Models for Animation

The inverse problem to visual acoustic speech recognition is the speech animation problem. Traditionally, such systems are based on musculoskeletal models of the face that are driven by hand-coded dynamics [232]. Off the shelf text-to-speech systems produce phoneme categories that control the sequence of face model dynamics. Some systems are driven by input video data of tracked lips [26] or audio data [196] instead of handcoded heuristics, and some systems output modified video data [200, 268] instead of rendered graphics images.

We describe a system *VideoRewrite*† that uses visual acoustic stock footage to build a video model of the face, and uses that model to repurpose video sequences of talking people so they can say new words. In the current version of the system we assume that the new acoustic utterance is given. The visual frames are generated such that they match the arbitrary new spoken sentence (visual dubbing). The system draws on the techniques that we introduced earlier for our visual-acoustic recognition and interpolation tasks. *VideoRewrite* can be described as an appearance based animation technique that is an alternative to traditional 3D face model and hand-coded dynamical model based graphics techniques.

14.6.1 Viseme Models

Our new experiments are applied to news cast and movie scenes with unconstrained vocabulary. This requires a more general decomposition of our visual acoustic speech models. If we wanted to recognize what has been said in the stock footage sequence, it would require modeling more than 60,000 words and we still would get a high error rate even with the best speech technology currently available. Instead to generate lip images synchronized to a new audio track we only need to model a small set of speech units that cover a basis set of lip movements. We developed a decomposition of 9 *viseme* categories that group together visual similar phonemes. This categorization is in part derived from a *viseme* set introduced by [231]. For example the voiced plosive /b/ and the unvoiced plosive /p/ and the lip position of /m/ have a similar visual appearance and therefore are grouped together in one viseme category. The shape of the lips also depend on the contex (coarticulation). Therefore our models are indexed with respect to bi-visemes (or visual diphones). A bi-viseme is a pair of consecutive visemes. For example, saying a /na/ or saying a /ma/ results in different /a/ lip positions. Fig. 14.8 shows 3 example categories.

Besides a different speech decomposition the new domain also puts different requirements on our visual acoustic feature representation and estimation.

HMMs are generative models of speech. We could generate likely trajectories through the state space and emission probability distribution and then backproject manifold coefficients to image space using techniques that we developed for the constrained image interpolation task.

† *VideoRewrite* is developed at Interval Research Corp.

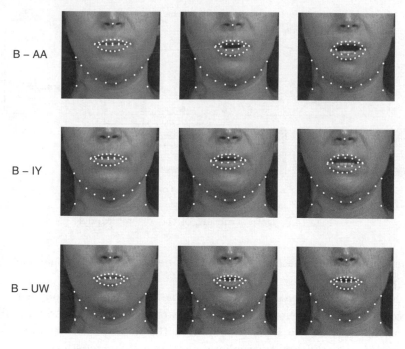

B – AA

B – IY

B – UW

Fig. 14.8. Characteristic diphone example images.

Unfortunately, the range of lip configurations covered by a single HMM state is very large. This is alright for recognition but it is an obstacle for animation. In our experiments it produced very blurry images (the average of many possible poses and appearances for one viseme). For a limited domain, [60] demonstrated a related technique on low resolution lip images. To achieve higher resolution and to cope with the large pose and appearance variance, we also store the explicit lip-space coefficients or complete input images with tracked geometric control points for each viseme model. Interpolating these images produces sharper images then picking random (but likely) points in the HMM emission probability distribution. Another advantage of the explicit storage of a set of images and their control points is that in animation mode we have a choice between different pose modes. We describe in detail such techniques in the next subsection. Fig. 14.9 illustrates the modified datastructure for our new viseme models. In some cases we model control points at the inner and outer lip contours and in some cases we also model points at

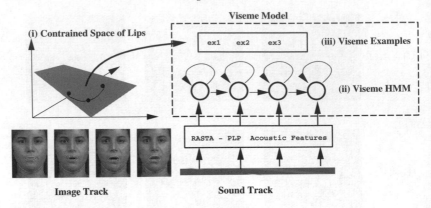

Fig. 14.9. Data structure of the Viseme Model

the chin and neck, because they need to be animated for visual speech as well.

For acoustic features, we use the same front-end as in our earlier recognition experiments. The channel invariant coding of RASTA-PLP is useful because the stock footage and the new spoken utterance is recorded using different microphone and room characteristics.

Fig. 14.9 illustrates our new visual acoustic speech models. Like the earlier models it consists of three main parts: (i) a constrained space for the lip configurations used for tracking, (ii) class based acoustic features modeled by the emission probability distribution of the HMM states, (iii) class based visual features modeled as a set of explicit image coefficients and control points.

14.6.2 Model Estimation

The estimation of the model parameters is done using two speech databases. To build the constrained lip/face tracking space and the viseme class based example set we use a stock-footage sequence of the desired person that we would like to animate. To estimate the acoustical parameters we decided to use a much larger speaker-independent database that contains phonetic labels (TIMIT). The reason why we use two different datasets for the different modalities is to compensate for two problems: (a) some of the stock-footage sequences are too small to have enough training data for robust recognition, (b) usually we only have full-sentence "close captions" for the stock footage available, but no detailed phonetic labels that are necessary to train our viseme models.

The training of the constrained lip/face space using the stock-footage and the training of the acoustical parameters using the phonetic labeled TIMIT database is done using techniques described earlier. Based on the partially trained models we can estimate the viseme class-based example lip configurations. The sentence based close-caption of the stock-footage is automatically transformed into a multiple pronunciation phonetic transcription using a pronunciation dictionary. The stock footage is decomposed into viseme sequences using the sound track and the trained acoustic HMMs in forced-viterbi mode. The lip and facial feature control points for each viseme image sequence are estimated using the trained lip/face space.

14.6.3 Appearance Based Animation

Now our visual acoustic speech model is ready for animation. It contains the trained acoustic features to transcribe the new input utterance, and a collection of example lip configurations for each viseme class to form an interpolated sequence of lip movements that fit the new audio track.

For the background, we need to pick an image sequence out of the stock footage that has at least the same length as the new utterance. The "background" stock-footage sequence is processed with the same constrained lip/face tracking algorithm as the training stock-footage to estimate the locations where we would like to change the facial parts.

We could just use a single background image that contains the rest of the non-moving facial parts, but we achieve a much more realistic video sequence if we retain the natural dynamics of the original scene. The sequences that we work with usually do not contain any drastic movements, but they never stay still. The head usually tilts to some extent and the eyes blink and produce various expressions. So far, we have made no attempt to synchronize these expressions to the new audio track. We replace just the lips or the lips, jaw, and neck to fit the new audio track. Potentially we could drive the other facial parts based on simple acoustic features.†

While the HMM models transcribe the new audio track, they index a corresponding sequence of example lip configurations. In the case a set of alternative lip-examples is available, we can choose among different lip sequences. In that case, the one that best fits the estimated background sequence is choosen, using a metric for pose similarity and dynamic

---

† For example the position of the eye-brows might change with pitch [229]. The system described in [83] models this finding.

programming. Once we have the sequence of key-frames, we need to interpolate missing frames dependent on the rate of speech. We integrate the new lips into the original background sequence using the tracked contours of lips, chin, and neck. We call this "stitching". Fig. 14.10 shows the flow chart with example images. Fig. 14.10(a) and (d) are two example key-frames. The images are spatially warped [25] in such a way that pixels along source contours are mapped to pixels along target contours. The two key frames have two different sets of source contours, but are mapped to the same set of target contours. To compute the target contour, we build the weighted average of the two key frame source contours and align the center and orientation of the upper lip contour with the original background lip contour. The lower lip contour and chin contour are rotated and shifted to the same extent, but not aligned to the contours of the background image. The neck contour is set equal to the background neck contour. Since the database includes the control-points the entire process is automatic.

Fig. 14.10(b) and (c) shows the warped versions of the two key frames. The warped images are cross-faded and multiplied with a soft spatial mask, Fig. 14.10(e)), before they are integrated into the background image.

A related technique based on optical flow measurements and image morphing was demonstrated for view interpolation of human faces by [29].

14.6.4 Experiments

Fig. 14.11 shows example frames extracted from *VideoRewrite* output footage. To create this footage, we recorded video of an actor saying 27 sentences and 135 vowel-consonant triples – about 6 minutes of footage. The system was trained on all the data *except* one of the sentences to create a video model. The system was then given the remaining sentence (the one that was not included in the training data) and asked to construct the corresponding image sequence.

As can be seen in Fig. 14.11, the synthesized footage is surprisingly good. There are only a few spots where our limited coarticulation model creates unrealistic sequences of mouth shapes and movements.

The perceived realism also depends on the viewers lip-reading skills and the actor's articulation skills. Highly trained lip-readers might have more objections to our dubbed video sequence than inexperienced viewers.

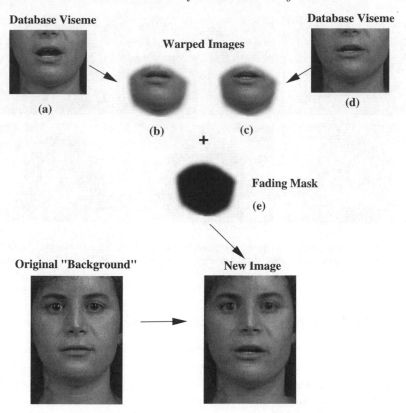

Fig. 14.10 Flow chart for morphing and stitching new lip images into the original movie sequence

Overall, we think the dubbed video sequences are more realistic than other animations produced by rendered 3D models, text-to-speech systems, and hand coded articulators. An important feature of our system that increases the realism is the way we morph and blend the example database images into a background image sequence. Even if the rest of the face (eyes, eyebrows) moves in an uncorrelated way, the human observer usually gets the impression that such expressions fit the new utterance. So far we have only modeled co-articulation with a very simple bi-viseme set. We believe a better treatment of co-articulation [83] would add another degree of realism.

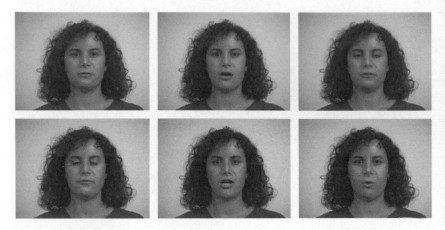

Fig. 14.11 Examples of sythesized ouput frames. These frames show the quality of our output after stitching diphone segments into different background
video frames.

14.7 The Next Step: Recognizing Body Gestures

We have described methods to represent and learn low-level feature constraints and temporal models of feature configurations. We applied these
techniques to the domain of lip and facial features. The representations
of geometric and appearances that we used are related to many other
techniques applied to the same domain [291, 41, 333, 190]. Although
faces and lips span a very complex set of configurations, the features
generated lie on a relatively small constrained subspace.

This is different in the domain of articulated objects like human bodies
or hands. Clothes generate a large range of appearance features due to
difference in color and texture. The large numbers of degrees of freedom
and self-occlusion produce a large range of geometric-based features. We
believe that manifold-based representations and Hidden Markov Models can be applied to learn constraints, higher level representations of
articulated objects, like joint-angles, or body configurations over time.
Lower level representations should be based on much weaker constraints,
or more general properties.

We describe extensions to our gesture recognition approach that employ such low-level probabilistic constraints to image sequences of articulated gestures, and we outline how these new techniques can be
incorporated into high-level manifold and HMM based representations.

The human body can be approximated by an assembly of rigid segments that are linked together at joints. While performing an action or gesture most of the body segments move most of the time. This is a single strong cue. The image region corresponding to a body segment contains a single coherent motion field. Two segments can be disambiguated by detecting two different coherent motion areas in the image. Joints can be detected if the pose and motion fields of a segment pair comply with the constraints associating with a body joint. Over multiple frames, characteristic sequences of jointed motion can be detected. For example, the process of walking consists of four connected body segments that traverse with three very characteristic periodic joint angle curves over time.

We introduce two low-level "layers" that represent single coherent motion blobs and jointed body segment pairs, and we describe how these representations are integrated into higher-level *kinematic manifolds* and HMM based dynamical models in a probabilistic framework. The problem of constrained estimation of body segments and their actions is described as a maximum a posteriori estimation. The low-level hypothesis of coherent motion areas are the likelihood terms, and the higher-level kinematic and dynamical constraints are coded as priors.

Motion Coherence Likelihoods: A collection of body segments are described with a multi-dimensional mixture of Gaussian *Blobs*. For each blob model, the means describe the center of mass in the image and its affine motion parameters. Part of the covariance describes the spatial distribution, and one variance describes the graylevel deviation of the motion prediction given the previous image frame. Without the spatial parameters, this approach is similar to layered motion estimation using EM search [159, 12].

Each pixel has a *hidden random variable* that assigns this pixel to one of the motion blob models or a background model. We initialize these models with optical flow clustering and then perform a few EM steps. Figure 14.12 shows some examples.

A similar representation based on *Blob* models for coherent color regions is applied to the human body domain by [320].

Simple Kinematic Priors: To further constrain the blob estimation and to incorporate high-level domain knowledge, we introduce body joint hypotheses and *score* coefficients for body segments and joints. General constraints can be coded straightforwardly as quadratic log-prior terms that give high values to body joint hypotheses at locations that are

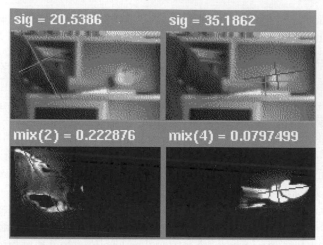

Fig. 14.12 Motion Coherence Blobs: Given two consecutive images we are able to group pixel regions with coherent motion and spatial proximity using Expectation Maximimzation (EM) search.

"compatible" with body segment pose and motion. The score parameter for each segment or joint is proportional to the fit of these constraints. For a more detailed description of the constraints see [54]. Fig. 14.13 shows the top four ranked hypothesis of body segments and joints of an arm sequence.

Complex Kinematic Priors: A set of connected body segments with more than one joint, like a pair of legs, or the torso and arms complies to further constraints. Certain joint-angle configurations are not possible or occur less frequently than others. We can model and estimate such configuration scenarios with the manifold learning techniques described previously. A mixture of linear patches in the joint-angle space provides additional kinematic priors. Additional hidden random variables must be introduced to assign each of the body joint hypotheses to one of the linear patches. Another level of EM can be used for a feasible estimation process.

Dynamical Priors: Constraints over multiple frames that are *action specific* can be modeled with Hidden Markov Models. As in the manifold representation, additional hidden random variables assign each joint model to a Hidden Markov State. A bottom-up process estimates the expected value for this state, and then a top-down process uses priors

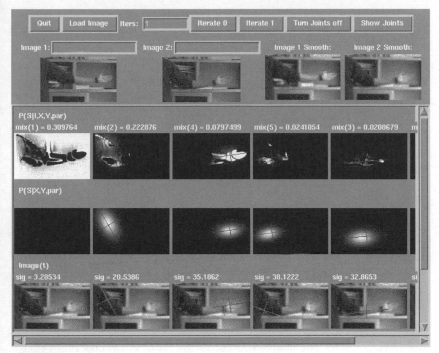

Fig. 14.13 One background model and four body segment hypotheses with joint constraints ranked with decreasing score values after two EM iterations. As you see, the last 2 blob hypotheses have significant lower score that the first 2 hypotheses, because no joint hypotheses with compatible motion could be computed.

from the Gaussian emission probability of the hidden states to further constrain the low-level estimation of body segment and joint models.

Fig. 14.14 shows a typical set of blob hypotheses. The top row shows the computed curve of rotation differences between two jointed body segments. Hidden Markov Models that are trained for typical angle curves detect primitive actions like arm swings. More extensive experiments using these high-level priors are currently in progress.

14.8 Conclusion

We have shown how constrained configuration subspaces and temporal models for configuration sequences can be estimated from example data and used for recognition and animation. We applied such models to the domain of visual acoustic speech recognition and synthesis.

Fig. 14.14 The bottom row shows two motion blob models found for the left arm of the person. The middle-row shows the posteriori probabilities that a pixel belongs to either the upper arm blob or the lower arm blob. The top row shows a history of rotation angles. Each angle is the difference between the rotation of the upper and lower arm blob.

We also outlined what additional low level feature constraints and mid-level articulated constraints are needed to estimate representations of articulated objects.

We believe that probabilistic modelling and learning such models from data is a crucial feature in our systems. Especially in the more complex domain of articulated human actions, we believe that bottom-up and top-down information flow, using iterative techniques like multiple EM optimizations, is another useful technique that shows how low and high-level models can interact and used to recognize non-trivial gestures.

15

Looking at Human Gestures

M. Yachida and Y. Iwai

Abstract

This chapter describes the work on human-computer interaction being carried out in our laboratory at the University of Osaka. Recognition of human expressions is necessary for human-computer interactive applications. A vision system is suitable for recognition of human expression since this involves passive sensing and the human gestures of hand, body and face that can be recognized without any discomfort for the user. The computer should not restrict the movements of the human to the front of the computer. Therefore, we study methods of looking at people using a network of active cameras.

15.1 Introduction

Sensing of human expressions is very important for human-computer interactive applications such as virtual reality, gesture recognition, and communication. A vision system is suitable for human-computer interaction since this involves passive sensing and the human gestures of the hand, body, and face that can be recognized without any discomfort for the user. We therefore use cameras for the sensors in our research to estimate human motion and gestures.

Facial expression is a natural human expression and is necessary to communicate such emotions as *happiness, surprise,* and *sadness* to others. A large number of studies have been made on machine recognition of human facial expression. Many of them are based on multi-resolution monochrome images and template pattern matching techniques [62, 293, 324]. This kind of approach needs some average operation on the face model or blurring of the input image to cope with the different appearance of faces in the images. This causes face detection to often fail by detecting false "faces" when the input images have complex backgrounds. We describe a method for face detection using fuzzy theory and a method for recognition of facial expressions by using a potential net.

Hand gesture is also one of the typical methods of non-verbal communication for human beings and we naturally use various gestures to express our own intentions in everyday life. Several model-based methods for the recognition of hand gestures from images have been proposed. Rehg et al. [253] used a kinematic model and fitted it to input images of fingers. Kuch et al. [186] used a calibrated 3D model and fitted the silhouette of this model to an input image. It is a good strategy to have a accurate model and a kinematic constraint of the known articulated or known complex object. We also describe how to acquire a shape model of an articulated object and how to fit the model to a real image.

Needless to say, considering some interactive systems requiring symbolic meanings of gestures, accurate joint angles are not necessarily required. Processing time is important rather than measurement accuracy in such an interactive system. From this point of view, Darrell et al. [102] presented a method for recognizing gestures directly from gray-scaled images instead of geometrical information of feature points. In the method, a gesture is represented by a set of images, and correlation scores between input images and models are calculated by special hardware. In this chapter, we also present a new method for recognizing gesture of arms and legs in real-time with multiple template models. In our method, the models for specific human body parts are used, and the disparity between an input image and the models is analyzed by a template matching method.

15.2 Facial Expression and Gesture Recognition

The face is an important object for extracting a lot of information about a person, so many studies have been made on facial image recognition. In particular, many researchers have paid considerable attention to facial expression. We describe a method for the recognition of facial expression as well as for the detection of faces. Detecting human faces in images is a key problem in human-computer interaction and is an essential step for face recognition.

15.2.1 Face Detection

It is difficult to detect human faces in an image with a complex background since the faces are not always distinct from others. We therefore propose a method for face detection by using color information and fuzzy pattern matching.

15.2.1.1 Uniform Chromatic System

In our research, we use the perceptually uniform color space proposed by Farnsworth to represent colors in an image. A non-linear color space such as Farnsworth's is called *perceptually uniform chromatic system* or UCS. The main advantage of UCS is that the distribution of "skin" color becomes concentric and can be expressed by a Gaussian distribution function, so we can reliably detect "skin" color.

We developed two models called the *skin color distribution model* and the *hair color distribution model*, where the values are between 0.0 and 1.0 since it is difficult to represent skin or hair color exactly. We can use these distribution models to estimate the degree of how well a color looks like skin or hair.

Selection of Face Candidates

We have currently prepared five basic head shape models, each of them containing $m \times n$ square cells of same size. There are two kinds information in each cell in a basic model:

 (i) the ratio of skin color area to total area,
 (ii) the ratio of hair color area to total area.

The basic models are scalable. Therefore we can use them to detect faces of any arbitrary size.

The faces in images are extracted by comparing the head shape models with the extracted skin color like regions and the hair color like regions using a fuzzy pattern matching method based on a *binary fuzzy relation*.

To detect regions containing faces, we use the face models to scan the entire image in order to estimate the matching degree between the face model and each rectangular region in the image. We use a matrix to represent the matching degrees of all the rectangular regions in the image. If a local maximum of matching degrees is greater than a certain threshold, we will consider that the rectangle may contain a human face and treat it as a face candidate.

Verification by Facial Parts

In most cases, the facial features are not clear in the image, thus eyes and eyebrows (also nose and mouth) cannot be detected separately from an image with high reliability. In our research, we first try to extract two regions that contain one eye and one eyebrow, and one region that contains the nose and the mouth.

Since the position and size of facial features such as eyes and mouth, do not differ that much between different persons, we can predict their position and size in the image when the position and the size of the face are known.

We build a simple model to represent the geometric relations among the two eye-eyebrow parts and the nose-mouth part of a human face. We call it the *relational facial model* or simply *RFM*. It is a scalable and rotation-independent model. The face verification is carried out by fitting the *RFM* to the extracted eye-eyebrow parts and nose-mouth part. It determines whether the face candidate is really a human face or not, based on the the estimation of difference between the model and the facial features.

The difference D between the *RFM* and the extracted facial features is estimated as the sum of the distances between the various *RFM* facial features and their corresponding extracted facial features divided by the distance between the two eye-eyebrow parts of the *RFM*. We consider that the face candidate is a true human face if D is less than a certain threshold value.

15.2.2 Recognition of Facial Expression

After detection of a face, recognition of facial expressions can be done. Conventional methods for recognition of facial expressions examine geometric relations established by facial features, such as eyes, eyebrows and a mouth, and variation of the locations of the features. However, estimation of their precise positions and shape attributes in real images is very difficult since abrupt rigid motion of the head including facial expressions degrades facial images.

We have suggested a new approach to treat facial images as whole patterns of potential fields induced on the retina of living things [218, 217]. The potential field is sampled by a potential net and analyzed in the principal pattern space by the Karhunen-Loève expansion method.

Potential Net and Netted Energy Model

To model the potential field, we used a physical model, called a potential net. The potential net is a two-dimensional mesh with each node connected to four neighbors by springs. We put this net on an edge image of human face; then the net is deformed by the image force from the potential field so as to reflect local deformation over the whole net through springs. The final configuration of the nodes represents the overall pattern of the potential field and can be used for various applications such as structural sampling of images [284]. We adopt an improved structure of the potential net model in which each node is connected to eight neighbors by springs to sample the potential field in detail.

Our new approach for modeling potential field is called the netted energy model, which is considered as an actualization of accumulated energy at the nodes of the potential net. The energy is easily calculated by the following equation:

$$F_{k,l} = \sum_{n_{i,j} \in N_{k,l}} \sum_{a=1}^{8} (S \frac{1}{2} k l_{i,j}^{a}{}^{2}) / N_{k,l} \qquad (15.1)$$

where $N_{k,l}$ is the number of nodes in a small block (k,l), $l_{i,j}^{a}$ is the expanded or contracted length of the springs which are connected to a node, and S is the sign of the deformed direction of the spring; plus for contraction and minus for expansion.

Fig. 15.1 shows a deformed net and gray-level conversion of its netted energy. In the figure, bright regions express highly accumulated energy induced by edge components of facial organs or furrows of facial expressions. The model is a very coarse representation for a facial image, but we can see that individuality disappears in the model, and useful information for determining facial expressions is well sampled from the input image.

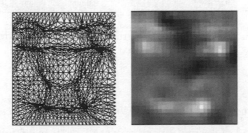

Fig. 15.1. A deformed potential net and an energy model

Representative Model for Facial Expressions

Our purpose in this work is to estimate the strength of facial expressions. However, it is very difficult even for human beings to recognize subtle changes in *anger, surprise,* and *sadness.* So here we restrict the object of recognition to one expression: *happiness* and attempt to roughly recognize its strength.

Facial expression is classified into four degrees of strength: *expressionless, minute, moderate,* and *maximum* happiness. From the training facial images, we first obtained the representative models according to the four degrees of expression strength with the following equation:

$$E_d = \frac{1}{h_d} \sum_{E_{k,l} \in \phi_d} E_{k,l} \qquad (15.2)$$

where ϕ_d is the set of energy models for the facial images in the dth strength grade training set which contains ϕ_d images. Fig. 15.2 shows the models represented in the netted energy model.

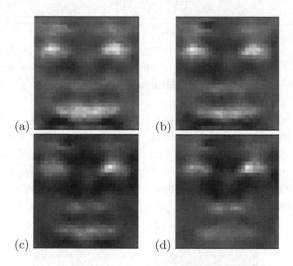

(a)

(b)

(c)

(d)

Fig. 15.2 The models represented in the netted energy model. The strength of the happiness expression: (a) maximum, (b) moderate, (c) minute, (d) expressionless

Principal Component Analysis on Netted Energy Models

We treat the net deformation as a overall pattern of facial feature. In other words, we extract the global features of the face in the potential net by the energy model and apply a principal component analysis to represent the expression strength in a low-dimensional vector space. The following summarize the procedure:

(i) compute the mean energy μ of the four representative energy models E_d;

(ii) compute the covariance matrix C of the training image set:

$$C = \frac{1}{4} \sum_{d=1}^{4} (E_d - \mu)(E_d - \mu)^T = AA^T; \tag{15.3}$$

(iii) compute the eigenvalue λ_f and the eigenvector U_f of the covariance matrix C;

(iv) Select G significant eigenvectors, $U_1, U_2, \ldots, U_G$;

(v) a G-dimensional vector $R_{df} = (r_{d1}, r_{d2}, \ldots, r_{dG})^T$, which is regarded as the feature vector for the netted energy model of facial expressions in the training set, is computed by

$$r_{df} = U_f^T (E_d - \mu) \qquad f = 1, \ldots, G. \tag{15.4}$$

Following the above PCA procedure, a low-dimensional space spanned by the G feature components is determined. We call this space *Emotion Space* because the projection of an energy model into this space reflects the global features of the facial expression in the training set.

15.2.3 Facial Gesture

Most existing face recognition systems such as facial expression recognition, personal identification system, require images containing faces in the frontal pose and at fixed size. Therefore, the camera must keep taking the frontal view of the face by changing the view point, view direction or zooming factor when the user's head moves.

In our system, we use active cameras which can follow the motion of the user's head. For this purpose, we need information about the pose of the face relative to the camera. The relative pose can be decomposed into the three rotation elements: the X and Y axes of the head coordinate system and the Z axis of the camera coordinate system.

We describe two approaches for estimating the rotational component of the Z and Y axes of the camera coordinate system.

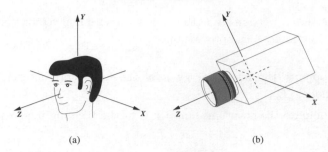

Fig. 15.3. The rotational components of a face

Tracking of Face

When a face in an image appears in frontal pose, the skin part will
be at the center and the hair will be around the edge since the face is
approximately symmetric. Thus the X coordinate of the center of the
skin area and that of the center of the hair area will be same. If the head
rotates from frontal to the left horizontally, the skin part will appear on
the right and the hair part on the left. If the X coordinate of the center
of the skin area moves to right, the center of the hair area will move to
the left relative to the center of the whole face area. Therefore, we can
determine whether a face is in frontal pose by checking the difference
between the x-coordinates of the center of hair area and the one of the
skin area.

Here we introduce a simple method for estimating the rotational component of the head around the Z axis of the camera coordinate system.
We can estimate the head rotation by inferring the direction of the face
pattern in the image since the rotation of the head around the Z axis
causes the rotation of the face pattern in the image. We therefore can infer the direction of the face pattern in the image by estimating the axis
of least inertia of the head region extracted from the image since the
shape of the head is symmetrical and can be considered as an elliptical
sphere.

15.3 Hand Gestures

We also use hand gestures to express our own intentions. Hand gestures
are also important in human-computer interaction.

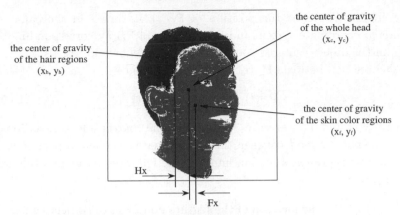

Fx: The x-coordinate of the center of gravity of the skin color regions
relative to the one of the whole head
Hx: The x-coordinate of the center of gravity of the hair regions
relative to the one of the whole head

Fig. 15.4. The relationship among head regions

15.3.1 3D Hand Motion and Position Estimation

Correct hand pose and position are sometimes needed in such applications as measurement systems, and robot learning systems. We describe a method for measurement of hand pose in this section.

Reconstruction of Hand Shape From a Monocular Image

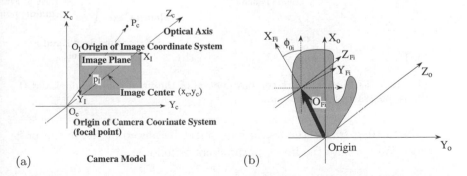

Fig. 15.5 (a) The camera coordinate system and (b) the hand model coordinate system

We consider that the object-centered coordinate system (X_O, Y_O, Z_O) whose origin O_O is fixed at the bottom of the palm as illustrated in

Fig. 15.5. We define the position of $P_C(t)$ at time t in the camera-centered coordinate system and the position of $P_O(t)$, corresponding to P_C, in the object-centered coordinate system (shown in Fig. 15.5).

The relation between $P_C(t)$ and $P_O(t)$ is given by

$$P_C(t) = R(t) \cdot P_O + T(t) \qquad (15.5)$$

where $R(t)$ and $T(t)$ are the 3×3 rotational matrix and translational components at time t between these coordinate systems, respectively.

Next, we represent a human hand by the following parameters shown in Fig. 15.6.

> $P_{Oi}(t)$ the location of the feature point i in the object-centered coordinate frame at time t,
> l_{ji} the length of the jth link of the finger i,
> W_{ji} the width of the jth link of the finger i,
> r_{Fi}, O_{Fi} the location of the tip r_F and the bottom O_F of the finger i in the object-centered coordinate frame.

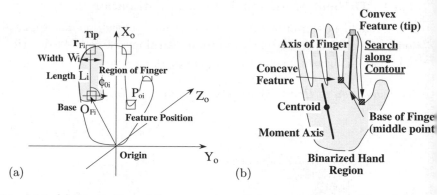

Fig. 15.6 (a) Illustration of the parameters of the hand shape model and (b) the reconstruction of hand shape

In the first frame, the user's hand must be placed at the initial position. We measure the finger parameters as follows:

Determination the X axis of the object coordinate system: First, we calculate the centroid and the moment axis of the binarized hand region. The moment axis of the binarized hand region is regarded as the X axis of the object coordinate system. At this stage, the direction of the X axis is not determined.

Generation of the finger tip and finger bottom triplets: We find
a triple of one convex feature point and two concave feature
points along the contour of the hand. The middle point between two concave feature points is the bottom of the finger
and the convex feature is the tip of the finger. Then we determine the length and the direction of this finger from the line
connecting this middle point and the finger tip.

Finding the thumb: We regard the tip-bottom pair which is nearest
to the centroid of the hand region as the thumb.

Determination of each finger: Then the tip-bottom pairs are considered as the forefinger, middle finger, ring finger, little finger
in order of the distance from the thumb.

Motion and Position Estimation From Monocular Sequence of Images

In general, we cannot estimate translational components of motion because of an inherent depth/speed scaling ambiguity in monocular vision.
To overcome this our system makes a shape model of the user's hand
from the input image at a known initial position. This is a reasonable
approach for the human interface, so as not to give the users any discomfort.

We assume that the initial position of the user's hand ($T(0)$ and $R(0)$)
is given in advance. Then, $P_{Oi}, l_{ji}, W_{ji}, r_{Fi}, O_{Fi}$, and $\phi_{ji}(0)$ can be
measured when the user places his hand at a certain distance from the
camera.

It is not easy to estimate the finger position analytically because the
degree of freedom of the fingers is too high. Therefore, to estimate the
finger position, we use the energy minimization method by using model
matching. To use this method we must define an evaluation function,
E_{total}, which consists of *the feature position constraint E_F, the contour
constraint E_C*, and *the finger position constraint F_B*.

We estimate the angles ϕ_0, ϕ_1, ϕ_2 and ϕ_3 by minimizing E_{total}.

Evaluation functions Let r_i be the position of each feature point i on
the image coordinate system and m_i be the position which corresponds
to r_i, on the model coordinate system. *The feature position constraint*
is defined as follows:

$$E_F = \frac{1}{2n} \sum_i^n (r_i - Pm_i)^T K_F (r_i - Pm_i) \qquad (15.6)$$

where K_F is the weight matrix, and P is the projection function from the model coordinate system to the image coordinate system.

The above equation (15.6) is minimal when the projected position of the model point and the position of the feature point are equal.

The contour constraint indicates when the contour of the model and the edge extracted from the real image are matched. Let n be the normal vector on the location c on the contour C generated from the shape model. *The contour constraint* is expressed by the following equation:

$$E_C = -\frac{1}{L} \int_C \left| \frac{\partial}{\partial \mathrm{n}} (G \star I) \right|^2 dc \qquad (15.7)$$

where $L(= \int_C dc)$ is the total length of the contour. This equation is minimal when edges actually exist on the generated contour.

The finger constraint binds the fingers so they cannot move freely. It is given by the following equation:

$$E_B = \frac{1}{2} \sum_{i \neq j} \left\{ (\mathrm{r}_i - \mathrm{r}_j) - (\mathrm{r}_i^0 - \mathrm{r}_j^0) \right\}^T K_B \left\{ (\mathrm{r}_i - \mathrm{r}_j) - (\mathrm{r}_i^0 - \mathrm{r}_j^0) \right\} \quad (15.8)$$

where r_i is the bottom position of the finger i, and r_i^0 is the bottom position, which was already estimated by the Initial Analyzer in the first frame.

Search algorithm We use a hill-climbing method to look for the minimal solution of each finger. The system ends the search if the iteration count is greater than a given value or the amount of the change of the energy cost function is less than a given threshold value.

Experimental Results

We show an experimental result on a real image sequence. We used 80 frames, some of which are shown in Fig. 15.7. The left-top image is the first frame and the right-bottom image is the 80th. The estimated shape model and position are superimposed on the input image.

15.3.2 Manual Alphabets Recognition Using Colored Glove

In the previous section, we described the method for correct measurement of hand pose. That method is not good for real-time applications. In this section, we describe a method for real-time recognition of hand gestures with savings in image processing time.

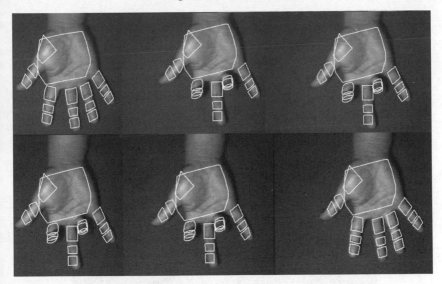

Fig. 15.7 The estimated shape model and position are superimposed on the input image.

Expression of manual alphabets

Fig. 15.8 shows the colored gloves used in our work. Each finger is divided into two regions by a PIP joint. Thus four fingers are divided into eight regions. The thumb is divided into two regions by an IP joint. We call each of the four finger regions and the thumb region "finger regions". The hand without fingers is divided into two regions: the wrist and the palm. In total, the hand is divided into twelve regions. We color all twelve regions differently, so that we can easily find each one.

The image features of a hand gesture acquired from a colored glove are shown in Fig. 15.9. We calculate the following features:

(i) the areas of the 10 finger regions;
(ii) the 10 vectors between the finger regions and the wrist part. We call these vectors "wrist vectors";
(iii) the 5 vectors between the base of the finger and the tip of the same finger. We call these vectors "finger vectors";
(iv) the 10 vectors between the tips of the fingers. We call these vectors "tip vectors".

We use the distance and angle of a vector as features, so we get two

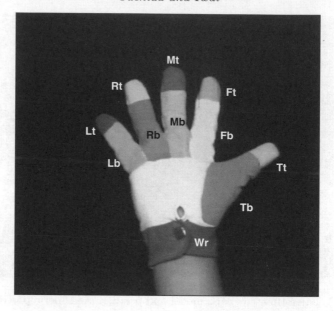

Fig. 15.8. The colored glove used in our experiments

features per vector. In total, 60 features are measured per hand gesture. When the area of a region is approximately zero, the features related to this region are treated as invalid.

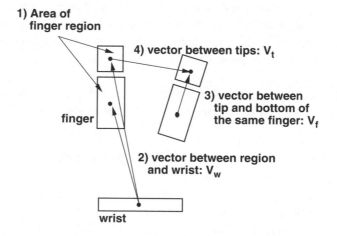

Fig. 15.9. Features acquired from real images

Recognition of Manual Alphabets by Decision Tree

Hand gestures are recognized by a decision tree made from the image features described above. We use the decision tree, as opposed to other pattern recognition methods (such as the nearest neighbor method), as it is efficient using only a few selected important features.

We automatically make the decision tree using an improved version of the ID3 method. The ID3 is a method for constructing a decision tree from positive examples which include pairs of features and values. We use the image features, described in the previous section, as ID3's attributes. ID3 classifies the example set C into clusters C_i by the threshold value v_i of the feature i which maximizes the gain of information. The ID3 method takes no account of the distance between clusters in classification, so the robustness grows worse as noise in the data increases.

We redefine the evaluation function F for feature selection as the following equation:

$$F = E \times D \tag{15.9}$$

$$E = -\sum_{k=1}^{patterns} P_{S,C_k} log_2 P_{S,C_k} - \sum_{v_j \subset Range(A_i)} \frac{|S_{ij}|}{|S|} I(S_{ij})$$

where E is the gain of information, D is the normalized distance between the two clusters, P_{S,C_k} is the frequency of the pattern C_k in the example set S, and S_{ij} is the subset consisting of the examples in which the feature A_i has value v_j.

In addition to the feature selection, we must determine the threshold value for dividing clusters for constructing the decision tree. When one cluster is divided by a certain attribute value, the number of the divided clusters becomes too large because ID3's attributes described in the previous section are numerical. Thus we need to gather attribute values into segments, and to regard each segment as one attribute value (like symbolization). Furthermore, we select only one threshold value to restrict division of the example set into only two clusters.

With the above idea, the feature and the threshold value are selected by the following procedure:

(i) for each image feature F_i ($0 \leq i \leq 59$), determine the threshold value T_i by the following procedure:

   (a) for each hand gesture j ($0 \leq j \leq 25$), make the minimum cluster L_j of all examples of the gesture j and calculate the maximum value $L_{j,max}$ and the minimum value $L_{j,min}$ of the image feature F_i for all examples in the cluster L_j. When either $L_{j,max}$ or $L_{j,min}$ is not available, the image feature F_i is excluded from the selection;

(b) sort the cluster L_j by $L_{j,min}$ in increasing order;

(c) compare $max(L_{k(0),max}, ..., L_{k(j),max})$ and $L_{k(j+1),min}$. If $max(L_{k(0),max}, ..., L_{k(j),max})$ is greater than $L_{k(j+1),min}$, the clusters $k(j)$ and $k(j + 1)$ are combined. repeat this procedure from $k(j) = 0$ to 24. (shown in Fig. 15.10);

(d) when the number of the clusters N is

$N = 1$ the image feature F_i is excluded from the selection.
$N = 2$ the threshold value T_i is given by $(L_{0,max} + L_{1,min})/2$
$N > 2$ select k which maximizes the distance between two clusters $D = (L_{k+1,min} - L_{k,max})$. The threshold value T_i is given by $(L_{k,max} + L_{k+1,min})/2$

(ii) calculate the gain of information E and the distance between two clusters D and the evaluation value F for each image feature F_i. Select the k-th feature F_k which maximizes the evaluation value F and select the threshold value T_k of the k-th feature;

(iii) divide the example set into clusters by the selected feature F_k and the threshold value T_k. If all leaf nodes of the decision tree contain examples of the same gesture, the procedure ends. Otherwise continue to (i).

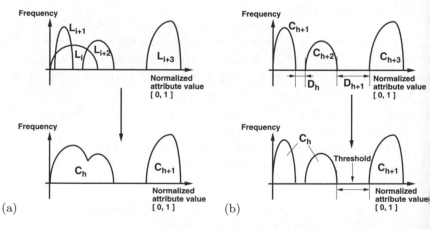

(a)   (b)

Fig. 15.10 Integration of the clusters (a) and determination of the threshold value (b).

Learning Manual Alphabets by CAD Model

Learning from positive examples needs many examples. It is difficult to take all the necessary examples from real scenes because it is tedious for humans to make many gestures. Thus we automatically make the example set using a CAD model.

We added Gaussian noise to the value of image features to take into consideration the noise of real images, by the following equation:

$$P'_{ij} = P_{ij} + 1.5\sigma_j n(area) \qquad (15.10)$$
$$= P_{ij} + \sigma_j n(distance, angle)$$

where P_{ij} is the image feature value, P'_{ij} is the image feature value added the Gaussian noise $N(0, \sigma_j)$, and σ_j is the standard deviation of the real image feature j of the example sets.

15.4 Body Motion and Gesture Recognition

Human body motions are also estimated by the same method for hand gesture recognition. The degree of freedom of arm motion is less than that of hand motion. Hence, we can apply simpler and faster methods for body gesture recognition than the ones above. We describe real-time body gesture recognition by using template matching.

15.4.1 Pose Estimation With Template Matching

Fig. 15.11. An example of left arm template models for difference poses.

Our method for gesture recognition is fundamentally based on template matching technique. The advantage of this technique is that the algorithm is very simple, so that a matching result can be calculated by a small scale hardware system like *ReMOT-M* [192]. In addition, since we compare similarities between a binarized input image and the template models, the influences caused by different persons or clothing can be ignored. Fig. 15.11 shows an example of template models employed in conventional template matching to estimate the poses of the left arm.

In template matching, we calculate the disparity between a partial region $R(x, y)$ in an input image I and a model image T_i as the result of the following equation:

$$d(R(x, y), T_i) = \sum_{m,n} |I(x + m, y + n) - T_i(m, n)|. \qquad (15.11)$$

In the above equation, $d(R(x, y), T_i)$ represents the disparity in $R(x, y)$, which is a partial region of I whose size is the same as T_i; and $I(x, y)$ and $T_i(m, n)$ show intensities of an input image and a model image respectively. Here we assume that the intensity of $I(x, y)$ and $T_i(m, n)$ is 0 or 1, that is $I(x, y)$ is obtained by binarizing a gray-scaled input image by a certain threshold value. By using d, we can obtain the disparity D between an input image I and a model image T_i by searching the smallest d in a search area S via the following equation:

$$D(T_i) = \min_{(x,y) \in S} d(R(x, y), T_i) \qquad (15.12)$$

where S represents the search area in the input image I.

When the disparity D is calculated for all model images $T_0, \cdots, T_{n-1}$, we can get the best pose number N as

$$N = \text{Pose}(T), \qquad (15.13)$$

where T is the ith template model and i minimizes $D(T_i)$. The function Pose() gives the pose number shown in Fig. 15.11, such as $\text{Pose}(L_{13}) = 3$. From this procedure, we obtain the best pose number. However, the conventional template matching has some problems in human gesture recognition. In the following section we describe them in detail.

Problems in Template Matching

The disparity calculated in the previous section is, however, very unstable since binarized input images have a lot of noise such as small dots and non-convex shapes caused by inadequate threshold values for various clothes in the binarizing process. This suggests that for estimating the pose of articulated objects correctly, the disparity should be calculated only in specific regions of interest, such as arms or legs in our case.

The other problem is how to calculate a disparity with odd shaped templates which are not adequately represented by rectangular patterns. In particular, to avoid interference from invalid regions such as the background, we should consider the non-rectangular decomposition of an object. For this problem, we usually employ a sequential masking operation.

Fig. 15.12 shows an example of a masked template. In the figure, (a) represents a masked template for an arm of the template model (b). Using mask templates and template models, the correct disparity in specific region can be calculated.

Although we can eliminate the influences of mismatch in template matching processing by using mask templates, the computation cost increases.

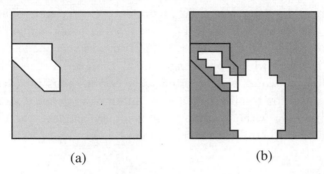

(a)   (b)

Fig. 15.12 An example of mask template and template model. (a) shows an example of mask template, (b) shows an example of a template model masked by (a).

15.4.2 Maskable Templates

In order to solve the problems in template matching for pose estimation, we propose a method for integrating the target template model and mask template into one — a maskable template model. Then, by selecting proper template intensities for the regions, (object region, non-object region and mask region), we derive that the matching process can be realized without obvious masking operation.

A maskable template model is generally defined as shown in Fig. 15.12; a rectangle-shaped template composing of an arbitrarily-shaped matching region Ω_p and a masking area Ω_m. A matching region Ω_p is composed of object regions and non-object regions, and it is the specific region in which we should obtain the disparity.

Assume that the value for region Ω_m is V_m, and Ω_p have binary values V_{p0} for non-object regions and V_{p1} for object regions. With this assumption, equation (15.11) can be rewritten as the sum of the disparity of the mask region Ω_m and matching region Ω_p,

$$d(R(x,y), T_{M_i}) = d_{\Omega_m}(T_{M_i}) + d_{\Omega_p}(T_{M_i}). \tag{15.14}$$

We can select the best model using the disparity in only matching regions.

15.4.3 Pose Estimation of Arms Using Maskable Template Models

When we use a conventional template matching method, it is impossible to prepare all the template models representing every state of a certain gesture. As shown in Fig. 15.11, we prepared a few models for the motion of raising and lowering arms. This means that models are very sparsely matched with input image and if the arm is placed between two models, matching will be often unsuccessful; thus we cannot get correct recognition results. In order to obtain more detailed and robust pose information without adding any template models, we adopt an interpolation method using maskable template models.

15.4.4 Application: Gesture game system

In this section, we explain a real-time interactive system which can recognize user's gesture and control a television game by using the recognition results. Fig. 15.13 shows the system's overview. It consists of the following units.

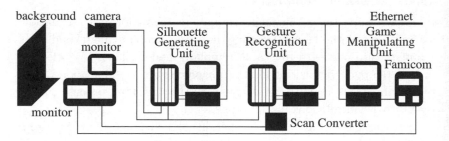

Fig. 15.13. Real-Time Gesture Game System

Silhouette Generating Unit: This unit generates the silhouette image by thresholding the intensity difference between the input image and the background image by using a Pipe-Line image processing system, MaxVideo 200 (Datacube Inc.). To avoid flickering due to the user's shadow, we use a black curtain as a background in our experiment.

Gesture Recognition Unit: This unit recognizes the user's gesture with the method described in the previous section. Template matching is performed with a specific hardware *ReMOT-M* system [192], and pose numbers of the arms and legs for every image frame are obtained in real-time. A sequential pose transitions are interpreted as a gesture and control codes are encoded and then transmitted to the *Game Manipulation Unit*.

Game Manipulation Unit: This unit emulates the button operation of a television game by a personal computer. It receives the control code and translates it to the practical button operation in sequence.

Acknowledgements

The editors are extremely grateful to David Tranah of Cambridge University Press. He has been an ideal editor, intellectually committed, enthusiastic and accommodating. We also acknowledge the a advice of William Newman and the help of Andrew Gee, Patrick Gosling and Simeon Keates. The design for the book cover (Lorenzo Lotto's *Creazione*, 1524) followed a suggestion by the Vicario family of Firenze. The picture was finally found hidden away in the church of Santa Maria Maggiore in Bergamo. The acknowledgements of individual contributors follow.

B. Bascle, A. Blake and J. Morris
The authors gratefully acknowledge the financial support of EPSRC and the Oxford Metrics company.

C. Bregler, S.M. Omohundro, M. Covell, M. Slaney, S. Ahmad, D.A. Forsyth, J.A. Feldman
The authors would like to thank Yochai Konig, Jitendra Malik, Nelson Morgan, Jianbo Shi, Alex Waibel and many others in the Berkeley Speech and Vision Group, the CMU and Univ. Karlsruhe Interact group, and Interval Research for support and helpful discussions.

R. Cipolla and N.J. Hollinghurst
The authors gratefully acknowledge the financial support of EPSRC, and the donation of a robot manipulator by the Olivetti Research Laboratory, Cambridge and the collaboration of Mr. Masaaki Fukumoto and Dr. Yasuhito Suenaga of the NTT Human Interface Laboratories, Japan.

J. Cassell
Some of this work is carried out, and all of it is informed by my interactions with Mark Steedman, Norm Badler, Catherine Pelachaud,

and the students of the Gesture-Jack group at the University of Pennsylvania, and Scott Prevost, Kris Thórisson, Hannes Vilhjalmsson, and the other members of the Gesture and Narrative Language group at the MIT Media Laboratory.

A. Gee and R. Cipolla

The authors are grateful for the help of Costi Perricos. Andrew Gee acknowledges the financial support of Queens' College, Cambridge, where he was a Research Fellow while undertaking this work.

C. Maggioni and B. Kämmerer

The authors wish to thank all people that contributed to the GestureComputer project: Subutai Ahmad, Daniel Goryn, Holger Kattner, Uwe Kusch, Christoph Pomper, Hans Rottger, Rolf Schuster, Sven Schroter and Brigitte Wirtz.

K. Mase

The Human Reader project was carried out at NTT Human Interface Laboratories in collaboration with Yasuhito Suenaga, Yasuhiko Watanabe, Masaaki Fukumoto, Atsushi Satoh and many other NTT researchers. The author would like to thank Alex Pentland for his support of lip reading research, which became a major thrust of this research work. The author would also like to thank Ryouhei Nakatsu and other ATR MIC members for their support and discussions.

E. Di Bernardo L. Goncalves and P. Perona

This work is supported in part by the California Institute of Technology; a fellowship from the "Ing.A.Gini" foundation; the Office of Naval Research grant ONR NOOO14-93-1-0990; an NSF National Young Investigator Award; the Center for Neuromorphic Systems Engineering as a part of the National Science Foundation Engineering Research Center Program; and by the California Trade and Commerce Agency, Office of Strategic Technology.

A.P. Pentland

This research was supported by ONR, ARL, and ARPA under the MURI and FERET contracts, and by BT (British Telecom) and Texas Instruments. Portions of this text have appeared in Scientific American [235].

C.J. Taylor, A. Lanitis, T.F. Cootes, G. Edwards & T. Ahmad

Most of the work described was supported by a University of Manchester Research Studendship and an ORS award to Andreas

Lanitis. Further research in the area is supported by EPSRC and British Telecom. Discussions with Professor J.F.W. Deakin and Dr. J.F. Whittaker from the Dept. of Psychiatry, Manchester Royal Infirmary, UK, have been particularly useful for the expression recognition experiments. We are grateful to all volunteers who provided face and hand images for our experiments.

K. Waters, J. Rehg, M. Loughlin, S.B. Kang and D. Terzopoulos
The authors would like to thank Tamer Rabie of the University of Toronto for making his color-based object tracking software available for our use.

J.J. Weng and Y. Cui
The authors would like to thank Dan Swets and Shaoyun Chen for providing us the programs for MEF and MDF computation. Thanks also go to Yu Zhong, Kal Rayes, Doug Neal, and Valerie Bolster for making themselves available for the experiments. This work was supported in part by NSF grant No. IRI 9410741 and ONR grant No. N00014-95-1-0637.

M. Yachida and Y.Iwai
We have summarized recent research projects (listed in the bibiliograhpy) in the Man-machine interaction group of Laboratories of Image Science & Technology and Computer vision & image media group of Department of Systems Engineering, Osaka University. We thank Haiyuan Wu, Takeshi Fukumoto, Satoshi Kimura, Ken Watanabe, Takahiro Watanabe, and Tsutomu Yabuuchi for their original contributions [304, 177, 321, 73, 72, 303] and Nels Benson for checking the English.

Y. Yacoob, L. Davis, M. Black, D. Gavrila, T. Horprasert and C. Morimoto
The authors gratefully acknowledge the support of the Defense Advanced Research Projects Agency (DARPA Order No. C635) under Contract N00014-95-1-0521.

Bibliography

[1] Adjoudani, A. and Benoit, C. (1996). On the integration of auditory and visual parameters in an HMM-based automatic speech recognition. In *NATO Advanced Study Institute on Speechreading by Man and Machine*, pages 461–472.

[2] Aggarwal, J. and Huang, T. (Editors). (1994). *Proc. IEEE Workshop on Motion of Non-Rigid and Articulated Objects*, Austin (TX), (November), IEEE Computer Society Press.

[3] Ahmad, S. and Tresp, V. (1993). Classification with missing and uncertain inputs. In *Proc. Int. Conf. on Neural Networks*, 3:1949-1954.

[4] Ahmad, S. (1994). A usable real-time 3D hand tracker. In *Proc. IEEE 28th Asilomar Conference on Signals, Systems and Computer*, (November), pages 1257–1261.

[5] Ahmad, T., Taylor, C.J., Lanitis, A. and Cootes, T.F. (1995). Recognising Hand Gestures Using Statistical Shape Models. In *Proc. 6th British Machine Vision Conference*, Birmingham, (September), volume 2, pages 403–412.

[6] Akamatsu, S., Sasaki, T., Fukamachi, H., Masui, N. and Suenaga, Y. (1992). An accurate and robust face identification scheme. In *Proc. IAPR Int. Conf. on Pattern Recognition*, Hague, pages 217–220.

[7] Akita, K. (1984). Image sequence analysis of real world human motion. *Pattern Recognition*, 17(1):73–83.

[8] Alibali, M.W., Flevares, L. and Goldin-Meadow, S. (1994). Going beyond what children say to assess their knowledge. Manuscript, Department of Psychology, University of Chicago.

[9] Aloimonos Y., (Editor). (1993). *Active Perception*, Lawrence Erlbaum Associates, Hillside (NJ).

317

[10] Argyle, M. and Cook, M. (1985). *Gaze and Mutual Gaze*, Cambridge University Press, Cambridge, England.

[11] Atkeson, C.G. and Hollerbach, J.M. (1985). Kinematic features of unconstrained vertical arm movements. *Journal of Neuroscience*, (September), 5(9):2318–2330.

[12] Ayer, S. and Sawhney, H.S. (1995). Layered representation of motion video using robust maximum-likelihood estimation of mixture models and mdl encoding. In *Proc. IEEE Fifth Int. Conf. on Computer Vision*, Cambridge (MA),(June), pages 777–784.

[13] Azarbayejani, A. and A. Pentland, A. (1996). Real-time self-calibrating stereo person tracking using 3D shape estimation from blob features. In *Proc. IAPR Int. Conf. on Pattern Recognition*, Vienna, (August), pages 136–145.

[14] Azarbayejani, A., Starner, T., Horowitz, B. and Pentland, A. (1993). Visually controlled graphics. *IEEE Transactions on Pattern Analysis and Machine Intelligence*, 15(6):602–605.

[15] Azarbayejani, A., Wren, C. and Pentland, A. (1996). Real-Time 3D Tracking of the Human Body. In *Proc. ImageCom96*, Bordeaux, France, (May).

[16] Bajcsy, R. (1988). Active Perception, In *Proc. of the IEEE*, 76(8):996–1005.

[17] Ballard, D. and Brown, C. (1982). *Computer Vision*, Prentice-Hall, Englewood (NJ).

[18] Barwise, J. and Perry, J. (1986). *Situation Semantics*, MIT Press, Cambridge (MA).

[19] Barnett, S. (1990). *Matrices: Methods and Applications*, Oxford University Press.

[20] Bartels, R.H., Beatty, J.C. and Barsky, B.A. (1987). *An Introduction to Splines for use in Computer Graphics and Geometric Modeling*, Morgan Kaufmann.

[21] Basu, S., Casey, M.A., Gardner, W., Azarbayejani, A., and Pentland, A. (1996). Vision-Steered Audio for Interactive Environments. In *Proc. ImageCom96*, Bordeaux, France, (May).

[22] Baudel, T. and Beaudouin-Lafan, M. (1993). Charade: remote control of objects with freehand gestures. *Communications of the ACM*, 36(7):28 35.

[23] Baumberg, A. and Hogg, D. (1994). An efficient method for contour tracking using active shape models. In *Proc. IEEE*

Workshop on Motion of Non-Rigid and Articulated Objects, Austin (TX), pages 194–199.

[24] Beckmann, N., Kriegel, H., Schneider, R. and Seeger, B. (1990). The r^* –tree: an efficient and robust access method for points and rectangles. In *Proc. ACM SIGMOD*, pages 322–331.

[25] Beier, T. and Neely, S. (1992). Feature-based image metamorphosis. *Computer Graphics*, 26(2):35–42.

[26] Benoit, C., Guiard-Marigny, T. and Adjoudani, A. (1994). A 3D model of the lips for visual speech synthesis. In *Proc. of the Second ESCA/IEEE Workshop on Speech Synthesis*.

[27] Bers, J. (1996). A body model server for human motion capture and representation. *Presence:Teleoperators and Virtual Environments*, 5(4):381–392.

[28] Besl, P.J. and Mckay, N.D. (1992). A method for registration of 3D shapes. *Transactions. Pattern Analysis and Machine Intelligence*, 14:239–256.

[29] Beymer, D., Shashua, A. and Poggio, T. (1993). Example based image analysis and synthesis. *MIT. A.I. Memo No. 1431*, (November).

[30] Beyer, H. (1992). Accurate Calibration of CCD Cameras. In *Proc. IEEE Conf. on Computer Vision and Pattern Recognition*, Champaign, Illinois, pages 96–101.

[31] Bichsel, M. (Editor), (1995). *Proc. Int. Workshop on Automatic Face and Gesture Recognition*, Zurich, Switzerland, (June).

[32] Bichsel, M. (1994). Segmenting Simply Connected Moving Objects in a Static Scene. *Transactions. on Pattern Analysis and Machine Intelligence*, (November), 16(11):1138–1142.

[33] Bichsel, M. (1994). Illumination Invariant Segmentation of Simply Connected Moving Objects. In *Proc. Fifth British Machine Vision Conference*, York, England, (September), pages 459–468.

[34] Bichsel, M. and Pentland, A. (1994). Human Face Recognition and the Face Image Set's Topology. *CVGIP:Image Processing*, 59(2):254–261.

[35] Bichsel, M. (1995). Human Face Recognition: From Views to Models - From Models to Views. In *Proc. Int. Workshop on Automatic Face and Gesture Recognition*, Zurich, (June), pages 59–64.

[36] Birdwhistell, R.L. (1970). *Kinesics and Context: Essays on Body Motion Communication*, Univ. of Pennsylvania Press, Philadelphia.

[37] Black, M.J. and Anandan, P. (1993). A Framework for the Robust Estimation of Optical Flow. In *Proc. IEEE Fourth Int. Conf. on Computer Vision*, Berlin, Germany, (May), 231–236.

[38] Black, M. and Yacoob, Y. (1995). Tracking and recognizing rigid and non-rigid facial motions using local parametric models of image motion. In *Proc. IEEE Fifth Int. Conf. on Computer Vision*, Cambridge (MA), (June), 374–381.

[39] Blake, A., Curwen, R. and Zisserman, A. (1993). A framework for spatiotemporal control in the tracking of visual contours. *Int. Journal of Computer Vision*, 11(2):127–145.

[40] Blake, A. and Isard, M. (1994). 3D position, attitude and shape input using video tracking of hands and lips. In *Proc. ACM SIGGRAPH*, pages 185–192.

[41] Blake, A., Isard, M. and Reynard, D. (1995). Learning to track the visual motion of contours. In *Artificial Intelligence*, 78:101–134.

[42] Blumberg B. (1994). Building Believable Animals. In *Proc. AAAI Spring Symposium on Believable Agents*, Palo Alto (CA), Morgan Kaufmann, San Mateo (CA), (March).

[43] Blumberg B., (1994). Action-Selection in Hamsterdam: Lessons from Ethology, In *Proc. Third Int. Conf. on the Simulation of Adaptive Behavior*, MIT Press, Cambridge (MA), (August).

[44] Bobick, A. and Wilson, A. (1995). A state-based technique for the summarization and recognition of gesture, In *Proc. IEEE Fifth Int. Conf. on Computer Vision*, Cambridge (MA), (June), pages 382–388.

[45] Bolinger, D. (1983). Intonation and gesture. *American Speech*, 58(2):156–174.

[46] Bolt, R.A. (1987). The integrated multi-modal interface. *Transactions. of the Insititute of Electronics, Information and Communication Engineers (Japan)*, J70-D(11):2017–2025.

[47] Bolt, R.A. (1980). Put-that-there: voice and gesture at the graphics interface. *Computer Graphics*, 14(3):262–270.

[48] Bolt, R.A. and Herranz, E. (1992). Two-Handed Gesture in Multi-Modal Natural Dialog. In *Proc. ACM SIGGRAPH Symposium on User Interface Software and Technology*,

Monterey, California, ACM Press, New York, (November), pages 7–14.

[49] Bonvillian, J., Nelson, K. and Charrow, V. (1976). Language and language related skills in deaf and hearing children. In *Sign Language Studies*, 12:211–250.

[50] Bookstein, F.L. (1989). Principal Warps: Thin-Plate Splines and the Decomposition of Deformations. *IEEE Transactions on Pattern Analysis and Machine Intelligence*, 11(6):567–585.

[51] Borghese, N.A. Di Rienzo, M. Ferrigno, G. and Pedotti, A. (1991). Elite: A goal oriented vision system for moving objects detection. *Robotica*, 9:275–282.

[52] Bornstein, H. and Saulnier, K. (1989). *The Signed English Starter*, Clerc Books, Gallaudet University Press, Washington, D.C..

[53] Bourlard, H.A. and Morgan, N. (1993). *Connectionist Speech Recognition, A Hybrid Approach*, Kluwer Academic Publishers.

[54] Bregler, C. (1996). Probabilistic recognition of human actions. Technical Report http://www.cs/bregler/actions.html, Computer Science Division, University of California, Berkeley.

[55] Bregler, C., Hild, H., Manke, S. and Waibel, A. (1993). Improving connected letter recognition by lipreading. In *Proc. IEEE Int. Conf. Acoustics, Speech, and Signal Processing*, volume 1, Minneapolis, pages 557–560.

[56] Bregler, C. and Omohundro, S.M. (1995). Nonlinear manifold learning for visual speech recognition. In *Proc. IEEE Fifth Int. Conf. on Computer Vision*, Cambridge (MA), (June), pages 494–499.

[57] Bregler, C. and Omohundro, S.M. (1994). Surface learning with applications to lipreading. In J.D. Cowan, G. Tesauro, and J. Alspector, (Editors), *Advances in Neural Information Processing Systems*, volume 6, Morgan Kaufmann, pages 43–50.

[58] Bregler, C. and Omohundro, S.M. (1995). Nonlinear image interpolation using manifold learning. In *Advances in Neural Information Processing Systems*, MIT Press, Cambridge (MA), volume 7, pages 973–980.

[59] Breiman, L., Friedman, J.H., Olshen, R.A. and Stone, C.J. (1993). *Classification and Regression Trees*, Chapman and Hall, New York.

[60] Brooke, M.N. (1996). Talking Heads and Speech Recognisers That Can See: The Computer Processing of Visual Speech

Signals. In *Speechreading by Humans and Machines, NATO ASI.*, Edited by Stork and Hennecke, Springer, pages 351–372.

[61] Brown, J.S. (1856). *A Vocabulary of Mute Signs*, Baton Rouge, Louisiana.

[62] Brunelli, R. and Poggio, T. (1993). Face recognition: features versus templates. *IEEE Transactions on Pattern Analysis and Machine Intelligence*, (October), 15(10):1042–1052.

[63] Bucy, R.S. (1965). Non-linear filtering theory. *IEEE Transactions Automation and Control*, AC-10:198.

[64] Bull, P.E. (1987). *Posture and Gesture*, Pergamon Press.

[65] Campbell, L.W. and Bobick, A.F. (1995). Recognition of human body motion using phase space constraints. In *Proc. IEEE Fifth Int. Conf. on Computer Vision*, Cambridge, pages 624–630.

[66] Carpenter, R.H.S. (1972). *Movements of the Eyes*, Pion Limited.

[67] Cassell, J., McNeill, D. and McCullough, K.E. (1996). Speech-gesture mismatches: evidence for one underlying representation of linguistic and nonlinguistic information. *Cognition*, (in press).

[68] Cassell, J., Pelachaud, C., Badler, N.I., Steedman, M., Achorn, B., Beckett, T., Douville, B., Prevost, S. and Stone, M. (1994). Animated Conversation: Rule-based generation of facial expression, gesture and spoken intonation for multiple conversational agents. In *Proc. ACM SIGGRAPH*, Orlando, (FL.), pages 413–420.

[69] Cassell, J., Steedman, M., Badler, N., Pelachaud, C., Stone, M., Douville, B., Prevost, S., and Achorn, B. (1994). Modeling the interaction between gesture and speech. In *Proc. Sixteenth Annual Conf. Cognitive Science Society*, Lawrence Erlbaum Associates, Hillside (NJ), pages 153–158.

[70] Chazelle, B. (1985). How to search in history. In *Inf. Control*, 64:77–99, 1985.

[71] Chellapa, R., Wilson, C.L. and Sirohey, S. (1995). Human and Machine Recognition of Faces: A Survey. *Proc. of the IEEE*, 83(5):705–740.

[72] Chen, Q., Fukumoto, T., Wu, H. and Yachida, M. (1995). Face observation using an active camera. In *Proc. Int. Conf. on Human Computer Interaction*, (July), pages 553–558.

[73] Chen, Q., Wu, H. and Yachida, M. (1995). Face detection by fuzzy pattern matching. In *Proc. IEEE Fifth Int. Conf. on Computer Vision*, Cambridge (MA), (June), pages 591–596.

[74] Cho, K. and Dunn, S.M. (1994). Learning shape classes, In *IEEE Transactions on Pattern Analysis and Machine Intelligence*, 16:882–888.

[75] Choi, C.S., Harashima, H. and Takebe, T. (1990). 3-Dimensional Facial Model-Based Description and Synthesis of Facial Expressions (in Japanese). *Transactions of the Insititute of Electronics, Information and Communication Engineers (Japan)*, (July), J73-A(7):1270–1280.

[76] Church, R.B. and Goldin-Meadow, S. (1986). The mismatch between gesture and speech as an index of transitional knowledge. *Cognition*, 23:43–71.

[77] Cipolla, R. and Blake, A. (1992). Surface shape from the deformation of apparent contours. *Int. Journal of Computer Vision*, 9(2):83–112.

[78] Cipolla, R. and Hollinghurst, N.J. (1996). Human–robot interface by pointing with uncalibrated stereo vision. *Image and Vision Computing*, 14(3):171–178.

[79] Cipolla, R. and Hollinghurst, N.J. (1997). Visually guided grasping in unstructured enviroments. *Robotics and Autonomous Systems*, 19:337–346.

[80] Cipolla, R., Okamoto, Y. and Kuno, Y. (1993). Robust structure from motion using motion parallax. In *Proc. IEEE Fourth Int. Conf. on Computer Vision*, Berlin, (May), pages 374–382.

[81] Cohen, A.A. (1977). The communicative functions of hand illustrators. *Journal of Communication*, 27(4):54–63.

[82] Cohen, A.A. and Harrison, R.P. (1973). Intentionality in the use of hand illustrators in face-to-face communication situations. *Journal of Personality and Social Psychology*, 28:276–279.

[83] Cohen, M.M. and Massaro, D.W. (1993). Modeling coarticulation in synthetic visual speech, synthesis of visible speech. In *Models and Techniques in Computer Animation*, (N. M. Thalmann, and D. Thalmann (Eds.)).

[84] Colombo, C., Andronico, S. and Dario, P. (1995). Prototype of a vision-based gaze-driven man-machine interface. In *Proc. Int. Conf. on Intelligent Robots and Systems, Pittsburgh*, (August), pages 188–192.

[85] Colombo, C. and Crowley, J.L. (1996). Uncalibrated visual tasks via linear interaction. In *Proc. 4th European Conference on Computer Vision (ECCV'96)*, Cambridge, England, (April), pages 583–592.

[86] Colombo, C. and Del Bimbo, A. (1997). Interacting through eyes. *Robotics and Autonomous Systems*, (in press).

[87] Cootes, T.F. and Taylor, C.J. (1992). Active shape models. In *Proc. Third British Machine Vision Conference*, Leeds, England, pages 265–275.

[88] Cootes, T.F. and Taylor, C.J. (1996). Locating objects of varying shape using statistical feature detectors. In *Proc. 4th European Conf. on Computer Vision*, Cambridge, 465–474.

[89] Cootes, T.F., Taylor, C.J. and Lanitis, A. (1994). Active Shape Models: Evaluation of a Multi-Resolution Method For Improving Image Search. In *Proc. of the Fifth British Machine Vision Conference*, York, volume 1, pages 327–336.

[90] Cootes, T.F., Taylor, C.J., Cooper, D.H. and Graham, J. (1995). Active Shape Models – Their Training And Application. *Computer Vision Graphics and Image Understanding*, 61(1): 38–59.

[91] Cottrell, G.W., Munro, P.W. and Zipser, D. (1987). Image compression by back propagation: A demonstration of extensional programming, In N.E. Sharkey (Editor), *In Advances in cognitive science*, Chichester, England, Ellis Horwood, vol. 2, pages 113–137.

[92] Cottrell, G.W. and Metcalfe, J. (1991). EMPATH: Face, Gender and Emotion Recognition Using Holons. *Advances in Neural Information Processing Systems*, volume 3, pages 564–571.

[93] Coze, P. (1980). *Quick Sketching*, Walter Foster Art Books, California, 1980.

[94] Craw, I. and Cameron, P. (1992). Face Recognition by Computer. *Proc. Third British Machine Vision Conference*, Leeds, pages 489–507.

[95] Craw, I., Tock, D. and Bennett, A. (1992). Finding Face Features. In *Proc. Second European Conference on Computer Vision*, Santa Margherita Ligure, Italy, pages 92–96.

[96] Cui, Y. and Weng, J. (1996). Hand segmentation using learning-based prediction and verification for hand-sign recognition. In *Proc. IEEE Conf. Computer Vision and Pattern Recog.*, San Francisco, pages 88–93.

[97] Cui, Y. and Weng, J. (1996). Hand sign recognition from intensity image sequences with complex backgrounds. In *Proc. Second Int. Conf. on Automatic Face and Gesture Recognition*, Vermont, pages 259–264.

[98] Cui, Y. and Weng, J. (1995). A learning-based prediction-and-verification segmentation scheme for hand sign image sequences. Technical Report CPS-95-43, Computer Science Department, Michigan State University, (December).

[99] Cui, Y., Swets, D. and Weng, J. (1995). Learning-Based Hand Sign Recognition Using SHOSLIF-M. In *Proc. IEEE Fifth Int. Conf. Computer Vision*, Cambridge (MA), pages 631–636.

[100] Curwen, R. and Blake, A. (1992). Dynamic contours: Real-time active splines. In A. Blake and A. Yuille, (Editors), *Active Vision*, MIT Press, chapter 3, pages 39–57.

[101] Dalton, B., Kaucic,R. and Blake, A. (1995). Automatic speechreading using dynamic contours. In *Proc. NATO ASI Conference on Speechreading by Man and Machine: Models, Systems and Applications*. NATO Scientific Affairs Division, (September).

[102] Darrel, T. and Pentland, A. (1993). Space-time gestures. In *Proc. IEEE Conf. Computer Vision and Pattern Recognition*, New York, (June), pages 335–340.

[103] Davey, G., (1989). *Ecological Learning Theory*, Routledge Inc., London.

[104] Davis, J. and Shah, M. (1994). Visual gesture recognition, In *IEE Proc. Vis. Image Signal Process*, (April), 141(2):101–106.

[105] Dempster, A.P. Laird, N.M. and Rubin, D.B. (1977). Maximum likelihood from incomplete data via the EM algorithm. *Journal of the Royal Statistical Society*, 39(B):1–38.

[106] Desain, P. (1989). The quantization of musical time: A connectionist approach. *Computer Music Journal*, 13(3):56–66.

[107] Dickmanns, E.D. and V. Graefe, V. (1988). Applications of dynamic monocular machine vision. *Machine Vision and Applications*, 1:241–261.

[108] Digital Equipment Corporation. *DECtalk Programmers Reference Manual*.

[109] Dobkin, D.P. and Lipton, R.J. (1976). Multidimensional searching problems. In *SIAM J. Comput.*, 5:181–186.

[110] Downton, A.C. and Drouet, H. (1991). Image analysis for model-based sign language coding In *Progress in image analysis and processing II: Proc. Sixth Int. Conf. on Image Analysis and Processing*, pages 79–89.

[111] Duda, R.O. and Hart, P.E. (1973). *Pattern Classification and Scene Analysis*, John Wiley and Sons, New York.

[112] Duncan, S. (1972). Some signals and rules for taking speaking turns in conversations. *Journal of Personality and Social Psychology*, 23(2):283–292.

[113] Eccles, J., (1989). Evolution of the Brain: Creation of the Self. Routledge and Kegan Paul, London.

[114] Efron, D. (1941). *Gesture and Environment*, King's Crown Press, New York.

[115] Ekman, P. (1977). Biological and cultural contributions to body and facial movement. In J. Blacking, (Editor), *The Anthropology of the Body*, Academic Press Inc., New York, pages 39–84.

[116] Ekman, P. and Friesen, W.F. (1975). *Unmasking the Face*, Consulting Psychologist Press, Inc., CA.

[117] Ekman, P. and Friesen, W.F. (1969). The repertoire of nonverbal behavioral categories – origins, usage, and coding. *Semiotica*, 1:49–98.

[118] Elman, J.L. and Zipser, D. (1988). Discovering the hidden structure of speech. *Journal of the Acoustical Society of America*, 83:1615–1626.

[119] Essa, I. and Pentland, A., (1994). A Vision System for Observing and Extracting Facial Action Parameters. In *Proc. IEEE Conf. on Computer Vision and Pattern Recognition*, Seattle, WA., (June), pages 76–83.

[120] Essa, I., and Pentland, A. (1995). Facial Expression Recognition Using a Dynamic Model and Motion Energy. In *Proc. IEEE Fifth Int. Conf. on Computer Vision*, Cambridge (MA), (June), pages 360–367.

[121] Etoh, M., Tomono, A. and Kishino, F. (1991). Stereo-based description by generalized cylinder complexes from occluding contours, In *Systems and Computers in Japan*, 22(12):79–89.

[122] Farkas, L.G. (1994). *Anthropometry of the Head and Face*. Second edition, Raven Press.

[123] Featherstone R., (1987). *Robot Dynamics Algorithms*, Kluwer Academic Publishers, Boston.

[124] Finn, E.K. and Montgomery, A.A. (1988). Automatic optically based recognition of speech. *Pattern Recognition Letters*, 8(3):159–164.

[125] Fischler, M.A. and Bolles, R.C. (1981). Random sample consensus: A paradigm for model fitting with applications to image analysis and automated cartography. *Communications of the ACM*, 24(6):381–395.

[126] Foley, J.D. (1987). Interfaces for advanced computing. *Scientific American*, 257:7.

[127] Foley, J., van Dam, A., Feiner, S. and Hughes, J. (1990). *Computer Graphics: Principles and Practice*, Addison-Wesley.

[128] Freeman, W. and Weissman,C. (1995). Television control by hand gestures. In *Proc. Int. Workshop on Automatic Face and Gesture Recognition*, Zurich, Switzerland, (June), pages 179–183.

[129] Freeman, W.T. and Roth, M. (1994). Orientation histograms for hand gesture recognition. Technical Report 94–03a, Mitsubishi Electric Research Labs., Cambridge (MA).

[130] Fukumoto, M., Mase, K. and Suenaga, Y. (1994). Finger-pointer: Pointing interface by image processing. *Comput. and Graphics.*,(May), 18(5):633–642.

[131] Gavrila, D.M. and Davis, L.S. (1996). 3D model-based tracking of humans in action: a multi-view approach. In *Proc. IEEE Conf. on Computer Vision and Pattern Recognition*, San Francisco, pages 73–80.

[132] Gee, A. and Cipolla, R. (1994). Determining the gaze of faces in images. *Image and Vision Computing*, 12(10):639–647.

[133] Gee, A. and Cipolla, R. (1996). Fast visual tracking by temporal consensus. *Image and Vision Computing*, 14(2):105–114.

[134] Gennery, D. (1992). Visual tracking of known three-dimensional objects. *Int. Journal of Computer Vision*, 7(3):243–270.

[135] Goldin-Meadow, S., Wein, D. and Chang, C. (1992). Assessing knowledge through gesture: Using children's hands to read their minds. *Cognition and Instruction*, 9(3):201–219.

[136] Goldschen, A.J. (1993). *Continuous Automatic Speech Recognition by Lipreading*, PhD thesis, Dept. Electrical Engineering and Computer Science, George Washington University.

[137] Goncalves, L., Di Bernardo, E., Ursella, E. and Perona. P. (1995). Monocular tracking of the human arm in 3D, In *Fifth Proc. IEEE Fifth Int. Conf. on Computer Vision*, Cambridge (MA), (June), pages 764–770.

[138] Goodwin, C. and Duranti, A. (1992). Rethinking context: An introduction. *Rethinking Context*, Cambridge University Press, Cambridge, England, pages 1–42.

[139] Guttman, A. (1984). R-trees: a dynamic index structure for spatial searching. In *Proc. ACM SIGMOD*, pages 905–910.

[140] Hajicova, E. and Sgall, P. (1987). The ordering principle. *Journal of Pragmatics*, 11:435–454.

[141] Halliday, M. (1967). *Intonation and Grammar in British English*, Mouton, The Hague.

[142] Hammond, K.J. (1989). *Case-Based Planning*, Academic Press, San Diego, 1989.

[143] Harris, C. (1992). Tracking with rigid models. In A. Blake and A. Yuille, (Editors), *Active Vision*, MIT Press, pages 59–74.

[144] Hauptmann, A.G. (1989). Speech and Gesture for Graphic Image Manipulation, In *Proc. Computer Human Interaction*, Austin, ACM Press, New York, pages 241–245.

[145] Heap, A. (1995). Robust Real-time Tracking and Gesture Recognition Using Smart Snakes. *Internal Report, Olivetti Research Ltd*, Cambridge.

[146] Hermansky, H., Morgan, N., Bayya, A. and Kohn, P. (1992). Rasta-plp speech analysis technique. In *Proc. IEEE Int. Conf. on Acoustics, Speech, and Signal Processing*, San Francisco, I:121–124.

[147] Hinrichs, E. and Polanyi, L. (1986). Pointing the way: A unified treatment of referential gesture in interactive contexts. In A. Farley, P. Farley and K.E. McCullough (Eds.), *Proc. of the Parasession of Pragmatics and Grammatical Theory at the Twenty-Second Regional Meeting of the Chicago Linguistics Society*, Chicago Linguistics Society, Chicago, pages 298–314.

[148] Hollinghurst, N.J. and Cipolla, R. (1994). Uncalibrated stereo hand–eye coordination. *Image and Vision Computing*, 12(3):187–192.

[149] Horprasert, T., Yacoob, Y. and Davis, L.S. (1996). Computing 3D Head Orientation from a Monocular Image Sequence. In *Proc. Second Int. Conf. on Face and Gesture Recognition*, Vermont.

[150] Hu, M.K. (1962). Visual pattern recognition by moment invariants. *IRE Transactions on Information Theory*, IT-8:179–187.

[151] Huang, T.S. and Pavlovic, V.I. (1995). Hand gesture modeling, analysis, and synthesis, In *Proc. Int. Workshop on Automatic Face and Gesture Recognition*, pages 73–79.

[152] Hutchinson, T.E. (1993). Computers that sense eye position on the display. *IEEE Computer*, 26(7):65–67.

[153] Hutchinson, T.E., White, K.P., Martin, W.N., Reichert, K.C. and Frey, L. (1989). Human-computer interaction using eye-gaze

input. *IEEE Transactions on System, Man and Cybernetics*, (November/December), 19(6):1527–1533.

[154] Huttenlocher, D.P. and Ullman, S. (1990). Recognizing solid objects by alignment with an image. *Int. Journal of Computer Vision*, 5(2):195–212.

[155] Ikeuchi, K. and Hebert, M. (1990). Task oriented vision. In *Proc. of DARPA Image Understanding Workshop*, Pittsburgh, (September), pages 497–507.

[156] Isard, M. and Blake, A. (1996). Contour tracking by stochastic propagation of conditional density. In *Proc. Fourth European Conference on Computer Vision*, Cambridge, volume 1, pages 343–356.

[157] Jacob, R.J.K. (1993). What you look at is what you get. *IEEE Computer*, 26(7):65–66.

[158] Jazwinski, A.H. (1970). *Stochastic Processes and Filtering Theory*, Academic Press.

[159] Jepson, A. and Black, M.J. (1993). Mixture models for optical flow computation. In *Proc. IEEE Conf. Computer Vision Pattern Recognition*, New York, pages 760–761.

[160] Jones, M., and Poggio, T., (1995). Model-Based Matching of Line Drawings by Linear Combinations of Prototypes. In *IEEE. Proc. Fifth Int. Conf. Computer Vision*, Cambridge, MA, (June), pages 531–536.

[161] Jordan, M.I. and Jacobs, R.A. (1994). Hierarchical mixtures of experts and the EM algorithm. *Neural Computation*, (March), 6(2):181–214.

[162] Kakadiaris, I. and Metaxas, D. (1995). 3D Human Body Model Acquisition from Multiple Views. In *Proc. IEEE Fifth Int. Conf. on Computer Vision*, Cambridge (MA), pages 618–623.

[163] Kakadiaris, I. and Metaxas, D. (1996). Model based estimation of 3D human motion with occlusion based on active multi-viewpoint selection. In *Proc. IEEE Conf. on Computer Vision and Pattern Recognition*, San Francisco, pages 81–87.

[164] Kalman, R.E. (1960). A new approach to linear filtering and prediction problems. *Transactions. of the American Society of Mechanical Engineers – Journal of basic engineering*, 35–45.

[165] Kämmerer, B. and Maggioni, C. (1995). GestureComputer: Research and Practice, In *Proc. Interface to real and virtual worlds*, Montpellier, France, (June), pages 251–260.

[166] Kang, S.B., Johnson, A. and Szeliski, R. (1995). Extraction of concise and realistic 3-D models from real data. Technical Report 95/7, Digital Equipment Corporation, Cambridge Research Lab, (October).

[167] Kang, S.B. and Szeliski, R. (1996). 3D scene data recovery using omnidirectional multibaseline stereo. In *Proc. IEEE Conf. on Computer Vision and Pattern Recognition*, San Francisco, (June), pages 364–370.

[168] Kang, S.B., Webb, J., Zitnick, L. and Kanade, T. (1995). A multibaseline stereo system with active illumination and real-time image acquisition. In *Proc. IEEE Fifth Int. Conf. on Computer Vision* , Cambridge (MA), (June), pages 88–93.

[169] Kass, M., Witkin, A. and Terzopoulus. D. (1987). Snakes: Active contour models. *Int. Journal of Computer Vision*, 1(4):321–331.

[170] Katayose, H., Imai, M. and Inokuchi, S. (1988). Sentiment extraction in music. In *Proceeding of Int. Conf. on Pattern Recognition*, Rome, (November), pages 1083–1090.

[171] Katayose, H. and Inokuchi, S. (1990). Intelligent music transcription system. *Journal of Japanese Society for Artificial Intelligence*, 5(1):59–66 (in Japanese).

[172] Kaucic, R., Dalton, B. and Blake, A. (1996). Real-time lip tracking for audio-visual speech recognition applications. In *Proc. Fourth European Conference on Computer Vision* , Cambridge, England, (April), pages 376–387.

[173] Kendon, A. (1993). Gestures as illocutionary and discourse structure markers in southern Italian conversation. *Linguistic Society of America Symposium on Gesture in the Context of Talk*, Los Angeles, (January).

[174] Kendon, A. (1980). Gesticulation and speech: two aspects of the process. In M.R. Key (Editor), *The Relation Between Verbal and Nonverbal Communication*, Mouton, The Hague.

[175] Kendon, A. (1972). Some relationships between body motion and speech. In A.W. Siegman and B. Pope (Eds.), *Studies in Dyadic Communication*, Pergamon Press, New York, pages 177–210.

[176] Kervrann, C. and Heitz, F. (1994). A hierarchical statistical framework for the segmentation of deformable objects in image sequences, In *Proc. IEEE Conf. on Computer Vision and Pattern Recognition*, pages 724–728.

[177] Kimura, S. Lee, C. and Yachida, M. (1995). Extended facial expression recognition using potential net. In *Proc. Asian*

Conference on Computer Vision, Singapore, (December), pages III:728–732.

[178] Kirby, M. and Sirovich, L. (1990). Application of the Karhumen-Loeve procedure for the Characterization of Human Faces. *IEEE Transactions on Pattern Analysis and Machine Intelligence*, 12(1):103–108.

[179] Kirby, M., Weisser, F. and Dangelmayr, A. (1993). A model problem in represention of digitial image sequences. *Pattern Recognition*, 26(1):63–72.

[180] Koch, R. (1993). Dynamic 3D scene analysis through synthesis feedback control. *IEEE Transactions on Pattern Analysis and Machine Intelligence*, 15(6):556–568.

[181] Koons, D.B., Sparrell, C.J. and Thórisson, K.R. (1993). Integrating simultaneous input from speech, gaze and hand gestures. In M.T. Maybury (Editor), *Intelligent Multi-Media Interfaces*, AAAI Press/MIT Press, Cambridge (MA), pages 252–276.

[182] Knuth, D. (1973). *The Art of Computer Programming III: Sorting and Searching*, Addison-Wesley, Reading (MA).

[183] Krauss, R., Morrel-Samuels, P. and Colasante, C. (1991). Do conversational hand gestures communicate? *Journal of Personality and Social Psychology*, 61(5):743–754.

[184] Krueger, M.W. (1983). *Artificial Reality*, Addison-Wesley.

[185] Krueger, M.W. (1990). *Artificial Reality II*, Addison Wesley.

[186] Kuch, J.J. and Huang, T.S. (1995). Vision based hand modeling and tracking for virtual teleconferencing and telecollaboration. In *Proc. IEEE Fifth Int. Conf. on Computer Vision*, Cambridge (MA), (June), pages 666–671.

[187] Lacquaniti, F., Soechting, J.F. and Terzuolo, S.A. (1986). Path constraints on point-to-point arm movements in three-dimensional space. *Neuroscience*, 17(2):313–324.

[188] Lades, M., Vorbruggen, J.C., Buhmann,J. Lange, J., Malsburg, C., Wurtz, R.P. and Konen, W. (1993). Distortion Invariant Object Recognition in the Dynamic Link Architecture. *IEEE Transactions on Computers*, 42(3):300–311.

[189] Lanitis, A., Taylor, C.J. and Cootes, T.F. (1994). Automatic Identification of Human faces Using Flexible Appearance Models. *Image and Vision Computing*, 13(5):393–401.

[190] Lanitis, A., Taylor, C.J., Cootes, T.F. and Ahmed T. (1995). Automatic interpretation of human faces and hand gestures using

flexible models. In *Proc. Int. Workshop on Automatic Face and Gesture Recognition*, Zurich (June), pages 98–103.

[191] Lanitis, A., Taylor, C.J. and Cootes, T.F. (1995). A Unified Approach To Coding and Interpreting Face Images. *Proc. IEEE Fifth Int. Conf. on Computer Vision*, Cambridge (MA), pages 368–373.

[192] Lee, C., Tsukamoto, A., Iirota, K. and Tsuji, S. (1994). A visual interaction system using real-time face tracking. In *Proc. 28th Asilomar Conference on Signals, Systems, and Computers*, California, pages 1282–1286.

[193] Lenarcic, J. and Umek, A. (1994). Simple model of human reachable workspace. *IEEE Transactions Systems, Man, and Cybernetics*, (August), 24(8):1239–1246.

[194] Leung, M.K. and Yang, Y.H. (1995). First sight: A human body outline labeling system. *IEEE Transactions on Pattern Analysis and Machine Intelligence*, 17(4):359–377.

[195] Levelt, W. (1989). *Speaking:From intention to articulation*, MIT Press, Cambridge (MA).

[196] Lewis, J. (1991). Automated lip-sync: Background and techniques. *Journal Visualization and Computer Animation*, 2:.

[197] Li, H. Roivainen, P. and Forcheimer, R. (1993). 3D motion estimation in model-based facial image coding. *IEEE Transactions on Pattern Analysis and Machine Intelligence*, 15(6):545–555.

[198] Li, B-C. and Shen, J. (1991). Fast Computation of Moment Invariants, *Pattern Recognition*, 24(8):807–813.

[199] Litwinowicz, P. and Henton, Viseme categories. *Private communications*,

[200] Litwinowicz, P. and Wiliams, L. (1994). Animating images with drawings. In *Proc. SIGGRAPH 94*, pages 409–412.

[201] Lorenz, K., (1973). *Foundations of Ethology*, Springer-Verlag, New York.

[202] Loeve, M.M. (1955). *Probability Theory*, Van Nostrand, Princeton (NJ).

[203] Lowe, D. (1992). Robust model-based motion tracking through the integration of search and estimation. *Int. Journal of Computer Vision*, 8(2):113–122.

[204] Luettin, J., Thacker, N.A. and Beet, S.W. (1996). Visual speech recognition using active shape models and hidden markov

models. In *Proc. IEEE Int. Conf. on Acoustics, Speech, and Signal Processing*, volume II, pages 817–820.

[205] Maes, P. (1991). *Designing Autonomous Agents: Theory and Practice from Biology to Engineering and Back.* Bradford Books/MIT Press, Cambridge (MA).

[206] Maes, P., Darrell, T., Blumberg, B. and Pentland, A. (1996). The ALIVE system: Wireless, full-body interaction with autonomous agents. *ACM Multimedia Systems*, Spring.

[207] Maggioni, C. (1995). Gesturecomputer – New ways of operating a computer. In *Proc. Int. Workshop on Automatic Face and Gesture Recognition*, Zurich, (June), pages 166–171.

[208] Maggioni, C. (1994). Non Immersive Control of Virtual Environments. In *Proc. Virtual Reality, Anwendungen und Trends*, Stuttgart, (February).

[209] Maggioni, C. (1993). A Novel Device for using the Hand as a Human Computer Interface In *Proc. Human Computer Interaction*, Loughborough, England, (September), pages 191–203.

[210] Maggioni, C. (1993). A Novel Gestural Input Device for Virtual-Reality, In *Proc. IEEE Virtual Reality Annual Int. Symposium*, Seattle, pages 118–124.

[211] Mase, K. (1991). Recognition of facial expression from optical flow. *Transactions. of the Insititute of Electronics, Information and Communication Engineers*, (October), E–74(10):3474–3483.

[212] Mase, K. and Pentland, A. (1989). Lip reading: Automatic visual recognition of spoken words. *Opt. Soc. Am. Topical Meeting on Machine Vision*, (June), pages 1565–1570.

[213] Mase, K. and Pentland, A. (1990). Lipreading by optical flow. *Transactions. of the Insititute of Electronics, Information and Communication Engineers of Japan*, (June), J73–D–II(6):796–803. (in Japanese, English version is available *Systems and Computers in Japan*, Scripta Tech. Inc., 22(6):67–76, July 1991).

[214] Mase, K., Suenaga, Y. and Akimoto, T. (1987). Head reader: A head motion understanding system for better man-machine interaction. *Proc. IEEE SMC*, (November), pages 970–974.

[215] Mase, K., Watanabe, Y. and Suenaga, Y. (1990). A real time head motion detection system. *Proc. SPIE*, (February), 1260:262–269.

[216] Massaro, D.W. and Cohen, M.M. (1983). Evaluation and integration of visual and auditory information in speech perception. *Journal of Experimental Psychology: Human Perception and Performance*, 9:753–771.

[217] Matsuno, K., Lee, C., Kimura, S. and Tsuji, S. (1995). Automatic recognition of human facial expressions. In *Proc. IEEE Fifth Int. Conf. on Computer Vision*, Cambridge (MA), pages 352–359.

[218] Matsuno, K., Lee, C. and Tsuji, S. (1994). Recognition of human facial expressions without feature extraction. In *Proc. Third European Conference on Computer Vision*, Stockholm, pages 513–520.

[219] McNeill, D. (1992). *Hand and mind: What gestures reveal about thought*, University of Chicago Press, Chicago.

[220] Metaxas, D. and Terzopoulos, T. (1993). Shape and nonrigid motion estimation through physics-based synthesis. *IEEE Transactions. Pattern Analysis and Machine Intelligence*, 15(6):580–591.

[221] Moghaddam, B., and Pentland, A., (1995). Probabilistic Visual Learning for Object Detection, In Proc. IEEE Fifth Int. Conf. on Computer Vision, Cambridge, (MA), (June), pages 786–793.

[222] Moghaddam, B., Nastar, C. and Pentland, A. (1996). Bayesian Face Recognition using Deformable Intensity Surfaces, In *Proc. IEEE Conf. on Computer Vision and Pattern Recognition,*, San Francisco (CA), (June), pages 638–645.

[223] Movellan, J.R. (1995). Visual speech recognition with stochastic networks. In G. Tesauro, D. Touretzky, and T. Leen, (Editors), *Advances in Neural Information Processing Systems*, volume 7, MIT press, Cambridge, pages 851–858.

[224] Mui, J.K. and Fu, K.S. (1980). Automatic classification of cervical cells using a binary tree classifier, *Pattern Recognition*, 16:69-80.

[225] Mundy, J.L. and Zisserman,A., (Editors), (1992). *Geometric Invariance in Computer Vision*, MIT Press, Cambridge (MA).

[226] Murase, H. and Nayar, S.K. (1995). Visual learning and recognition of 3D objects from appearance. *Int. Journal Computer Vision*, (January), 14(1):5–24.

[227] Nan, L., Dettmer, S. and Shah, M. (1995). Visual lipreading using eigensequences. In *Proc. Int. Workshop on Automatic Face and Gesture Recognition*, Zurich (June), pages 30–34.

[228] Niyogi, S.A. and Adelson, E.H. (1994). Analyzing gait with spatiotemporal surfaces. *Proc. IEEE Workshop on motion of non-rigid and articulated objects*, pages 64–69.

[229] Ohala, J.J. (1994). The frequency code underlies the sound symbolic use of voice pitch. In L. Hinton, J. Nichols, and J.J. Ohala (Editors), *Sound Symbolism*, pages 325–347.

[230] Otsu, N. (1979). A threshold selection method from gray-level histograms. *IEEE Transactions Systems, Man, and Cybernetics*, SMC9:62–66.

[231] Owens, E. and Blazek, B. (1985). Visemes observed by hearing-impared and normal-hearing adult viewers. In *J. Speech and Hearing Research*, 28:381–393.

[232] Parke, F. (1972). Computer generated animation of faces. In *Proc. ACM National Conference*, pages 451–457.

[233] Pavlidis, T. (1982). *Algorithms for Graphics and Image Processing*, Springer.

[234] Pavlović, V., Sharma, R. and Huang, T. (1995). Visual interpretation of hand gestures for human-computer interaction: A review. Technical Report UIUC-BI-AI-RCV-95-10, University of Illinois at Urbana-Champaign, (December).

[235] Pentland, A. (1996). Smart rooms. *Scientific American*, (April), 274(4):68–76.

[236] Pentland, A., (1976). Classification By Clustering, In *IEEE Proc. Symposium On Machine Processing Of Remotely Sensed Data.*, (June).

[237] Pentland, A. (Editor), (1993). *Looking at People Workshop*, IJCAI, Chambery, France, (August).

[238] Pentland, A. and Horowitz, B. (1991). Recovery of nonrigid motion and structure. *IEEE Transactions Pattern Analysis and Machine Intelligence*, 13(7):730–742.

[239] Pentland, A., and Liu, A., (1995). Toward Augmented Control Systems, *Proc. IEEE Intelligent Vehicle Symposium*, Detroit (MI), (September), pages 350–356.

[240] Pentland, A., Picard, R., Sclaroff, S. (1996). Photobook: Tools for Content-Based Manipulation of Image Databases, *Int. Journal of Computer Vision*, 18(3):233–254.

[241] Perricos, C. (1996). Jester - a head gesture recognition system for Windows 95. In *Proc. Rehabilitation Engineering and Assistive Technology Society of North America Annual Conference*, pages 304–306.

[242] Petajan, E.D. (1984). *Automatic Lipreading to Enhance Speech Recognition*, PhD thesis, University of Illinois at Urbana-Champaign.

[243] Poggio, T. and Edelman, S. (1990). A network that learns to recognize three-dimensional objects, *Nature*, 343:263–266.

[244] Poggio , T. and Girosi, F. (1990). Networks for Approximation and Learning, In *Proc. of the IEEE*, 78(9):1481–1497.

[245] Polana, R. and Nelson, R.C. (1994). Recognizing activities. In *Proc. IAPR Int. Conf. on Pattern Recognition*, Jerusalem, (October), A:815–820.

[246] Press, W.H., Flannery, B.P., Teukolsky, S.A. and Vetterling, W.T. (1986). *Numerical Recipes*, Cambridge University Press, New York.

[247] Prevost, S. (1996). An information structural approach to spoken language generation. In *Proc. 34th annual meeting of the Association for Computational Linguistics*, Santa Cruz, (June), pages 294–301.

[248] Quan, L. and Mohr, R. (1991). Towards structure from motion for linear features through reference points. *Proc. IEEE Workshop on Visual Motion*, Princeton, New Jersey, pages 249–254.

[249] Raibert M. and Hodgins J., (1991). *Animation of Dynamic Legged Locomotion, In Proc. SIGGRAPH '91*, ACM Press, (July), 25(4).

[250] Rashid, R.F. (1980). Towards a system for the interpretation of moving light displays. *IEEE Transactions on Pattern Analysis and Machine Intelligence*, 2(6):574–581.

[251] Rehg, J. and Kanade, T. (1994). DigitEyes: Vision-based hand tracking for human-computer interaction. In *Proc. IEEE Workshop on Motion of Non-Rigid and Articulated Bodies*, Austin (TX), (November), pages 16–24.

[252] Rehg, J. and Kanade, T. (1994). Visual tracking of high DOF articulated structures: An application to human hand tracking. In *Proc. Third European Conf. on Computer Vision*, Stockholm, Sweden, volume 2, pages 35–46.

[253] Rehg, J. and Kanade, T. (1995). Model-based tracking of self-occluding articulated objects. In *Proc. IEEE Fifth Int. Conf. on Computer Vision*, Boston (MA), pages 612–617.

[254] Reynard, D. Wildenberg, A. Blake, A. and Marchant, J. (1996). Learning dynamics of complex motions from image sequences. In

Proc. Foruth European Conf. on Computer Vision, Cambridge, England, (April), pages 357–368.

[255] Rheingold, H. (1991). *Virtual Reality*, Secker and Warburg.

[256] Rimé, B. (1982). The elimination of visible behavior from social interactions: Effects of verbal, nonverbal and interpersonal variables. *European Journal of Social Psychology*, 12:113–129.

[257] Roberts, L.G. (1965). Machine perception of three-dimensional solids. In J.T. Tippet, (Editor), *Optical and Electro-Optical Information Processing*, MIT Press.

[258] Rogers, W.T. (1978). The contribution of kinesic illustrators toward the comprehension of verbal behavior within utterances. *Human Communication Research*, 5:54–62.

[259] Rohr, K. (1993). Incremental recognition of pedestrians from image sequences. In *Proc. IEEE Conf. Computer Vision and Pattern Recognition*, New York, (June), pages 8–13.

[260] Rohr, K. (1994). Towards model-based recognition of human movements in image sequences. *CVGIP Image Understanding*, 59(1):94–115.

[261] Rosenblum, M., Yacoob, Y. and Davis, L.S. (1994). Human Emotion Recognition from Motion Using a Radial Basis Function Network Architecture. In *Proc. IEEE Workshop on Motion of Non-rigid and Articulated Objects*, Austin (TX), pages 43–49.

[262] Rosenfeld, A., (1969). *Picture Processing by Computer.* Academic Press, New York.

[263] O'Rourke, J. and Badler, N.I. (1980). Model-based image analysis of human motion using constraint propagation. *IEEE Transactions on Pattern Analysis and Machine Intelligence*, 2(6):522–536.

[264] Saitz, R.L. and Cervenka, E.J. (1972). *Handbook of Gestures: Columbia and the United States.* Mouton & Co., The Hague, Netherlands.

[265] Sakai, T., Nagao, M. and Kanade, T. (1972). Computer analysis and classification of photographs of human faces. In *Proc. First USA–JAPAN Computer Conference*, 2–7.

[266] Samal, A. and Iyengar, P. (1992). Automatic Recognition and Analysis of Human Faces and Facial Expressions: A Survey. *Pattern Recognition*, 25(1):65–77.

[267] Sato, A., Mase, K., Tomono, A. and Ishii, K. (1993). Pedestrian counting system robust against illumination changes. In *Proc. SPIE*, (November), 2094:1259–1270.

[268] Scott, K.C., Kagels, D.S., Watson, S.H., Rom, H., Wright, J.R., Lee, M. and Hussey, K.J. (1994). Synthesis of speaker facial movement to match selected speech sequences. In *Proc. of the Fifth Australian Conference on Speech Science and Technology*, (December).

[269] Segen, J. (1993). Controlling computers with gloveless gestures. In *Proc. Virtual Reality Systems Conf.*, (March), pages 2–6.

[270] Segen, J. (1991). GEST: an integrated approach to learning in computer vision, In *Proc. of the First International Workshop on Multistrategy Learning*, Harpers Ferry, USA, pages 403–410.

[271] Seki, S., Takahashi, K. and Oka, R. (1993). Gesture recognition from motion images by spotting algorithm. In *Proc. Asian Conference on Computer Vision*, Osaka, pages 759–762.

[272] Sellis, T., Roussopoulos, N. and Faloutsos, C. (1987). The r+-tree: a dynamic index for multidimensional objects. In *Proc. of 13th Int. Conf. on VLDB*, pages 507–518.

[273] Sethi, I.K. and Savarayudu, G.P.R. (1982). Hierarchical classifier design using mutual information. *IEEE Transactions. Pattern Analysis and Machine Intell.*, 4:441–445.

[274] Short, J., Williams, E. and Christie, B. (1976). *The social psychology of telecommunications*, Wiley, New York.

[275] Silsbee, P.L. (1994). Sensory integration in audiovisual automatic speech recognition. In *Proc. 28th Annual Asilomar Conf. on Signals, Systems, and Computers*, (November), pages 561–565.

[276] Simard, P., LeCun, Y. and Denker, J. (1993) Efficient pattern recognition using a new transformation distance. In *Advances in Neural Information Processing Systems*, Morgan Kaufman, pages 50–58.

[277] Sparrell, C.J. (1993). *Coverbal iconic gesture in human-computer interaction*, Master's thesis, Massachusetts Institute of Technology. Cambridge (MA).

[278] Starner, T. and Pentland, A., (1995) Visual Recognition of American Sign Language Using Hidden Markov Models, In Proc. Int. Workshop on Automatic Face and Gesture Recognition Zurich, Switzerland, (June), pages 189–194.

[279] Stokoe, W. (1960) Sign language structure: an outline of the visual communication system of the American deaf. *Studies in Linguistics Occasional Paper No. 8.*

[280] Sturman, D., Zelter, D. and Pieper, S. (1989) Hands-on interaction with virtual environments. In *Proc. of the ACM*

Symposium on User Interface Software and Technology, Williamsburg, Virginia, (November), pages 19–24.

[281] Suenaga, Y., Mase, K., Fukumoto, M. and Watanabe, Y. (1993) Human reader: An advanced man-machine interface based on human images and speech. *Systems and Computers in Japan,* (February), 24(2):88–102.

[282] Swain, M. and Ballard, D. (1991) Color indexing. *Int. Journal Computer Vision,* 7(1):11–32.

[283] Szeliski, R. and Kang, S.B. (1994) Recovering 3D shape and motion from image streams using nonlinear least squares. *Journal of Visual Communication and Image Representation,* 5(1):10–28.

[284] Terzopoulos, D. and Casileascu, M. (1991) Sampling and reconstruction with adaptive meshes. In *Proc. IEEE Conf. Computer Vision and Pattern Recognition,* Maui (HI), pages 70–75.

[285] Terzopoulos, D. and Waters, K. (1993) Analysis and Synthesis of Facial Image Sequences Using Physical and Anatomical Models. *IEEE Transactions on Pattern Analysis and Machine Intelligence,* 15(6):569–579.

[286] Thompson, L.A. and Massaro, D.W. (1986). Evaluation and integration of speech and pointing gestures during referential understanding. *Journal of Experimental Child Psychology,* 42:144–168.

[287] Thompson, D.W. and Mundy, J.L. (1988) Model-based motion analysis – motion from motion. In R. C. Bolles and B. Roth, (Editors), *Robotics Research: The Fourth International Symposium,* pages 299–309, MIT Press, Cambridge (MA).

[288] Thórisson, K.R. (1995). Multimodal Interaction with Humanoid Computer Characters. In *Proc. Conf. Lifelike Computer Characters,* Snowbird, Utah, (September), page 45.

[289] Thórisson, K.R. (1996). Communicative Humanoids: A Computational Model of Psychosocial Dialogue Skills. Ph.D. Thesis, Media Arts and Sciences, MIT Media Laboratory.

[290] Toelg, S. and Poggio, T. (1994) Towards an Example-based Image Compression Architecture for Video-conferencing. *Technical Report CAR-TR-723,* Center for Automation Research, University of Maryland.

[291] Turk, M. and Pentland, A. (1991) Eigenfaces for recognition. *Journal of Cognitive Neuroscience,* 3(1):71–86.

[292] Tsai, R.Y. (1987) A Versatile Camera Calibration Technique for High-Accuracy 3D Machine Vision Metrology Using Off-the-Shelf TV Cameras and Lenses, *IEEE Journal on Robotics and Automation*, (August), RA-3(4):323–344.

[293] Tsukamoto, A., Lee, C.W. and Tsuji, S. (1993) Detection and tracking of human face with synthesize templates. In *Proc. Asian Conference on Computer Vision*, Osaka, (November), pages 183–186.

[294] Ullman, S. (1979) *The interpretation of visual motion*. MIT Press.

[295] Ullman, S. and Basri, R., (1991) Recognition by linear combinations of models. *IEEE Transactions. Pattern Analysis and Machine Intelligence*, 13:992–1006.

[296] Väänänen, K. and Böhm, K. (1993). Gesture-driven interaction as a human factor in virtual environments – an approach with neural networks. In R.A. Earnshaw, M.A. Gigante and H. Jones (Eds.), *Virtual Reality Systems*, Academic Press, London, pages 73–106.

[297] Valentin, D., Abdi, H. O'Toole, A. and Cotrell, G.W. (1994) Connectionist Models of Face Processing: A Survey. *Pattern Recognition*, 27(9):1209–1230.

[298] Vargas, M. (1987) *Louder than words*, Iowa State University Press.

[299] Vincent, V.J. (1993) Mandala: Virtual Village. In *ACM SIGGRAPH Visual Proc.*, Computer Graphics, (July).

[300] Wahlster, W., Andre, E., Graf, W. and Rist, T. (1991). Designing illustrated texts. In *Proc. Fifth European Chapter of the Association Computational Linguistics*, pages 8–14.

[301] Warme, S. (1994) The Mandala Virtual World System. *Virtual Reality World*, 2(2):65–71.

[302] Ware, C. and Balakrishnana, R. (1994) Reaching for objects in VR displays: Lag and frame rate, *ACM Transactions on Computer-Human Interaction*, (December), 1(4):331–356.

[303] Watanabe, K., Iwai, Y., Yagi, Y. and Yachida, M. (1995) Manual alphabet recognition by using colored gloves. *Transactions. of the Insititute of Electronics, Information and Communication Engineers of Japan*, (September), PRU 95–134.

[304] Watanabe, T., Tsukamoto, A., Lee, C-W. and Yachida, M. (1995) Gesture recognition using multiple silhouette models for a

real-time interactive system. In *Proc. Asian Conference on Computer Vision*, volume 2, pages 235–239.

[305] Waters, K. (1987) A muscle model for animating three-dimensional facial expressions. *Computer Graphics (SIGGRAPH '87)*, (July), 21(4):17–24.

[306] Waters, K. and Levergood, T. (1994) An automatic lip-synchronization algorithm for synthetic faces. *Multimedia Tools and Applications*, Kluwer Academic Publishers, (October), 1(4):349–366.

[307] Webber, B. (1994). Instruction Understanding for Human Figure Animation. In *Proc. American Association for Artificial Intelligence Spring Symposium on Active Natural Language Processing*, Stanford (CA), (March).

[308] Webber, B., Badler, N., DiEugenio, B., Geib, C., Levison, L., and Moore, M. (1995). Instructions, Intentions and Expectations. *Artificial Intelligence Journal*, 73:253–269.

[309] Wellner, P. (1993) Interacting with paper on the DigitalDesk. *Communications of the ACM*, 36(7):86–96.

[310] Wellner, P. (1991) The DigitalDesk Calculator: Tangible Manipulation on a Desk Top Display, In *Proc. ACM Symposium on User Interface Software and Technology*, Hilton Head (SC), (November), pages 27–33.

[311] Williams, E. (1977). Experimental comparisons of face-to-face and mediated communication: A review. *Psychological Bulletin*, 84:963–976.

[312] Weng, J. (1994) On comprehensive visual learning. In *Proc. NSF/ARPA Workshop on Performance versus Methodology in Computer Vision*,Seattle (WA), pages 152–166.

[313] Weng, J. and Chen, S. (1995) SHOSLIF convergence properties and MDF version of SHOSLIF-N. *Technical Report CPS-95-22*, Department of Computer Science, Michigan State University, East Lansing (MI).

[314] Weng, J. (1996) Cresceptron and SHOSLIF: Toward comprehensive visual learning. In S. K. Nayar and T. Poggio (eds.), *Early Visual Learning,* Oxford University Press, New York.

[315] Wilson, A., Bobick, A. and Cassell, J. (1996). Recovering the Temporal Structure of Natural Gesture. In *Proc. Second Int. Conf. on Automatic Face and Gesture Recognition*, Vermont.

[316] Wilks, S.S. (1963) *Mathematical Statistics*, Wiley, New York.

[317] Wirtz, B. and Maggioni, C. (1993) ImageGlove: A Novel Way to Control Virtual Environments, In *Proc. Virtual Reality Systems*, New York, pages 7–12.

[318] Wolf, C.G. (1992) A comparative study of gestural, keyboard and mouse interfaces, *Behaviour and Information Technology*, 11(1):13–23.

[319] Wolff, G.J., Prasad, K.V., Stork, D.G. and Hennecke, M.E. (1994) Lipreading by neural networks: Visual preprocessing, learning and sensory integration. In J.D. Cowan, G. Tesauro, and J. Alspector, (Editors), *Advances in Neural Information Processing Systems*, Morgan Kaufmann, volume 6, pages 1027–1034.

[320] Wren, C., Azarbayejani, A., Darrell, T. and Pentland, A. (1995), Pfinder: Real-time tracking of the human body. In *Proc. SPIE Conference on Integration Issues in Large Commercial Media Delivery Systems*, (October), volume 2615.

[321] Wu, H., Chen, Q. and Yachida, M. (1995) An application of fuzzy theory: Face detection. In *Proc. International Workshop on Automatic Face and Gesture Recognition*, Zurich, (June), pages 314–319.

[322] Yacoob, Y. and Davis, L.S. (1994) Recognising Facial Expressions by Spatio-Temporal Analysis. In *Proc. of the 12th Int. Conf. of Pattern Recognition*, Jerusalem, volume 1, pages 747–749.

[323] Yacoob, Y. and Davis, L.S. (1996) Computing Spatio-Temporal Representations of Human Faces. *IEEE Transactions on Pattern Analysis and Machine Intelligence*, 18(6):636–642.

[324] Yang, G. and Huang, T.S. (1993) Human face detection in a scene. In *Proc. IEEE Conf. Computer Vision and Pattern Recognition*, New York, pages 453–458.

[325] Young, J. (1993) *Head and Face Anthropometry of Adult U.S. Citizens*, Government Report DOT/FAA/AM-93/10, (July).

[326] Young, S.J. (1996) Large vocabulary continuous speech recognition: a review, *IEEE Signal Processing Magazine*, (September), 13(5):45–57.

[327] Yuhas, B.P., Goldstein, M.H., Sejnowski, T.J. and Jenkins, R.E. (1990) Neural network models of sensory integration for improved vowel recognition. *Proc. IEEE*, (October), 78(10):1658–1668.

[328] Yuille, A., Cohen, D. and Halliman, P. (1992) Feature Extraction From Faces Using Deformable Templates. *Int. Journal of Computer Vision*, 8:104–109.

[329] Yuille, A. and Halliman, P. (1992) Deformable templates. In A. Blake and A. Yuille, (Editors), *Active Vision*, MIT Press, pages 21–38.

[330] Zhang, Z. (1994) Iterative point matching for registration of free-form curves and surfaces. *Int. Journal of Computer Vision*, 13:119–152.

[331] Zeltzer D. (1991) Task-level graphical simulation: abstraction, representation and control. In N.I. Badler, B.A. Barsky and D. Zeltser (Editors), *Making them move: mechanics, control and animation of articulated figures*, Morgan Kauffman, pages 3–33.

[332] Zhou, Z., Smith, K.C., Benhabib,B. and Safaee-Rad, R. (1989) Morphological Skeleton Transforms for Determining position and orientation of Pre-Marked Objects, In *Proc. IEEE Pacific Rim Conference on Communication, Computers and Signal Processing*, pages 301–305.

[333] Zhu, S.C. and Yuille, A.L. (1995) Forms: a flexible object recognition and modelling system. In *Proc. IEEE Fifth Int. Conf. Computer Vision*, pages 465–472.

[334] Zimmermann, T.G., Lanier, J., Blanchard, C., Bryson, S. and Harvill, Y. (1987) A Hand Gesture Interface Device, In *Proc. ACM Conf. Human Factors in Computing Systems and Graphics Interface*, pages 189–192.

Contributors

Subutai Ahmad
Interval Research Corporation, 1801 Page Mill Road, Building C, Palo Alto, CA 94304, USA.

Tariq Ahmad
Department of Medical Biophysics, Stopford Building, Oxford Road, Manchester, M13 9PT, England.

Benedicte Bascle
Department of Engineering Science, University of Oxford, Oxford OX1 3PJ, England.

Michael Black
Xerox Palo Alto Research Center, 3333 Coyote Hill Road, Palo Alto, CA 94304, USA.

Andrew Blake
Department of Engineering Science, University of Oxford, Oxford OX1 3PJ, England.

Christopher Bregler
Department of Computer Science, University of California, Berkeley, CA 94720, USA.

Justine Cassell
The Media Laboratory, MIT, 20 Ames Street, Cambridge MA 02139, USA.

Roberto Cipolla
Department of Engineering, University of Cambridge, Cambridge CB2 1PZ, England.

Carlo Colombo
Department of Electronics for Automation, University of Brescia, Via Branze, 38, 25123 Brescia, Italy.

345

Tim Cootes
Department of Medical Biophysics, Stopford Building, Oxford Road, Manchester, M13 9PT, England.

Michele Covell
Interval Research Corporation, 1801 Page Mill Road, Building C, Palo Alto, CA 94304, USA.

Yuntao Cui
Siemens Corporate Research, 755 College Road East, Princeton, NJ 08540, USA.

Larry Davis
Computer Vision Laboratory, Center for Automation Research, University of Maryland, College Park, MD 20742, USA.

Alberto Del Bimbo
Department of Systems and Informatics, Via Santa Marta, 3, 50139 Firenze, Italy.

Silvio De Magistris
Department of Systems and Informatics, Via Santa Marta, 3, 50139 Firenze, Italy.

Enrico Di Bernardo
California Institute of Technology, MS 136-93, Pasadena, CA 91125, USA.

Gareth Edwards
Department of Medical Biophysics, Stopford Building, Oxford Road, Manchester, M13 9PT, England.

Jerome Feldman
Department of Computer Science, University of California, Berkeley, CA 94720, USA.

David Forsyth
Department of Computer Science, University of California, Berkeley, CA 94720, USA.

Dariu Gavrila
Computer Vision Laboratory, Center for Automation Research, University of Maryland, College Park, MD 20742, USA.

Andrew Gee
Department of Engineering, University of Cambridge, Cambridge CB2 1PZ, England.

Luis Goncalves
California Institute of Technology, MS 136-93, Pasadena, CA 91125, USA.

Nicholas Hollinghurst
Department of Engineering, University of Cambridge, Cambridge CB2 1PZ, England.

Thanarat Horprasert
Computer Vision Laboratory, Center for Automation Research, University of Maryland, College Park, MD 20742, USA.

Yoshio Iwai
Department of Systems Engineering, Faculty of Engineering Science, Osaka University, Machikaneyama, Toyonaka, Osaka 560, Japan.

Bernhard Kämmerer
Siemens AG, Corporate Research and Development, Otto Hahn Ring 6, 81739 Munich, Germany.

Sing Bing Kang
Digital Equipment Corporation, Cambridge Research Lab, One Kendall Square, Cambridge MA 02139, USA.

Andreas Lanitis
Department of Medical Biophysics, Stopford Building, Oxford Road, Manchester, M13 9PT, England.

Maria Loughlin
Digital Equipment Corporation, Cambridge Research Lab, One Kendall Square, Cambridge MA 02139, USA.

Christoph Maggioni
SIEMENS AG, Corporate Research and Development, Otto Hahn Ring 6, 81739 Munich, Germany.

Kenji Mase
ATR Media Integration and Communications Research Laboratories, Seika-cho, Soraku-gun, Kyoto 619-02, Japan.

Carlos Morimoto
Computer Vision Laboratory, Center for Automation Research, University of Maryland, College Park, MD 20742, USA.

Julian Morris
Oxford Metrics, Unit 14, 7 West Way, Oxford OX2 0JB, England.

Stephen Omohundro
NEC Research Institute, 4 Independence Way, Princeton NJ08540, USA

Alex Pentland
The Media Laboratory, MIT, Cambridge MA 02139, USA.

Pietro Perona
California Institute of Technology, MS 136-93, Pasadena, CA 91125, USA.

Jim Rehg
Digital Equipment Corporation, Cambridge Research Lab, One Kendall Square, Cambridge MA 02139, USA.

Malcom Slaney
Interval Research Corporation. 1801 Page Mill Road, Building C, Palo Alto, CA 94304, USA.

Chris Taylor
Department of Medical Biophysics, Stopford Building, Oxford Road, Manchester, M13 9PT, England.

Demetri Terzopoulos
Department of Computer Science, University of Toronto, 10 King's College Road, Toronto, ON, M5S 1A4, Canada.

Masahiko Yachida
Department of Systems Engineering, Faculty of Engineering Science, Osaka University, Machikaneyama, Toyonaka, Osaka 560, Japan.

Yaser Yacoob
Computer Vision Laboratory, Center for Automation Research, University of Maryland, College Park, MD 20742, USA.

Keith Waters
Digital Equipment Corporation, Cambridge Research Laboratory, 1 Kendall Square, Cambridge MA 02139, USA.

John Weng
Department of Computer Science, Michigan State University, East Lansing, MI 48823, USA.